D0893520

BROOKLYN
TO BAGHDAD

BROOKLYN TO BAGHDAD

>>>

AN NYPD INTELLIGENCE COP
FIGHTS TERROR IN IRAQ

CHRISTOPHER STROM

WITH JEROME PREISLER AND MICHAEL BENSON

CHICAGO
REVIEW
PRESS

Published by Chicago Review Press Incorporated
814 North Franklin Street
Chicago, Illinois 60610
ISBN 978-1-64160-102-3

Library of Congress Cataloging-in-Publication Data

Names: Strom, Christopher, author. | Preisler, Jerome, author. | Benson,
    Michael, author.
Title: Brooklyn to Baghdad : an NYPD intelligence cop fights terror in Iraq
    / Christopher Strom with Jerome Preisler and Michael Benson.
Description: Chicago : Chicago Review Press, [2019] | Summary: "The true
    story of a retired NYPD intelligence sergeant who applies his street-cop
    tactics and interrogation skills against a lethal insurgency that had
    infected Iraq"— Provided by publisher.
Identifiers: LCCN 2019030375 (print) | LCCN 2019030376 (ebook) | ISBN
    9781641601023 (cloth) | ISBN 9781641601030 (adobe pdf) | ISBN
    9781641601054 (epub) | ISBN 9781641601047 (kindle edition)
Subjects: LCSH: Strom, Christopher. | Iraq War, 2003–2011—Personal
    narratives, American. | Insurgency—Iraq. | Terrorism—Iraq.
Classification: LCC DS79.766.S87 A3 2019 (print) | LCC DS79.766.S87
    (ebook) | DDC 956.7044/342 [B]—dc23
LC record available at https://lccn.loc.gov/2019030375
LC ebook record available at https://lccn.loc.gov/2019030376

All images from the author's collection
Typesetting: Nord Compo

Printed in the United States of America
5 4 3 2 1

This book, written in memory of Matt Pucino,
is dedicated to my wife, Debbie,
and my children, Stephanie and Christian,
for their undying support and love—and for believing in me.

CONTENTS

FOREWORD

YOU'RE IN GOOD HANDS

I FIRST MET CHRIS STROM in the winter of 2002. I was interviewing him for a very sensitive assignment within the Intelligence Division of the New York City Police Department. Between the flood of endorsements from his peers, the accolades from his supervisor, and the research I had done on my own, I had gotten a pretty clear picture of the man who was sitting before me. It took only a few minutes to confirm all of my positive preconceptions.

Here was someone who was modest, intelligent, diligent, and able to work well with others. A person who was dedicated not only to his job but also to performing quality work and excelling in his career at a rapid speed. Most important, I saw a man who was willing to give his all to protect the city of New York.

The position was for a field intelligence officer, and it required a person who was highly motivated and had excellent knowledge of investigations and a willingness to work in the gray areas of law enforcement. There was no rule book for this job. Not even rough guidelines. The job was what you made of it, and Chris exceeded all expectations for a candidate.

Although Chris was being interviewed for a position working in one of the city's seventy-six precincts as a solo field investigator, I already had an idea that he would be a natural fit for supervising one of our investigation teams. Shortly after being picked up as a field intelligence officer, Chris was shifted to supervise a team.

In the wake of September 11, the Intelligence Division had transformed, and Chris's team had a huge task to perform. Its sole responsibility was to investigate tips generated by the community. If you were one of the thousands of people who took the "See something, say something" slogan as a call to action, be content in the knowledge that Chis and his team investigated each and every tip to its fullest.

The key to Chris's success in this role was his dedication, which motivated his team to be diligent. He understood that one of these tips could be the only indication of another attack. Although most investigations led to a reasonable explanation with no nexus to terrorism, no stone was left unturned. Some of these tips were passed on for their intelligence value, and a few of them became the catalyst for bigger terrorism cases. His team investigated tip number twenty thousand with the same sense of dedication and importance as tip number one. He led by example and always looked out for his guys.

When Chris retired from the NYPD, it was of little surprise to find out he wasn't taking it easy on a beach down in Florida. He wasn't on a suburban backyard deck flipping burgers while wearing a chef's hat and an apron. He was instead in harm's way, as he had always been. Keeping us safe from a distance, overseas. For this and countless other reasons I will always regard him as truly one of New York's finest and one of those guys I could always count on to have my back.

And now he has gifted us with this book, an exhilarating and infuriating look at busting bad guys on both sides of the Earth. Feel secure that the man about to tell you his story of law enforcement from Brooklyn to Baghdad is of the utmost character. You are in good hands.

NYPD DEPUTY INSPECTOR VINCENT MARRA,
OPERATIONS COMMANDER, INTELLIGENCE DIVISION, RET.

AUTHOR'S NOTE

THIS IS A TRUE STORY. When possible, spoken words have been quoted verbatim. However, when that was not possible, conversations have been reconstructed as closely as possible to reality based on the recollections of those who spoke and heard the words. In places speech has been slightly edited, but only to improve readability. The denotations and connotations of the words remain unaltered. In some cases, witnesses are credited with verbal quotes that in reality occurred only in written form.

Some locations have been changed for security reasons, and the names and other identifying details of some individuals and organizations have been fictionalized. This is sometimes to protect them, but also sometimes because I've forgotten a name, or knew the person only by a nickname, or knew someone's name but haven't got a clue how to spell it. Please don't assume that a fictionalized name means something sinister. I've always made the changes with your reading ease in mind. Fictionalized names will be *italicized* on first mention. Any resemblance between fictionalized names and the names of real persons is strictly coincidental.

ABBREVIATION KEY

2IC	second-in-command
AA	arming agreement
AAR	after action report
ACU	army combat uniform
AO	area of operation
BATS	Biometrics Automated Toolset
BIP	blow in place
BFT	Blue Force Tracker
CAV	cavalry
CHOPS	chief of operations
CHU	containerized housing unit
CI	confidential informant
COP	combat outpost
CSI	crime scene investigation
DIR	detainee interrogation reports
DO	desk officer
DOMEX	document and media exploitation
EFP	explosively formed projectiles
EOD	explosive ordnance disposal
FIO	field intelligence officer
FNG	Fucking New Guys
FOB	forward operating base

GAF	ground assault force
HUMINT	human intelligence
HVI	high-value individual
ID	infantry division
IED	improvised explosive devices
INP	Iraqi National Police
ISR	intelligence, surveillance, and reconnaissance
IZ	International Zone
JAG	Judge Advocate General
JAM	Jaysh al-Mahdhi
JERRV	joint EOD rapid response vehicle
JIEDDO	Joint Improvised Explosive Device Defeat Organization
JSS	Joint Security Station
JTTF	Joint Terrorism Task Force
KIA	killed in action
LEA	law enforcement adviser
LEP	law enforcement professional
LN	local national
MNSA	Ministry of National Security Affairs
MPRI	Military Professional Resources Inc.
MRAP	mine resistant ambush protected carrier
NCO	noncommissioned officer
NSA	National Security Agency
NVG	night vision goggles
OGA	other government agencies
OSC	on-scene commander
PB	personal business
PBA	post-blast analysis
PID	positive identification
POC	point of capture
PSYOPS	psychological operations
PT	physical training
PX	post exchange
QRF	quick reaction force
RIP/TOA	relief in place / transfer of authority

RTB	return to base
SCIF	sensitive compartmented information facility
SF	Special Forces
SIGINT	signals intelligence
SOI	source of information *or* Sons of Iraq militia
TC	tactical commander
TCN	third country nationals
TEO	technical exploitation operations
TOC	tactical operations center
TQ	tactical questioning
TS/SCI	Top Secret / Sensitive Compartmented Information
TSE	tactical site exploitation
TST	time sensitive targeting
TTP	tactics, techniques, and procedures
UAV	unmanned aerial vehicle
USCF	United States coalition forces
VBIED	vehicle-borne improvised explosive device
WIT	weapons intelligence team

1

LIFE AS A COP

I'M CHRIS. I AM THE INTERROGATOR, the Q in Q&A. One of the best. Not to brag, but merely to point out that I am a worthy narrator for this important story, a story both inspiring and frustrating. Before Iraq, I was one of the skilled interrogators of the New York City Police Department, a member of its elite Intelligence Division. I have more than twenty years of experience getting the truth out of hard-core liars.

My experience as an interrogator dates back to 1996, but even before then I knew that I had instinctive skills as a judge of character. One of the keys to interrogating someone is to be able to tell a couple things right away, and I mean in the first thirty seconds. One, is this basically a good person? And two, is he guilty of what he's been accused of?

One of my favorite side effects to being a good judge of character is my friends tend to be folks of excellent character.

I cannot count the number of criminals I questioned as a cop in New York City. First as a street cop, then as a member of a narcotics detail in South Brooklyn, I was good at getting criminals to gab. In Iraq, I upped the ante, questioning terrorists: "Who are your friends? Where did you hide the bombs?"

And this is my book. With it, I hope to accomplish several things. I will take you with me as I crash through the front door of evil with the most effective counterinsurgency team ever assembled. I will share some tough secrets and expose the forces that eventually compromised our leadership and shut us down, putting soldiers' lives at risk with the complicity of the CIA, FBI, and US Army. And I will tell you about a dedicated husband and father—me!—separated from my wife and kids by thousands of miles, torn between my love for them and a mission I knew was saving countless American (and Iraqi) lives.

While many books about the war in Iraq have been written from the point of view of journalists embedded in a military unit on a restricted and temporary basis, my story tells of a civilian contractor, not just embedded within a conventional army unit but entering right beside them as the structural target is assaulted, the gates and doors shotgunned off their hinges.

And it's a story about the importance of human intelligence. Today's intelligence-gathering techniques being what they are, people can easily be distracted by the high-tech toys: electronic gadgets, surveillance devices, satellite communications. Who doesn't love that part in a James Bond movie when Q introduces 007 to all-new tech? Future-shock technology is fun, but it is still HUMINT—human intelligence—that drives the intel picture.

And the key to HUMINT is to take subjects alive. In wartime, it might feel efficient to kill bad guys whenever you get the opportunity, but in most cases a live captive beats a body. If the target of an investigation is killed, the intel picture also dies. If the target is captured, the role of interrogation in gathering human intelligence becomes critical.

But I'm getting ahead of myself. My story begins in peacetime, if you can ever call New York City peaceful. The five boroughs had their own war zones, and as a cop I prowled some of the most dangerous streets in America.

The events of my life before I joined the NYPD molded me as much as or more than anything that happened after. There were kids who had a lot tougher time than I did, but my youth was nonetheless tumultuous. My parents divorced when I was three. My dad was in and out of my life, mostly because my mother had remarried in disastrous fashion. My stepdad had seven kids from a previous marriage, most of whom had gone through their own trauma/drama in life. As a bonus, my mother and stepdad had twins.

When that marriage ended, my two sisters and I moved to Garden City, Long Island, to live with our grandfather. My mom worked nights at a bar in Glen Cove, and my poor grandfather was on the verge of a nervous breakdown because of all the turmoil. My sisters and I were basically left to fend for ourselves.

I struggled in school, not because I wasn't capable—my grades were fine—but because I was listless, feeling angry and abandoned. One day when I was sixteen I passed by the US Marine Corps recruiting station at the Roosevelt Field shopping mall and asked about joining. They told me I had to wait until I was seventeen, and even then I'd need the permission of both parents. I couldn't sit around anymore and watch the family deteriorate even further, so I got my mother and father to sign off. Five days after turning seventeen, I was in Marine Corps boot camp in Parris Island, South Carolina.

When I graduated fourteen weeks later, I was sent to aviation mechanics school in Tennessee, and after completion I was stationed at New River Air Station in Jacksonville, North Carolina. From there, I traveled all over the world courtesy of the US Navy: Scandinavia, elsewhere in Europe, Africa, and the Caribbean.

After four years I reentered civilian life, moved to Texas, and was a police officer in Plano for two years. Then I moved back to New York and was hired by the NYPD. It was the best career decision I ever made. In 1993 I met Deborah, my Debbie, and in December 1994 we were married, both of us for the second time.

In April 1996 I was reassigned to the Queens Robbery Task Force, a unit designed to combat violent felony crimes including robberies, car thefts, gun crimes, and serious assaults. I remained in the robbery unit for four years, until my promotion to sergeant in May 2000. At that point I was assigned to the Seventy-Sixth Precinct—the Seven-Six—in Carroll Gardens / Red Hook, Brooklyn. Not long after my arrival, the captain reviewed my career folder and put me in charge of the narcotics unit. Within six months of my taking over, the team had eclipsed the previous year's activity, doubling the felony arrests and narcotics seizures.

———————

September 11, 2001, happened to be my daughter Stephanie's fourth birth-day. I had intentionally changed my shift to a daytime tour of duty to be there for her on her special day. Before leaving home that morning, I kissed her and wished her a happy birthday and told her that when she came home from school, we would have a cake.

When I got to the Seven-Six, I grabbed my detective Ginger Velazquez and headed to the local diner for breakfast. Since we were both in plain-clothes and not in the running for jobs from Central Communications, I had intentionally turned down my radio so as to not attract attention from patrons inside the diner. After finishing breakfast, we headed west on Atlantic Avenue toward the East River when I saw the first tower of the World Trade Center erupt into flames. My first thought was that it was an accident, a plane crash, tragic but not necessarily a national security issue. I turned up the volume on the police radio, but there was so much traffic it was hard to discern what was happening.

I called Debbie, who was working in the X-ray department at St. John's Episcopal Hospital in Far Rockaway, Queens. Debbie was five foot four, 105 pounds, and 100 percent Italian. Debbie grew up on the South Shore of Long Island, in a town called North Woodmere. In a neighborhood known for large homes and great affluence, Debbie's attitude was hard to miss. Not because she flaunted any wealth—hell, I was a civil servant, not a trader for Goldman Sachs. More because of the way she spoke and her choice of words, sharp and direct. Debbie could trade verbal jabs with the best, and choosing to spar with her could prove very embarrassing. She was tough on the inside and beauti-ful all at the same time.

I told her that I still intended to be home later for dinner and some birthday cake. I was still on the phone when I saw the sun glint off a jet in the sky and watched in horror as it slammed into the South Tower. The explosion was so violent that it shook my police vehicle, causing my partner Ginger to scream out loud. Gray ash sprinkled down over Lower Manhattan like a hellish snowstorm.

"What was that?" Debbie asked.

I knew we were under attack, but I didn't say that. "I have to go," I said, and hung up.

Easterly winds carried the airborne debris across the water until it was falling on the hood of my car. I saw small portions of photographs, presumably pictures of loved ones from someone's workstation.

In the three days that followed, I was first stationed at the entrance to the Brooklyn-Battery Tunnel, then as security at Ground Zero, and later digging on the pile looking for survivors. One of the eeriest things I saw were the hundreds of pairs of ladies' high-heeled shoes and empty baby strollers abandoned on the street, presumably so that their owners could run away faster from the falling debris.

On the third day, I finally got to go home to see my family. Driving along on the Belt Parkway, I was initially numb, exhausted from the past seventy-two hours of work, trying to process what had just happened. As I entered my house, I tried to compose myself for Debbie and my daughter, Stephanie, who would have to live with the fact that her birthday was forever associated with unthinkable carnage. My son Christian was still too young to understand any of this, but he was on my mind, too. Who knew at that point what his future would hold?

In the weeks that followed, Intelligence's counterterrorism unit investigated each tip that came in and responded to everything from an explosion to a report of a suspicious package. They covered the whole city, a world unto itself, from the uppermost Bronx to Coney Island, from Staten Island to the far eastern reaches of Queens. That was where the action was, and where I wanted to be.

The events of 9/11 were acts of war, an attack on American ideals and freedom. That, and the fact that we didn't know what would happen next, with perhaps more attacks to come, kept us all on the ball. We took our work very seriously, and it kept us busy.

The entire city was on edge, a level of communal anxiety I'd never encountered before. Because of the attack from the outside, folks who would normally have nothing to do with one another, folks from different neighborhoods, of different colors, different religions, were banding together. They had terror in common. For a time, the city was as one. It didn't last, of course.

But the nervous edge persisted everywhere, including in my house, where you could accurately gauge the anxiety of the day by the number of cigarettes Debbie smoked. She was a moderate smoker on relatively calm days but chained them if there was a major incident in the city. The threat of anthrax made us crazy for a while.

As the weeks turned into months, I restarted the narcotics team as a way of bringing about some normalcy and routine. During the summer of 2002, my old captain David Barrere called me on my cell phone and asked me how my son was doing. In January 2001, Christian had been in intensive care for nine days with a deadly virus. Concerned about Christian's recovery, Captain Barrere had gotten me reassigned to Employee Relations, allowing me to stay home for eight weeks with my son. An incredible gesture. I was pleased to say Christian was now doing great.

"Chris, I need a favor."

"Anything, boss."

"I need you to take the FIO [field intelligence officer] spot for Captain Harris." Thomas Harris was the commanding officer of the Seventy-Sixth Precinct. "I need you to please take it. After six months, if it doesn't work out, I'll try to give you a soft landing at the 114th Precinct."

"For you, boss, anything," I said.

By October 2002, I was reassigned to the Intelligence Division, specializing in interrogations, debriefing of prisoners, and criminal investigations. Because I had developed a reputation among the criminal element, people would reach out to me directly to give me information on illegal activity or to help themselves get out from under a pending court case.

One time we received a walk-in at the Seven-Six, a guy who presented himself as a confidential informant. *Joey the Junkie* came through the door out of the blue, went right up to the desk officer, and told him he was interested in speaking directly with me. When the DO asked why, he clammed up. I don't know how he got my name, but he insisted it was either me or nobody.

A few minutes later, Joey was at my desk telling me he had information about a cold-case double homicide—presumed to be a gangland crime—that was closing in on six years old. I hadn't expected that, but

I knew he wasn't a crank, because he mentioned some accurate details about the investigation that we hadn't released to the public. Joey confirmed our long-held suspicions that there was Mafia involvement in the killings, specifically by a wiseguy in the Gambino crime family—John Gotti's old outfit—which controlled all the rackets in the Cobble Hill–Carroll Gardens neighborhood.

Joey was not only from the neighborhood but also a stone-cold heroin junkie and errand boy for Stephen Borriello, a tough wiseguy who'd also grown up nearby on Clinton Street in Red Hook. It occurred to me that we could use Joey to get close to the supposed shooter, and that was exactly what happened. Basically, we gave him cash to buy guns and drugs from Borriello's partner, *Pedro "Pete" Medina*, who had inherited the drug trade from his *papi* and was now the exclusive dealer for Borriello. Medina dealt out of his apartment above a social club in Red Hook, as well as out of his girlfriend's apartment in the Fort Greene section of Brooklyn and his locker at the hospital where he worked as an aide. *And* he was the suspect in the old double murder. Before long we were introducing NYPD undercover officers into the mix and buying guns and heroin from the target by the kilo.

We ran the case for five months, conducting video surveillance of the dealer and an NYPD undercover cop who'd been introduced to him courtesy of Joey the Junkie. When we finally took the case down, I interrogated the dealer. Medina saw himself as a hard case and refused to talk. "I'll do the time," he said adamantly.

"Oh really?" I said. "Well, let me show you a movie. You like movies, right?"

"Sure," he said. "Who don't like movies? Everybody likes fucking movies."

"Good, because I've got an Academy Award–winning performance to show you, and guess who has the starring role?"

I played Medina the surveillance video. Again and again there he was, selling firearms and drugs to our undercover man and Joey the Junkie. When the recording was finished I gave him some mock applause. For good measure, I had the undercover cop walk into the office and give Medina a bright, toothy smile worthy of Hollywood.

Just like that, the dealer wasn't acting so tough. He looked about ready to crumble. I counted off the A-I felony charges we were slapping on him. "They carry twenty-five to life—*each*," I said. "We are putting the case in the hands of the US Attorney's Office, and recommending the prison sentences run consecutively, not concurrently."

That was it. He mentally and physically collapsed, dropping his head into his hands.

I moved in for the kill. "Listen up, bro. Before you say 'I'll do the time' again, think about this: Your kids will be married and have children of their own before you get out of prison. Most likely your grandchildren will be calling someone else grandpa. Is that what you want? Or do you want to help yourself?"

I let up after that, giving him some space. I was trying to inflict as much emotional trauma as possible without being too over-the-top or insulting. Awareness is key in interrogations. You need to know how far to push.

I knew I had the guy—but then, after everything we'd done to build the case, the US attorney stepped in and essentially stole it. I never learned what Medina may have given up about the double murder. But I did get to see our bust of Medina on the front pages of the *New York Post* and *Daily News* for two full days in April 2004. And I learned a key lesson during my interrogation, though it wouldn't be until years later in Iraq that I would reap the dividends.

———————

Because of the case's high profile, I was promoted to the "leads desk," from which I ran all of Brooklyn, as well as Manhattan south of Fifty-Ninth Street from river to river, on any case that involved a nexus to terrorism. We looked into any activity that made city citizens nervous, especially if it involved Middle Eastern men.

My normal day started at 8:00 AM and ended at 10:30 PM and involved suspicious packages, explosions, and stolen chemicals. Because of the nature of the jobs, I was called upon frequently, regardless of the territory or even the state line. New Yorkers remained safe as I became an expert in the use of the Patriot Act.

When I was in the field and Debbie was home, I always kept her informed, to let her know I was OK and what was going on. We spoke in a code that only a cop's wife could understand.

"Gonna be late tonight?"

"Probably," I usually replied.

My boss at the time was Deputy Commissioner David Cohen, who'd been a CIA analyst for thirty-six years before being brought into the Intelligence Division by NYPD commissioner Ray Kelly. Cohen was a creative man who could think both in three dimensions and outside of the box when combating terrorism.

My Job phone was a Nextel Direct Connect device with international capabilities. (The term "Job" here is not generic, thus the uppercase. It refers to all things NYPD. "On the Job" means you are a cop.) I was required to keep it on at all times, and Commissioner Cohen had a knack for calling at the most inconvenient times: on my day off, just as I was arriving home after a long shift, during dinner, during my nap, always awkward. Regardless of the timing, I would respond directly to the particular incident.

I also worked frequently with our counterparts in the FBI as part of the JTTF (Joint Terrorism Task Force). I'd heard the feds were glory hogs, but I was still astonished at FBI spokespersons who unabashedly stood at any available podium, ready at a moment's notice to take full credit for the hard work of an NYPD detective.

Nonetheless, I loved my work, and I became very adept at handling it, mostly because I was surrounded by smart and dedicated people. I developed a solid reputation as a problem solver and was selected for challenging assignments in which intensity was always high. Many of our counterterrorism successes were splashed on the front page of the New York papers—*Times*, *News*, and *Post*—or broadcast over local TV and radio news outlets. Other incident responses were kept on the down low, clandestine in nature.

But after four years of running cases and live responses, I was ready for a change. Retirement looked great. I knew I would miss the Job and, more important, the people, but I also knew from experience that one bad day could change everything. I was leaving on a high note.

2

LAST DAYS

I CERTAINLY WASN'T DREADING RETIREMENT. I had plans. But it *was* a major milestone, and the concept caused the usual restless nights. The official date of my retirement was February 28, 2007, but I had accrued more than fifteen hundred hours in sick days, vacation, and personal days, so my last day was April 29, 2006.

On the night of April 28, I barely slept. I'd had a great career, but after twenty years it was time to hang 'em up. I got up around five and turned on the coffeepot and TV. It was going to be a beautiful day. How could it be otherwise? It was my day and nothing could ruin it.

I packed a suit and some gym clothes. Not knowing exactly how the day was going to unfold, I figured better safe than sorry. I showered, and by the time I had finished, Debbie was up in the kitchen fixing us both a cup of coffee.

Debbie and I had been married for twelve years, and she was my anchor of sanity amid NYPD Intelligence Division madness. We both went out on the porch and she lit up a cigarette. She'd tried to quit, many times, but in the end how could I blame her for lighting up? She was a cop's wife, and that takes a strong woman.

"So, how's it feel?" she said with an exhale of smoke and a smile.

"Great."

"No second thoughts?"

"A little late for that," I said, then, "No, none."

"Good. What time will you be home? In time for dinner?"

The question surprised me. "I'll call you."

I finished my coffee and got dressed. In the Intelligence Division, you were expected to wear, at minimum, business casual. But today was my last day, and all I could think of was getting it started. I threw on a pair of jeans, a collared shirt, and a pair of highly shined black leather shoes. Fuck 'em if they couldn't take a joke. I hung my sergeant's shield around my neck and strapped on my Glock 9 mm. The shirt was left untucked to conceal my firearm.

I was almost ready to leave when my beautiful eight-year-old daughter Stephanie awoke from our bed. She came out of the bedroom and gave me a great big hug and kiss. My Kryptonite. Stephanie could melt me with words or just a look.

I gave her a kiss and said, "I love you, Monkey. I'll see you later."

"I love you too, Daddy." She had long blonde hair and bright blue eyes. The complete opposite of my wife's features. My son Christian, my five-year-old, also blond and blue-eyed, was fast asleep, also in our bed. Christian wasn't a morning kind of guy. I kissed him on the cheek.

"I love you, buddy. I'll see you later," I said. Christian hated when I kissed him, and it became a game for me to pull the covers away so I could sneak one in.

My Siberian husky Juneau came running up to say good-bye. The dog, like me and the kids, had blue eyes. Debbie was the only one in the family with brown eyes. Having two blue-eyed children and a 100 percent Italian wife is quite a genetic achievement. Turned out Debbie's maternal grandmother had blonde hair and blue eyes. She had a Sicilian background, and it was from her that Debbie inherited her sharp tongue and no-nonsense personality.

My wife followed me out onto the porch. "Have everything?"

A quick mental checklist. "Yes."

We exchanged "I love yous," and as I left I heard her say, "See you later. Call me!"

———————

I hung my suit up on the coat hook and climbed into my company car. Sadness radiated from everything I touched. All the Job stuff would have to be turned in: my car, my phone, my ID card, even my shield. So much of my stuff, it turned out, wasn't mine anymore.

No big deal, I kidded myself. I'd been to several retirement parties. Some of my closest friends. I knew the drill. Before I hit my first toll at the Atlantic Beach Bridge, my Nextel Job phone rang. It was my partner, Sergeant Mike O'Neil.

One of my best friends, Mike was an Italian-mannered Irishman. New York is like that: people pick up a grab bag of ethnic mannerisms depending on their upbringing and where they went to school. Growing up in Marine Park, Brooklyn, Mike absorbed Italian culture—to hear him on the phone you'd swear he was Italian—yet he was as Irish-looking as they come. He was also a sharp dresser, hair perfectly coiffed, with a penchant for fine dining and expensive wristwatches. He owned several Breitlings and Movados. Mike was a true street cop, a reputation earned working the housing projects in Brooklyn. Being known as a street cop was better than any Job commendation. It was a tag placed only on real deals. Poseurs were quickly exposed. Putting yourself out as a street cop when you weren't could have severe career and health consequences. It could get a guy killed.

"Where the fuck are ya, Skillet?" Mike asked. I don't know why he called me Skillet, but he always said it affectionately, so I went with it.

"Just hitting the toll right now," I replied.

"So, what you're saying is, if I'm hungry I should get something to eat now, because it'll be lunchtime before you get here?"

"Jeez. Last day. Where's the love, man?"

"Oh, that's right. I guess it's all about you today, huh? All right, I'll wait, but hurry the fuck up. We got lots of PB today." PB was code for "personal business."

"Four," I said. Code for *I hear you.*

The Job revolved around code words and cursing. We knew that our phones were monitored and were careful to discuss sensitive things only in person. I knew of the surveillance technology used in the Intelligence

Division and the data-mining bases used with cellular and electronic communications.

Traffic on the Belt Parkway was fucking horrendous as usual. I was making a list of things I wasn't going to miss. The drive would take a minimum of an hour, but who cared? It was not as if I had anything scheduled. I merged onto the Belt, passed JFK Airport on my left, and pulled off the parkway just past the Verrazano-Narrows Bridge exit. My office was inside a warehouse at the Brooklyn Army Terminal. "Security" at the gate was provided by jackasses with square badges. There was no telling how closely they would scrutinize your parking permit. Sometimes they were hungover and didn't care. I had a nondescript Job vehicle and a "pool plaque" that allowed me to park anywhere within reason in New York City. Those who didn't have a pool plaque wanted one badly. I flashed mine at the square-badged jackass and began my search for a parking space.

In my building's lobby I saw John behind the newsstand counter. He and his son were Chinese immigrants. They always greeted me with a smile and a friendly hello. Since I'd made Mike wait, I grabbed a copy of the *Post* and *News*, dropped a dollar bill on the counter, and strode toward the elevators.

I burst into Mike's office with a sarcastic "I'm here!"

"About fucking time. I was about to pass out from fucking starvation."

"Let me put my shit away and take a piss and I'm ready."

Once I was squared away, we went out and climbed into Mike's car. If you thought you might like to ride shotgun in the Indy 500, then hitching a ride beside Mike is right for you. He lived by the creed "control and speed." Our destination was the diner on Eighty-Sixth Street in Bay Ridge. We were there in seconds.

"So how's it feel, Skillet?"

"Great. I never thought it would ever get here."

"We got some PB to take care of today, so let me lay it out for you. First, we have to work out, and then we have to meet a guy regarding a security gig in Manhattan for a walk-through and threat assessment."

As part of Mike's daily duties, he performed security checks at area hotels and venues for high-profile dignitaries visiting New York. These visiting guests would have NYPD detectives and sergeants providing 24-7 "dignitary protection," known outside the Job as bodyguarding.

Mike continued: "Then there's lunch at Volare." Perfect. Italian food, Greenwich Village, where the service was as incredible as the menu. "Any problem with the schedule?" Mike asked.

"One," I said. "I need to stop by Lou's to pick up my ring."

Lou was a top-level investigator—a detective first grade—who worked out of the Seventeenth Precinct detective squad, but he was fast approaching mandatory retirement. Lou loved being a detective, and leaving the Job was going to be tough for him. He had a side business selling jewelry, with a shop on Canal Street in Chinatown. I had ordered from Lou a sergeant's ring bearing my shield number, made of white gold with a yellow-gold shield attached to the top. I didn't want to wear it until I was actually retired.

We finished breakfast and headed back to the office. "Where is everybody?" I asked.

"Out on cases and a response by the Marriott Hotel in downtown Brooklyn." Mike said.

Strange, I thought. My phone hadn't rung about the Marriott job. My Job phone was never off, even when I was on vacation. If the Job called, I was expected to answer. (On the other hand, the Job allowed me to make personal calls on my work phone—I hadn't had a phone bill for four years.) Maybe there was a reason my phone didn't ring. Maybe a courtesy from the operations desk. My buddy Sean Gelfand ran the desk from a discreet location in Chelsea, so perhaps he figured I'd be preoccupied with PB.

Sean was a sergeant, half Irish, half Jewish, and another best friend. He was six two, 220, all muscle. Sean was also a street cop, experienced in martial arts. Those who tried to exploit Sean's easy demeanor were quickly corrected.

On one occasion, I was working with Sean in plainclothes near the United Nations during a World Trade Organization demonstration. There were more than a million people there, so there were bound to be a few assholes. One scumbag decided to push down a barricade manned by three rookie cops and cross into the frozen zone. Without hesitation, Sean grabbed the interloper by the seat of his pants and scruff of his jacket collar and tossed him back over the top of the reerected barrier. From that day on, Sean was known affectionately as "the Dwarf Tosser"—no offense to actual little people.

Impressive, and fucking hilarious, but Sean wasn't finished. He pulled a telescoping baton from his pants pocket and swung it with great velocity, extending it like an antenna into the ready position. The metallic whipping sound of the baton caused a grown man to shriek like a little girl, "Look out, he's got a weapon!"

If the shit hit the fan, you wanted to be standing beside Sean.

I changed into my workout clothes and made my way toward the gym. Mike met me in the hallway.

"What do you want to do today?" Mike said.

"Chest," I said.

One of the Job's greatest perks was being able to get in a workout on department time. We finished our routine in about an hour. After showering, I put on a suit. Volare was on the fancy side.

Mike and I sat in traffic on the Gowanus Expressway because of the never-ending construction. Road construction and traffic was one of the primary reasons I'd decided to move my family out of New York.

We got to Lou's shop in about forty minutes. As soon as I walked in, Lou greeted me with a big smile and went to the safe to bring out my ring.

"What do you think?" Lou asked.

It looked beautiful. "Fantastic, Lou," I said. I put it on and showed it to Mike.

"Nice, man. Congratulations—you earned it."

I attempted to settle up, but Lou said, "It's taken care of," and shot a glance at Mike.

"Wear it well. It's from the boys," Mike said, meaning him, Sean, and our retired buddy Jimmy Harkins.

I was like a little kid, looking at my ring over and over again.

We left and continued on to our next stop, the Ritz-Carlton in Battery Park City. There we met with Carlos Mendes, the director of hotel security. Carlos was a retired NYPD lieutenant whom Mike knew from his days in the Three-Two squad in Harlem. Mike explained that the dignitary would be arriving the following week and that we were here for the walk-through and to tighten up loose ends. The last thing the Job wanted was a guest of New York City falling victim to a crime. Mike went through a mental checklist of deficiencies and manpower needs and explained to Carlos that a complete security detail would be finalized by week's end.

The whole consultation took a half hour. "We'll be in touch," he concluded. We shook hands and left the hotel.

Mike said, "Well, I don't know about you, but all this work shit has made me hungry."

"Twist my arm, let's go," I said.

Mike made a quick call to the office, then we went to Volare and found a parking spot right out front. Not that the spot was legal, but we had a pool plaque, which Mike threw on the dashboard.

Going in, Mike grabbed the door and said, "Age before beauty."

The instant I got my head in the door I heard it.

"*SURPRISE!*"

There were about thirty-five of them, grins as shiny as high beams.

I shook my head at Mike, who gave me a hug and said, "Congratulations, man."

Everyone there was someone I really cared about. One by one they came up to me, let me know I was appreciated and would be missed. With each embrace, each shared personal memory, I felt a strong sense of family, and I started to feel sad.

This was it.

Mike brought me a glass of Glenlivet scotch on the rocks and said, "Here, Skillet, no fuckin' Dewar's today, my friend." He'd been busting my balls about my taste in scotch for years, and he wasn't about to stop now.

I took the glass and said thanks. The scotch was magical, aged and perfected into a hypnotic flavor by the love in the room. I took a seat at the head table and felt like I was in a scene from *The Godfather*. The waiters treated me like a king. The attention made me feel a little uncomfortable. Appetizers and antipasto came. The smell from the kitchen was making my mouth water. I ordered lamb chops.

Mike banged his glass with a spoon and asked that everyone please take a seat. Mike remained standing.

"First of all, I want to thank everyone for coming here to Chris's retirement party. It says a lot by your attendance here. I know I speak for all of you when I say I have never met anyone nicer. It wasn't long after first meeting Chris that I knew he was a stand-up guy. Most of you have witnessed how loyal and committed Chris was to his friends and coworkers. I just want to say . . ." He paused, because he was getting emotional.

I was thinking, *Don't do it, man, or I'm gonna do it.*

Mike continued: "I consider Chris my best friend and one of the finest guys I've ever met. The Job is truly losing one of its finest. So, Chris, it gives me great pleasure to present you with this plaque, from your friends in the Intelligence Division."

There was an eruption of applause and a standing ovation. I stood up and gave Mike a big hug and a kiss on the cheek and said, "Thanks so much."

The plaque was a shadow box with a crushed blue velvet background. It contained replicas of my police officer and sergeant's shields. In the center were replicas of my medals and commendations. Below the medals was an engraved inscription. Mike read it aloud: "To a steadfast leader and true friend, Congratulations on your retirement. From your friends at the Intelligence Division." On the back were signatures and notes written by the guys and gals at the party. Mike handed me the plaque and said again, "Congratulations."

I was at a complete loss for words. I looked out at the room full of hopeful faces. They were hoping I would say *something*. I futzed with the plaque for a moment, hoping I'd think of something. I finally set the plaque down and opened my mouth, praying words would come out.

Luckily, they did. "Wow, first of all, I want to thank all of you for making this day so special for me. I am truly touched by your presence here. I also want to thank Mike for his friendship and guidance. If it wasn't for Mike I would have never gotten this far in my career, and that's a fact. I also want to thank you all for your hard work. You guys made me look like a superstar, and believe me when I say the credit belongs to you.

"I'd like to tell you a story about my daughter, Stephanie, that happened the other day. I was watching the news and a heated debate was going on with one of the talking heads and a guest. My daughter walked up to me and said, 'Daddy, can I read you a story?' Now, most of you have met my daughter, or at least been forced to see a picture of her. I turned the TV off and pulled her up on my lap and said, 'Sure, Monkey . . .'"

I tried to continue, but my mouth just sort of sagged open noiselessly. A wall of emotions hit me. My eyes started to well up. Mike sensed my distress and stood up, put his arm around me, and in a comforting way gave me a shake. After a moment I got my act together.

"The reason I'm telling you this story is because life is short. Never let what's really important in your life get pushed aside. Thank you again." I gave Mike a big hug and felt a sudden sense of relief and satisfaction. Sean Gelfand gave me a big hug and asked to see the ring. Jimmy Harkins gave me a firm handshake, and my mind flooded with memories. . . .

Harkins was a retired detective second grade, one of the smartest cops I've ever had the pleasure to work with and learn from. His partner Tommy Dades was a first-grade detective, recently retired as well, now working with the Brooklyn district attorney prosecuting two crooked cops who iced guys for the mob. Tommy and Jimmy were like the Odd Couple, but together they were brilliant. Their cases were legendary in the NYPD's Organized Crime Investigation Division. The two of them were responsible for locking up more murderers than the whole rest of the division combined. They ate mobsters for breakfast.

Because every night for Tommy and Jimmy was like a scene out of a Marty Scorsese picture—on the mean streets up to their knees in cannoli—they were relentlessly courted by the crime beat reporters from all the city rags. Their phones were always ringing from people who wanted to take rather than give. But that was the price they paid for taking on cases they knew were going to be sensational and controversial.

There were times, however—not often—when dealing with the press was less painful than usual. One of their favorite reporters was a woman named Michele McPhee with the *Daily News*. She had a nose for Italian organized crime. She was a trusted friend, and she never revealed her sources.

Michele was so impressed by Tommy and Jimmy that she wrote the book *Mob over Miami* about one of their cases. I'd finally gotten to meet Michele one day for lunch at the Pearl Room in Bay Ridge, Brooklyn. Tommy and Jimmy arranged the whole thing. The Pearl Room was an Italian restaurant, and back then a known hangout for wiseguys and their friends. Within the police department there was a list of off-limits locations, places where a cop was not to be seen. It included restaurants, of course, but the Pearl Room never made the list. Maybe it was the

Tommy Dades's retirement. That's Jimmy Harkins on the left, Dades in the middle, and me on the right.

squid-ink linguine, a specialty. But probably it was because the average cop was too cheap—i.e., poor—to pay $100 for lunch.

At the restaurant, Tommy had introduced me to Michele, who was both a beautiful woman and a reporter with tons of crime-beat game. Given the location and the numerous hoods Tommy and Jimmy had sent to prison, we sat facing the door so we could keep track of who was entering. Michele thanked us for the juicy info on Pete Medina; when we finally took the case down, Michele had gotten the "wood"—that is, the front-page story. This expensive lunch was a way for Michele—and the *Daily News*, which picked up the tab—to show their gratitude. It was fun to see how the other half lived.

My retirement party was about over, and folks were starting to say their good-byes. I stopped by the bar with Mike and my close friend Freddy Rodriguez for one last scotch. Freddy was Dominican, handsome and intelligent, a magnet for the ladies, and one hell of a detective.

For the last two years, Freddy had been my steady driver, and he was my ride back to my home in Long Beach that night. My Job car was gone forever. I climbed into Freddy's personal car. We crossed the Brooklyn Bridge in rush-hour traffic, barely beating a pedestrian who seemed to be alongside us the entire time. Freddy pulled into a bodega and bought a six pack. He was worried that I'd get thirsty on the ride home. I needed another drink like a hole in the head—but what the heck. I cracked one open.

We headed east down Atlantic Avenue through East New York, Brooklyn. This was neither the fastest nor the most scenic route, but it did get the cop memories flowing again. East New York was the homicide capital of New York City, the Seventy-Fifth Precinct. Freddy and I couldn't stop laughing as we remembered this and that. He kept calling me Sarge, and I asked him to call me Chris.

"Not today, Sarge. Not today."

Freddy's loyalty and friendship were unshakable, something you'd think would be necessary in police work but that is actually rare. We talked about the move I was about to make, that I was excited but sad at the same time. Saying good-bye to police work would be an easy transition. Saying good-bye to the friendships and memories would be hard.

Freddy pulled down my street and parked a few houses away from my home in the west end of Long Beach, a community of civil servants, mostly in the city, living in zero-lot, one-story bungalows.

As Freddy and I walked down the block, Debbie was standing on the porch, cigarette lit. I could see she'd been in on the surprise party thing. She hugged me first, but quickly went to Freddy, and I could hear her softly say, "Thanks for taking such good care of Chris. He's really gonna miss you, you know."

"I'll be down to visit," Freddy said. "When you're working on the house, you need a good Mexican."

We laughed. Freddy left and Debbie helped me get inside.

3

MOVING

The plan was to move my family to a quiet, rural Roanoke, Virginia, where in the summer of 2004 I had purchased a twenty-eight-hundred-square-foot house on a three-acre lot with a million-dollar view of the Blue Ridge Mountains. For work, I was going to be a home improvement and remodeling contractor.

Moving day arrived, and Freddy Rodriguez and Vinny DiMare came over to help load the rental truck. Vinny was a close friend and a detective who worked for me in the Intelligence Division. It's amazing that a house with less than a thousand square feet of space could hold so much crap. It was August and hot, and some of Debbie's coworkers also came by to help.

I came up with the five-second rule: if I had to spend more than five seconds wondering whether an item should be packed, it was discarded at the curb. Debbie is a pack rat and hated to part with some of the most arcane stuff, like twenty-year-old recipe books on how to cook by microwave. She put up a fuss over my rule but in the end reluctantly relented. When it was over we had a pile of trash twenty-five feet long and four feet high. The town garbagemen loved me, because I paid well. This pickup was going to cost me at least $100.

All this moving made us very thirsty. Luckily, I had picked up a case of Coors Light. I don't even remember drinking the first beer.

It was 10:00 PM and we were all exhausted. Something about moving just wears people out both mentally and physically. I said good night and thanked everyone for their help.

We were on the road by 9:00 AM. Stephanie and Christian were very excited and fighting over where the dog should ride. Juneau ended up riding in the truck with me. Nine hours later we pulled into our long, long driveway in Roanoke. Unpacking could wait. Debbie heated up a frozen pizza and I quickly got the television set working to avoid drama from the kids. Debbie and I retreated to the back deck to take a moment to decompress. We both reached for each other at the same time with an embrace and a kiss.

Later I poured a scotch; Debbie lit a Marlboro Light. Her mom called, and I stayed on the deck. I could hear Debbie from the kitchen telling her mother everything was OK and that we all made it in one piece. I looked out at the trees and sighed. I could see the stars and hear the crickets. Retirement was going to be great!

After we settled into the house, it was time to start my new job. I had begun doing construction with a guy in New York. He offered to buy into a business doing the same in Roanoke, Virginia. The plan on paper seemed simple enough; working with my hands gave me great satisfaction, and it was a welcome change from dealing with the stress of counterterrorism.

My business partner was *Robert Mason*, whom we knew through my good friend and the pastor of my church since I was four years old: Father Brown, a man touched by God. He married Debbie and me, and it was Father Brown that I called when Christian was sick. I didn't really know my partner during Father Brown's life. Oh, I'd seen him around in church once or twice, but I didn't get to know him until after Father Brown was stricken by a massive stroke.

I went to visit him in the hospital. He said, "This was not part of my retirement plan."

I tried to keep it positive and talk about the future. "Speaking of which, I heard about the house you bought and that it needs some work. I'm pretty good with a hammer—I'd be very insulted if my services were not used." I said.

"I'll take you up on that," he said.

Sadly, that was the last time I saw or spoke to Father Brown, who died on his birthday.

I spent the next two years, mostly on Sundays, renovating Father Brown's house. For much of that time, I was working alone with Robert, my future business partner, who seemed determined to punish me for doing a favor by making mad structural changes, moving walls, and rerouting staircases. As we neared the end of the project, I was sad and relieved at the same time. Two years' worth of Sundays away from my family.

Father Brown's wife was another very special person. She talked about paying me for the work I'd done on the house, but I wouldn't hear of it. "It was a labor of love," I said.

So Bob Mason was my partner in the Roanoke construction business. Right away there were signs of trouble. On the very first day I was painting a six-panel colonial door when my partner came by, stroked his paintbrush in one of the door's corners, and said, "Watch for the drips."

The comment infuriated me—the condescending prick. Yet it wasn't attitude that ended up being the problem but rather Bob's character. He was slow to pay me and tended to take on new jobs before finishing the ones we had. He was late and absent often, many things in his life taking priority over work. When he finally showed up, he bragged about his advanced education. It was his common refrain when trying to impress clients. If only that scholarly achievement translated into solid business practices.

After ten months, I'd had enough. My word and integrity were the two nonnegotiable constants in my life. I asked Robert for a check covering my stake in the business. He shortchanged me by $1,000—but I figured I still came out ahead.

I was once again out of work.

My new game plan was two pronged. I was studying for my Class A contractor's license while keeping as many irons as I could handle in the fire and distributing my résumé electronically. While waiting for responses that summer, I took the three best vacations I ever had with Debbie and the kids. By the end of the summer, Stephanie and Christian were thoroughly spoiled. Debbie and I didn't care. After spending three summers without any real vacation, it was long overdue. While driving back home from our trip to Florida, both Stephanie and Christian were already asking when we were going back.

When it came time to take the license test, the information was pouring out of my head. I finished with fifteen minutes to spare, and easily passed.

As a retired cop, I was also set up for a number of other opportunities, including any supervisory position in security. I had sent in an application to the human resources department at Virginia Tech for director of campus security, but they misunderstood and thought I wanted to be a campus security guard. I applied with the Roanoke County Police Department for a position as a police officer. The job paid meager wages, $32,000 to start, but I needed a backup plan in case all other fired irons cooled. I eventually withdrew my application after they insisted I contract to work for at least three years.

I also tackled projects around the house, but I constantly battled boredom. I'm the kind of guy who runs on adrenaline—and there wasn't much adrenaline in puttering around. I especially disliked painting, and so it was wholly appropriate that one afternoon I was in the basement perched on a ladder with a drippy paintbrush in my hand when the phone rang.

For a moment I thought, *Should I answer it or not?* After fumbling with the brush and wiping the paint from my hand, I decided to pick up.

The voice on the other end belonged to someone named Tim Clemente—a recruiter with an outfit called MPRI, Military Professional Resources Inc.—and asked for Chris Strom.

"Speaking," I said.

4

RECRUITED

Tᴍ Cʟᴇᴍᴇɴᴛᴇ ꜱᴀɪᴅ ᴛʜᴀᴛ ʜᴇ ᴡᴀɴᴛᴇᴅ to discuss my résumé. He'd cold-called me at 4:00 ᴘᴍ. I apologized for not recognizing his company, explaining that I'd filled out several applications during the past month.

"Not a problem," he said. "Because of your background in the NYPD's elite Intelligence Division, you have been cherry-picked for a job."

"What kind of a job?"

"We're embedding law enforcement personnel with US forces in Iraq and Afghanistan."

For the first time in many weeks I could feel my adrenal glands starting to pump. I could sense my dreams of a peaceful life and a new career as a home improvement and remodeling contractor slipping away. I didn't struggle. I let go. "You have my attention," I said.

"You will be responsible for analyzing intelligence regarding the bombs responsible for killing our US forces in Iraq or Afghanistan. Looking at your résumé, I can see that you're well qualified for this mission. And oh, by the way, did I mention the job pays $220,000 for a one-year commitment?"

I squeezed the phone. "I'm very interested," I said. "But I need to discuss it with my wife."

Boy, did I ever. A year was a long time. During my time with the US Marine Corps, I'd spent sixteen months at sea living on an aircraft carrier in close proximity to sailors and fellow marines, so I knew what I'd be getting myself into.

After dinner, Debbie and I went out on the deck to discuss MPRI's offer.

Debbie said, "Chris, I heard parts of your conversation on the phone, and I have to tell you, you haven't sounded that excited about anything since you left the police department. I say go for it, but only if you want to."

I went for it.

I was having trouble sleeping—nightmares. New anxieties were conjuring up old ones. My mom and I were estranged. I hadn't spoken to her in ten years. Some family members sided with her and maintained their own wall of silence. It was a mess.

My biggest concern was knowing that I would eventually have to say good-bye to Stephanie and Christian. I knew Debbie could handle it, but my heart was already aching from the thought of leaving the kids. I felt dread. Guilt. After all, I had persuaded Debbie that moving to Roanoke would be a good thing for the family.

On this night I got out of bed and went out on the deck. In a minute Debbie joined me.

"What's wrong?" she said.

"I'm sorry," I said.

"For what?"

"For all of this—the move, the business, everything."

"Chris, are you kidding me? It's not your fault. No one could have predicted this. You could've sat around and felt sorry for yourself and said let's move back to New York. That would've been the easy way out. But you chose to stick it out. This job is who you are, it's what you do, and you're very good at it."

Debbie grabbed my face with both hands. "Listen to me: God's plan and your plan are not always the same thing. We have a lot to be grateful for. Most importantly, two beautiful children."

"You're right," I said. My eyes started to well up. "I'm really gonna miss them, though."

"I know, Chris, I know. I love you and am so proud of you," Debbie said.

"I love you too. If I die in Iraq I'm OK with it, because I'll know I died doing something worthwhile for my country."

"How would you've felt if you died in the NYPD?"

"I'd've been really pissed—because it would have meant somebody fucked up." I asked, "If I don't come back, how will you and the kids manage here in the country?"

"No worries," Debbie said. "If something happens to you overseas, we are all moving back to New York."

October 29, 2007. Roanoke, Virginia. I got up at 5:00 AM. Everyone was still asleep, even the dog. I made a travel mug of coffee and shook Juneau's leash. That got her up. My husky and I headed out the door in search of deer and field mice. Right away there was action: three deer on the front lawn. Juneau woofed and they bounded away. After ten minutes of sniffing around, she did her business, I grabbed the newspaper, and we headed back inside. Debbie was on the deck, smoking.

"How long is the ride?" she asked.

"I don't know," I said. "Three hours."

"Did you MapQuest it?"

"Debbie, please."

Stephanie was up next, groggy on her way to the couch. "Mom, I need coffee!" she moaned.

"Mom, I need coffee, *please*," Debbie reminded her. In the mornings, she made the kids warm milk with sugar and a splash of coffee, which made it easier to get them up and out of the house.

"*Pleeeease*," Stephanie begged.

Debbie made sandwiches for the kids' lunches and helped them get dressed and ready. These mundane morning machinations were now so precious to me. I would soon be going away. I had decided that I would say good-bye to the kids at the school bus. My plan was to make each departure as normal as possible, so when the final one came and I was gone for a year, it would be like any other good-bye.

When all appeared to be ready, we again leashed up Juneau and headed out the five of us to the bus stop—but there was a bit of a false start as Christian said he had to go back in the house and use the bathroom one more time. "Go behind the tree," Debbie said. He happily, even joyously, complied. Christian was a mama's boy. There was no doubt that Debbie was his mother, a fact that made us all laugh.

By the time we got to the end of the driveway we could hear the school bus struggling its way up the mountain. I felt a sinking feeling in the pit of my stomach as I hugged and kissed the kids and managed to smile and wave as they disappeared.

Debbie and I were quiet. Even Juneau sensed the emotion. I took care of my morning hygiene and packed. When I was done, I found Debbie putting together a folder of my medical, dental, and passport information. She was very efficient. Twenty-nine years in the medical field had made her a stickler for detail.

"You should have everything you need," she said.

I did the only thing a man could do at that moment: I made out with my wife. Then I broke it off and said, "I gotta go."

"Call me when you get checked in."

I climbed into my truck and waved good-bye. I made calls while on the road, I-81 North—more good-byes. Before I knew it, I'd pulled up to the security booth of the National Conference Center in Lansdowne, Virginia. I gave the guard my name and identification.

"Company?"

"MPRI, ma'am."

The place was so huge that I parked my car in Lot C and had to take a four-minute bus ride. The complex was designed to host events for corporations in the government security sector, with more than a thousand guest rooms and a hundred conference rooms. The guy at the front desk gave me a name tag and a map.

A bunch of guys from the St. Louis police department showed up, and we became fast friends. I went to my room, unpacked, called Debbie, and went back to the lobby to order pizza with the St. Louis boys. The guy I talked to most was *Keith*, who said they'd grown unhappy with their department, which was jerking them around over raises, back pay, and the working environment. They hadn't retired like me. "We just quit last Friday," Keith said, and they all laughed.

After pizza we went to our initial orientation in a big room half full of obvious cops, some young, some old. For a moment I felt negative vibes, that I wasn't ready to start all over again like this—but I shook the feeling off. There were round tables and assigned seating, like at a banquet. I found my name card at one table in the back and sat down.

Bill Lloyd, the lead recruiter for MPRI, spoke first, giving a few introductory remarks and introducing the dais: "Starting from my left, Tim Clemente, Scott Marcy, and Bill Hart." Lloyd was a sixteen-year FBI veteran who had been working for the company for a little over three years. Tim Clemente was a California boy who'd worked as a cop in St. Louis, rolled over to the FBI, and resigned after fourteen years before signing on with MPRI. Scott Marcy was a retired army colonel and program manager for the law enforcement professional program. Bill Hart, the recruiting program manager, was another retired army colonel.

I wondered why anyone would leave the FBI after fourteen or sixteen years. The stories struck me as off. Something was missing. In my mind, if you had invested that much time in a law enforcement agency, you should stick it out and get a pension out of it.

After talking about the company and the benefits, Bill stressed that we were all handpicked and now part of a family. We were expected to take care of each other and uphold the family name. Most of what Bill said was obviously canned, but it was too early in the process to become cynical.

We were instructed to stand up and give our own introductions. When it was my turn, I delivered my bio in fifty words and the crowd gave me a hand. One guy at my table was Doran Michels. He'd done five years in the army, five in the FBI. Again, I didn't get it. Why split the FBI to do this? FBI guys being as they are, storytellers, I figured I'd get the details soon enough.

When the formalities were over, Bill invited us all to the conference center bar. Those who indulged were bought a drink and offered a cigar from a box Bill passed around. After a beer I went out with Bill and a few others for a smoke. I pushed the subject toward the FBI. I said I'd had bad experiences, found FBI guys to be podium poseurs, quick to take credit for other people's cases.

Bill said, "Guys at the bureau are short on field experience and interpersonal skills." He sensed my question. *Why were guys giving up pensions to be at this orientation?* Bill said the answer was easy: "We are all in for *one hell of an adventure* in Iraq."

For two weeks we were immersed in training: everything from Basic Terrorism 101 to marksmanship skills. Every day we were having new things thrown at us. Physical fitness training covered ninety minutes every day.

I was forty-six years old, and some questioned if I could keep up. I said I was a triathlete and would run with any man a decade younger. That got me volunteered to run some intensive workouts, but none of the younger guys took me up on my challenge. I would start out running with the others, but I would always kick and leave them in my dust. They finished their four-mile runs sucking wind on a cool day in November. Not good.

During the second week, we'd been promised a weekend off, and I was looking forward to a visit home. That Friday I was walking back to class with El, a former New Yorker now with the Brevard County Sheriff's Office in Florida. He was Egyptian, fluent in Arabic. We hadn't quite made it to class when we were met by law enforcement program manager Scott Marcy, who told us to follow him.

El and I looked at each other. This couldn't be good. We went to the adjacent office and were asked to close the door. It felt like school, having to go to the principal's office.

"You are fine. You are here because you've been selected for a top-secret mission," said Marcy. "Do not discuss this with anyone outside this room, are we clear? Do not go home and discuss it with your family, friends, or talk about it on the phone," he said.

Tim Clemente was standing behind me when he said, "The assignment involves investigating improvised explosive devices and explosively formed projectiles. This project was just approved by the Joint Improvised Explosive Device Defeat Organization [JIEDDO] only a few weeks ago. You guys were selected because of your experience and also because of your physical condition."

El and I accepted the assignment, sealing the deal with a handshake.

Marcy was beaming. "You guys are either as good as your résumés say you are, or you're the best bullshit artists I ever met. You'll finish out next week and be given final instructions on additional schools and departure dates next week. When you come back, you'll be considered 'subject matter experts.'"

Tim said, "You'll be able to teach anywhere in the country. You could even write a book about your experiences."

I couldn't wait to tell Debbie.

––––––––––

"I got a promotion from the company," I said to my wife.

"Really, that's great, what kind of promotion?"

"Well, without going into any great detail, they asked me to help with the improvised explosive device problem going on over in Iraq."

"Explosives?" she asked, taking a deep drag on her cigarette. "Who are you, fucking Jack Bauer from *24*?"

I was quiet. She knew I was not telling her the whole story.

"I'm getting another cigarette," she said.

That night, there we all were, two kids and two adults in one king-size bed. That was fine with me.

The next day my dad came to visit, to see me one more time before I went overseas. I gave him a three-quarters version of my future, just enough to worry him.

"I know you have to do this," he said.

––––––––––

Those of us chosen for the secret mission drove to Arlington, Virginia, to an office complex called Crystal City, the regional equivalent of California's Silicon Valley. The major military contractors involved in computer software and the security industry were based here. It was also a big recruiting area for former military personnel with skills and security clearances.

I parked my truck in a parking lot directly across from the headquarters of a major communications firm, an ultramodern building with a stone and glass facade. As each one of us entered, we handed over our driver's licenses and were cross-checked against a roster that contained our pedigree information and level of security clearance. Instead of getting our licenses back, we were each issued a temporary identification tag that said in bold red lettering ESCORT REQUIRED and were instructed to place the identification tag on our outermost garment, above the waist. We were ferried by elevator, our escort using a security badge attached to his jacket pocket by a retractable string to open the elevator door. When we got out on the sixteenth floor, there was another set of doors that required a magnetic badge and a key-punch code to open. Security cameras were everywhere, except inside the bathrooms—I think.

I was introduced to a Lieutenant Colonel Corrigan from the Australian Army. He sat at the head of a huge boardroom table while the rest of us formed a semicircle on the left and right sides. I reached for a pen and paper and was abruptly told to put them away. "There'll be no notes, boys. No copies, and definitely no conversation about this briefing, understood?"

We were given folders that outlined our mission. Inside were satellite maps of Iraq with colored arrows pointing in various directions. This is what I'd gotten myself into: In 2007, the US government's JIEDDO established a highly classified program by which law enforcement and military personnel, chosen for their varied yet complementary skills, would track down insurgent groups responsible for the roadside bombs that were killing our soldiers and marines and local civilians in Iraq and Afghanistan. I was assigned to a forensic exploitation team, code-named *Phoenix*, that would swiftly respond to IED events in Iraq. We would analyze the scene using techniques familiar to viewers of the TV show

CSI—except we would be surrounded by real-world destruction, and the equally real bodies of soldiers and innocent civilians. Maintaining a small, highly mobile footprint and coordinating our operations via state-of-the-art electronic surveillance and communications techniques, Phoenix would speed into Iraq's deadliest neighborhoods on lightning kill/capture raids, tracking the terrorists to their hiding places and bomb factories.

As Phoenix's lead tactical debriefing officer, I would be specifically tasked with questioning insurgents at the point of capture (POC). That meant withering New York cop–style interrogations done under the most primitive, dangerous, and challenging conditions. Afterward, the information I extracted would be turned into actionable intelligence for follow-on targeting and elimination of the remaining cell members.

"I apologize for the last-minute briefing," Lieutenant Commander Corrigan concluded. "The ink's barely dry with funding approval from Congress—hence the rush to get you guys on board. Any questions?"

Questions? Where the fuck do I begin? I thought. Here I was, sitting in a conference room in America getting a top-secret briefing from a total stranger—one in an Aussie military uniform with a matching accent— for a project supporting our military forces. I searched my psyche for indications of ambivalence but found none. I suddenly realized I was *all in*. I felt the adrenaline racing though my veins as I imagined taking it to those Iraqi bomb-makers New York City–style. I was excited about the mission but knew I couldn't tell Debbie about it. Operational security, as Corrigan put it. Besides, I really was a little bit like Jack Bauer in *24*, and I didn't want to add to her worries.

"No, sir," I ended up saying. I had no questions.

"Right, then, boys, here's my number in Washington. Once you get in-country, you'll be supported by a green-suiter from Canada named Major Dufour. He'll be running support and top cover on this project— here's his number. Good luck, gents, and Godspeed."

5

CSI FOR IEDS

After another weekend at home in the warm pocket of domestic bliss, I drove to Aberdeen, Maryland. It was a beautiful, crisp fall day. The hotel was brand new with all the amenities: restaurant, bar, and indoor pool. My room was an efficiency with a stove, refrigerator, and sitting area with cable TV. I had dinner with El and Doran, the former army/FBI guy from my table at orientation (he'd also worked as a scuba instructor on a cruise ship).

I tossed and turned all night, and in the morning I had a bagel and coffee in the lobby. El told me my ride to the Aberdeen Proving Ground was a gray Ford Expedition and my driver was named Tom. By 8:00 AM I was at my first class, which began with a video clip of IEDs blowing up US troop vehicles. It was disturbing to watch, knowing whoever was inside the vehicles probably died a horrible death. From time to time the instructor would freeze and replay the video, highlighting how devious these cowards were when placing their bombs. They used dead animals and live donkeys pulling carts to disguise their deadly devices.

We learned that bombers worked on a sliding fee scale depending on the type of vehicle and the number of soldiers killed. For a bomber to get paid, he had to provide the supplier with a proof-of-death video. That footage would make its way to Iraqi TV within minutes.

As the class went on, we were given instruction on electrical schematics and the different types of detonation devices used to set off the bomb. The lessons were very sobering. Most of the electrical components I was familiar with from my days in the Marine Corps. The level of sophistication varied, but every type of IED was lethal.

The biggest problem in Iraq and Afghanistan was the influx of explosively formed projectiles from foreign nations, in particular Iran and Syria. EFPs were far and away the deadliest type of device being used. Our primary objective was to learn as much as possible about the construction and implementation of these devices while taking down and disrupting the network responsible for their spread.

Easier said than done. We were dealing with a cowardly enemy unwilling to engage in a gunfight. It was so much less risky to detonate a roadside bomb from a hide.

We drilled on simulated post-blast scenes, learning CSI forensics. We would arrive at the scene of a blast, put the pieces back together, and analyze them. I had been the first responder to many explosions while with the NYPD's Intelligence Division, but the Phoenix procedures differed somewhat.

In the NYPD, I had been responsible for coordinating resources and establishing a safety cordon around the explosive device, either pre- or post-detonation. I gathered intelligence from potential witnesses and sought out video recordings of the area of concern. In terms of handling evidence, my primary responsibility was to make sure nothing was compromised—or, worse, taken as a souvenir by some jackass civilian.

In contrast, my responsibilities now included physically recovering evidence, capturing the scene with my own video and still photography, and interviewing and, if necessary, interrogating witnesses, who under my authority could instantly become detainees.

The instructors asked questions as we went along. In this way, we sharpened our skills, mentally and verbally. There was no script or limitation on the questions we could be asked. You were on your own and had to defend your answers. I was good at it—but not perfect.

Once, I was three-quarters of the way through presenting my case when the instructors began chiming in with questions. I answered their first two inquiries without a hitch. The third one referenced a trigger device, and I incorrectly identified the type. It was a minor mistake but one that sounded funny when made by a retired cop from New York City. Hell, I thought their accents were funny, too. We took great delight in imitating one another. It was never mean, just a way to keep it light.

At last we came to the final exam. I scored an 88 out of 100. The highest score was a 94. We all passed. At the end of the day we were all issued diplomas from the instructors. With each name read there was applause from the classroom.

I learned that after Thanksgiving break, there would be at least three more weeks of training in the Southwest. That would bring us close to Christmas, and I still had no deployment date for Iraq.

I met Debbie and the kids in Phoenix, Arizona, for Thanksgiving at my sister Kelly's house. Kelly's husband, Brent, wanted to know what I was up to, of course, and I had my vague answers down by this time.

"Stop asking him questions," Debbie eventually said. "He's fucking Jack Bauer."

It was a football house, and Thanksgiving dinner had to be timed to follow the Texas bowl game. Their daughters and our kids got along great. The latest thing on Brent's computer was something called Skype. I had to get this technology for when I was in Iraq. We ate till we were stuffed and napped in front of football.

The next day we took a sightseeing trip to Sedona. Brent and Kelly pointed out the large cacti called saguaros. They grew like big forks, with a middle tine and two end ones. They were beautiful and reminded me of old black-and-white western movies. We got into town and toured the little shops and eateries. In one store they had a cowboy outfit complete with a sheriff's star and two chrome plastic pistols. Christian immediately spied them but knew my feelings about guns of any sort, even toys.

Christian knew that the mere pointing of a finger simulating a gun was enough to draw my attention.

Debbie said, "You're gonna be gone for a long time. He's never had a toy gun. It would mean a lot to Christian if you bought it for him."

I didn't argue. I bought the outfit, and Christian was ecstatic. He could barely contain himself.

I set out the rules: "First, if I see you pointing this directly at anyone, I'm taking it away. Do you understand?"

"Yes, Daddy."

"OK then, just remember if you misbehave I'll take it away," I said.

"All right, Dad," Christian said.

After I handed the guns to Christian, Debbie squeezed my hand as a sign of affirmation. When we got back to my sister's house it was time for me to start packing for my next training session.

At the airport I pulled up the departures ramp and told everyone to stay in the car. I was feeling it and wanted to keep the good-byes short. I was efficient—kissing, shaking hands, love you, love you, love you, thanks to our hosts, and *boom*: my backpack was on my shoulders and I was walking away without looking back.

I might've looked calm and determined, but my mind raced as I thought not just about this good-bye but also about the big one still to come. Did the family understand why I was going away—for them, not just for myself? How would they remember me if I were killed over there? Who would walk my princess Stephanie down the aisle should I not make it back? I told myself to suck it up. I was just going to have to accept the fact that I would miss my family and get over it and move on. My mind still had a tendency to race, but I managed to focus. I believed God had a plan for me.

6

ROSWELL

Roswell, New Mexico, of course, is best known for UFOs, so as I headed for my training there I wondered if I'd run into any extraterrestrials. I had booked a direct eighty-minute flight to Albuquerque on a twin-engine prop plane. A puddle jumper.

In the airport, I spotted guys who I suspected were heading to the same training as me. One guy was wearing an Elvis jacket, complete with glitter, rhinestones, and embroidery of guitars and pianos. He was sporting large sideburns and dark black sunglasses that seemed simultaneously appropriate and odd. The guy sitting beside him was busy playing with a video camera phone. The third guy was older. He needed a haircut, scowled, and made no sound. (That third guy turned out to be *Zack Conte,* our second-in-command during my first months in Iraq. I ran into the cameraman later on, too, transferred because at his old base he couldn't keep it in his pants.)

We spotted each other but no one offered a greeting. That was partly due to the socially awkward situation and partly tradecraft, as there would be plenty of time for conversation once we were all sure who everyone else was. What was I supposed to say? *Hey, my name's Chris. Are you guys part of the Phoenix program?* No. We kept our mouths shut. But they were Phoenix. *We* were.

Sure enough, they all got on the plane with me. We flew to Albuquerque and moved to a narrow prop plane for the last leg of the trip.

In Roswell we discovered six inches of fresh snow, and the residents had all gone underground or something. It took a half hour, but a shuttle bus finally picked us up. After I checked in at my hotel, the guy at the desk told me a party of five men was waiting for me in the restaurant next door.

One turned out to be my team lead from Aberdeen. I also recognized another guy named Brian, and there were three other guys I hadn't met before. I got the lowdown on the training schedule. One guy mentioned they'd be ferrying people from the airport to the barracks.

I listened a lot more than I spoke and made a snap judgment that these guys were soft. They might have been Special Forces at one time, but they looked like they hadn't seen the inside of a gym for years. At dinner, some of them ate gluttonously. I was both the oldest and in the best shape by far.

After dinner, I excused myself, saying that I was beat from the flight and was turning in.

———————————

The next morning, I was driven down Roswell's main strip toward our training center. The street was lined with mostly abandoned shops that once catered to military personnel—tattoo parlors, pawn shops, liquor stores, and an adult video store. Some had been shuttered for so long that their signs were sun-bleached, their wood cracked, their facades a canvas for aspiring graffiti artists.

The training facility was an old US Air Force barracks for B-52 crew members. It was nestled on the grounds of an active airport that had itself been converted into a *larger* training facility. It was like some weird Chinese puzzle, a box within a box within a box. As we approached the gate, Brian entered a four-digit code into a keypad and we passed through. I could hardly believe my eyes. The barracks were largely underground, surrounded by active runways and mothballed airplanes.

So much for flying saucers.

The planes reminded me of a scene from *Mad Max* in which the skeletal remains of fuselages and jet engines are scattered haphazardly for miles around. It was sad and eerie. Some of these planes once flew combat missions. Now they were discarded like trash, home to wild animals, birds, and rust.

There were active hangars where commercial passenger planes were maintained by caring mechanics while their orphaned counterparts sat in rotting neglect. Military and civilian aircraft took off and landed on the same runways, simulating touch-and-go in some mysterious, coordinated training exercise.

We were directed to our "billeting"—that is, our rooms. Unpacking, I placed my clothes inside one of the green steel wall lockers that looked to have been built during the Eisenhower administration. The bunk beds were identical to the ones I'd used as a young marine in 1978. The floor was battleship-gray concrete, the walls off-white cinder block.

At the foot of each bunk bed were fresh linens, complete with blankets and pillows. As the day wore on, the beds filled up. These guys would all eventually be assigned to one team or another, but for now we were strangers feeling our way through awkward introductions.

At the mandatory after-dinner briefing, there was a lot of noise coming from the room, everyone talking at once. Old friends were reuniting; new friends were meeting. Mike Judy stood at the front of the class and asked that everyone take their seats. Mike was my team lead, a retired Special Forces operator with a gentle way about him: confident, friendly, and very intelligent. He also limped, which I assumed was due to a combat injury.

Mike introduced me to *Carl Solo*, a top executive at one of the other defense contractors involved in our mission. I spotted a couple other new faces. Guys were cracking open beer cans, tossing one to the guy against the wall. I was used to more civilized behavior. We were here to learn important shit. Why be loud, rough, drunken? Why the *Animal House* routine?

Carl ignored the beer drinkers. "You want a beer, Carl?" one guy said.

"No, thanks," Carl said, seriously. As it turned out, Carl was a former Special Forces sergeant major with an excellent reputation. He was about fifty, five nine, 230, with a thick neck and hands, rough around the edges, a master of profanity and sexism, not a guy that hung out with the country-club crowd, a guy who talked to soldiers.

He started by thanking us for volunteering, because "it took balls." He referenced our huge salaries: "Anytime you feel down in the dumps, you can look at your bank account and go *ca-ching*!" That got a laugh.

Concerned about our mental well-being, Carl told us about someone he'd had in his squad once, a guy named *Nelson Leon*. Whenever Nelson got depressed, he would start to shave off all his body hair. "I came into the room we shared one day, and there he was with a bucket of water and a razor, buck fucking naked, all lathered up with shaving cream, working his way around to his asshole, just shaving away. I said to him, 'What the fuck are you doing, Nelson?' You know what Nelson said to me? He said, 'My wife left me and is fucking my next-door neighbor. I can't believe it. The guy used to come over—with his *wife*—and have dinner with us. Can you believe it? This is the same fucking guy used to come over with his wife and kids and eat dinner with me.' I told him I was having trouble hearing him because he was shaving his ass. He asked me what the fuck he should do, so you know what I told him?"

The group said it as one: "*What?*"

"I told him, 'Keep thinking *ca-ching*!'"

Everyone fell out laughing.

"So," he continued, "whenever you sorry bastards think your life is over because your wife left you to go fuck your neighbor, just think of all the money that you'll be putting into your own personal savings account while you are over there. Me, I got two ex-wives, each one of them I bought fake tits for while I was overseas. I'm not saying you shouldn't buy your old lady fake tits, but I'm saying if you like her and she's a good woman, then don't be stingy with all that fucking money you'll be making when you're downrange and buy her a new set of tits for Christmas, that's all."

So I learned quickly that he was an aficionado of the inappropriate, and I'm a guy who once ate lunch and watched TV in the same room as a cadaver while waiting for the medical examiner to arrive. I'm a guy who once decorated a Christmas tree with photos of men who had resisted arrest and were bleeding from the head. I believe I know inappropriate when I hear it.

The oddity for me was that this was the opening speech from a top defense executive, who I imagined was a lot of laughs outside of work and an accomplished soldier, but for now seemed more like a stand-up comedian than a trained killer. Funny as hell, though.

––––––––––––––

A lot was crammed into the next three weeks. The majority of our instructors were former Special Operations Forces—Delta Force, top of the food chain when it came to difficult training, assignments, and operations—with little patience or respect for civilian law enforcement types like me. But when we got to the shooting range and field exercises, I showed them there's no replacement for twenty-plus years with the NYPD.

After the first week of training, we were transferred to a place called the Ranch. Over 250,000 acres in size, it was an actual working ranch in the middle of the desert. There we put on camouflage uniforms and grabbed our weapons. Everything we did had a single purpose, and that was to replicate the treacherous situations we would face on the ground in Iraq. We practiced breaching buildings and shooting from organized movements in a team framework. We engaged in combat weapons training and a full seven days of flat-range shooting with domestic and foreign rifles and pistols. We learned how to drive in a convoy formation and repel an assault from an opposing force. We did high-speed combat driving and "driver-down" maneuvers, which simulated riding in a vehicle with a killed or wounded driver. The vehicles were equipped with a remote kill switch that unexpectedly disabled them while in motion— chaos if you weren't keeping an eye on your formation and teammates. Finally, we learned more about how to respond to a post-blast site and apply our diverse skill sets to analyzing the scene. When that exercise was finished, we returned to the hangar and wrote up a report that drew on our various disciplines.

I'd had hopes that Roswell would be my final three weeks of training before going overseas, but Carl dispelled that notion. After Christmas break, there would be another month in Fort Hood, Texas, the army's top installation for training heavy forces.

When the meeting was over I called Debbie and gave her the headline: "I'm going to get a Christmas break."

7

FORT HOOD

FORT HOOD TRAINING DRONED. At the end of each day, right after dinner, Rob Lambert, a retired US Army Special Forces warrant officer, would announce the next day's schedule. We only had one question: When are we leaving? The answer was always the same: it's being worked out.

It didn't seem that complicated to me—get a military plane to fly us overseas so we could get the show on the road—but I wasn't an expert in the subject, so I kept my mouth shut. I suspected a problem, a delay or something, the cause of which Rob was keeping secret. I thought it was a bad move on his part. Keep your men informed. That's good leadership. On the other hand, we could tell Rob was genuinely frustrated by the lack of logistical support, and to avoid idle hands, he kept our days filled with training. But since we could sense that the training was just killing time, it dragged on to the point of being obnoxious.

I had no doubt Rob was in there plugging. He was as eager to get downrange as the rest of us. I could hear him striding down the hotel hallway with his Bluetooth affixed to his ear, yelling at some green-suiter: "Where's the *goddamn* plane? I got sixty fucking guys sitting on their asses. What's it going to take to make this happen? Wait a second. Ears." Then he'd wait for a stranger to pass before continuing the tirade.

Not everything remained static. We were joined by some new members during this period; the timing made me wonder if their arrival had been the cause of the delay.

One of the new guys was named *J.R.*, and right away he rubbed me the wrong way. I'd known him for a matter of seconds when I knew my quality of life had just taken a hit. He was a recently retired sergeant major from Army Special Forces who was still running out his terminal leave. He stood five ten with his pencil-thin Dick Dastardly 'stache. He was loud, brash, and a braggart, the kind of guy who'd elbow his way uninvited into a group of senior teammates at the bar, causing the conversation to come to a halt. Everything he said had a can-you-top-this feel to it.

One of the most obnoxious things about J.R. was he was friends with the management, including Carl Solo, and he was quick and skillful at mentioning it. It was his way of telling you that you couldn't fuck with him. He was a Puerto Rican New Yorker with an accent that made me sound like I was from Ohio.

During our introduction, I let J.R. know that I was the team's law enforcement adviser (LEA). Without missing a beat, J.R. snarled, "Cop, huh? Most of the cops I knew in New York were stupid."

"Do you base that on personal relationships or personal experience?" I asked.

"*Oooooh*, burn," said several bystanders.

He sputtered a little and then ran down his CV for me. With limited vocabulary and interpersonal skills, he made it clear he considered himself the best of the best. For me, the question was how the hell he had made it into the position he was now in.

The most aggravating part was that J.R. was replacing Mike Judy, who'd been with us throughout training. What the fuck—this asshole was here not even five minutes and already he was replacing Mike, a man in whom I had complete confidence, a true leader who possessed all the tools needed to move a team of type A personalities through a war zone, treacherous terrain, and *combat*.

It only got worse. Zack Conte, our second-in-command—I remembered him in the airport waiting for the puddle jumper to Albuquerque—would be working hand in hand with J.R. as his underling, the blind leading the blind, two village idiots careening their way through the town square, drunk with ego.

Another newcomer was a former Navy SEAL and combat medic, *Dr. Lester Theron*, whom we called Sawbones. He was fifty-one years old and fighting the horrors of a full-blown midlife crisis, constantly bringing up his age, quaffing compulsively at a variety of theoretical fountains of youth.

Sawbones's stories sometimes featured him—in the deep past, presumably—receiving the gentle attentions of fresh-faced and barely legal women, which struck me as grisly despite the locker room atmosphere we were in. It was hard to separate fact from fiction, as Sawbones volleyed effortlessly between the two. Made a fortune in the stock market. Was a tenured high school English teacher with bubble gum–snapping coeds staying after class for some private tutoring.

Sawbones claimed to have become disabled while in the navy, yet he remained in an active reserve unit as an officer. I know because I saw Sawbones's ID card one day. I recognized it from when I was in the Marine Corps, a Common Access Card for active duty personnel. Another inconsistency I would file away under "Bullshit."

Last of the new arrivals was *Jesse Hamlin*, a guy we called Hammy, forty-five years old, five eight, 190. He wore black Ray-Ban Wayfarer sunglasses regardless of the time of day. He most amazing stat was that he'd managed twenty-six years in the army without being kicked out.

Hammy wasn't one of those ironic nicknames. It was accurate—unfortunately. He wasn't a flat-out braggart like J.R. and Sawbones. It was more of a stroll with him down a hall of shame. He'd retired from the Special Forces at the lofty position of staff sergeant with nineteen official letters of reprimand. Before that, he'd been an instructor at the army's Special Forces "Q" course. It sounded impressive on the surface, but I knew the army sent problem children like Hammy to the Q course as a form of punishment or isolation from harm. Q course limited his ability to join a Special Forces unit deploying to a combat zone while keeping him under a watchful eye at the same time. Now he was on my team. Yay.

Hammy's career path reminded me of an NYPD process whereby guys that fucked up—say, they were involved in domestic abuse or questionable shootings—were put into a work pool called the Rubber-Gun

Squad. These guys would find themselves in the bowels of a Central Booking facility in a particularly charred section of the South Bronx or East New York, processing another cop's arrests. The specific assignments were just as mean: as far from the cop's home as possible, preferably requiring a commute with tolls. The Job could dole out vindictive and harsh punishment like no other workplace. Investigations lasted years, holding up promotions and retirement.

Until this point, I'd had a lustrous notion of the Special Forces. They were trained killers, the true silent professionals. But when I met the newcomers at Fort Hood, my fantasy lost its luster. How the fuck did these guys get a top-secret security clearance? It boggled the mind.

"What the hell am I doing here?" I asked. I couldn't help but project. I imagined myself casing a dirty street in Iraq, one bad move and things could go badly, and J.R. or Hammy was at my side—my fucking "leader." We were dead meat.

———————

On January 29, 2008, Rob gave us the word: "We have manifested a flight for Sunday, February 3." That was Super Bowl Sunday, so at first we thought he was joking. Rob said no joke, be packed and ready to go at 0600.

"Tomorrow we finish the palletization of all the hard gear for the plane," he said. This task involved stacking items, and restacking already stacked items, according to military regulations. Prior to placing any equipment on the plane, a K-9 team with drug-sniffing dogs made sure no one was smuggling aboard any contraband. A month earlier I would have said the dogs were unnecessary, but considering the guys we picked up at the last second it was probably a good idea. I was rooting for Hammy to be caught holding the bag, but we all passed the preflight inspection with flying colors.

Some of the guys took a last trip to Austin, about an hour's drive. Others flew in their wives or girlfriends. I called Debbie to tell her we were reportedly leaving Sunday. We decided to hold off on telling the kids until we were sure.

The next five days moved with excruciating monotony. I could kill three hours a day in the gym, but that left twenty-one with nothing to do but wait. I packed my stuff, unpacked my stuff, packed it again. Eating became a chore—nerves, I guess. Sleep was troubled by bad dreams. In one recurring nightmare, I pulled the trigger on my M4 rifle only to hear a click. I tried to clear the problem again and again. *Click.* I tried pulling harder and harder, wrapping both of my index fingers around each other squeezing with all my might. *Click.*

I thought about dying. One thing was for sure: if I died, Debbie had things at home under control, no worries there. My worries were more selfish. I worried about the things I would miss. I thought about Stephanie, my angel. What would her first boyfriend be like? Would he break her heart? Would she remember the times I used to tease her saying she couldn't have a boyfriend until she was thirty-five, that I was always going to be her boyfriend, and she was always going to be my Monkey?

I thought about my relationship with Christian and how it had grown close over the summer. Would he even remember me? I thought about how sick he was when he was a baby and how it had aged Debbie and me, changed us really, strengthening our relationship. Not having had my father in my life growing up, I wondered if Christian would become angry as I had, suffering in silence, feeling abandoned, betrayed by a man he barely knew. Would Christian struggle in school like me, not because he wasn't smart but because of repressed feelings that interfered with socialization? Would he join the Marine Corps, fight in faraway lands, become a father, and have a son? Would he become a cop addicted to catching bad guys?

Would Debbie remarry? Would the kids call the new guy Dad?

Sunday came. I stood on the flight line watching the last pallet loaded onto the air force C-17 cargo plane. Some of the guys posed for photos with the plane. I made "This is it" phone calls: my best friend Steve, whom I'd known since I was four and whose brother died on 9/11; Gerard Ahearn, one of my detectives whose son had been stricken with cancer and made a miraculous recovery; Mary, who was more like a sister to me than my own, who told me she loved me and to be careful; Aisha, who was Mary's detective partner and about to get married and was hoping I'd be home in time for the wedding; my sisters Kelly, whose cell phone went directly to voice mail, Cindy, the same, and Diane, who spoke to me for five minutes before breaking down saying be careful. And my father, who struggled to find the right words. Of course, there was one call left, the one I dreaded most.

I told Debbie this was it, to put me on with the kids. I told Christian that his job was to take good care of Juneau. He asked if I'd buy him a BB gun when I got back. I said sure. Stephanie and Debbie told me to be careful. They all said their "I love yous," and that was it. I had a lump in my throat as big as a medicine ball.

As I was filling out some last-second paperwork, Sawbones asked if anyone wanted Ambien. "We're fourteen hours in the air with a layover in Germany," he said.

What I really wanted was a stiff drink—but I took the sleeping pill. In the meantime, we hurried up and waited. An hour passed, and I didn't feel anything. "Hey, Sawbones, give me another one of those pills," I said.

I'm a big guy, so he said OK. Just as I popped the second pill, we were told to walk out on the flight line toward the plane. The heat from the engines' exhaust warmed my face. The smell of burning jet fuel washed over my clothes. My heart raced. Finally.

I walked up a ramp and into the cargo hold of the massive plane. Forming an island at the center of the large space were all of our personal belongings and gear, stacked expertly in a ten-foot cube of the pallets we'd been constructing for days.

If you, like most people, have never been inside a C-17, know that it boggles the mind with its tremendous interior. It is an incredible aircraft capable of carrying eighteen pallets of equipment measuring twelve by twelve feet at the base and eight feet high, an M1 Abrams tank, and up to 102 troops—at the same time!

I followed my buddy Mike Sullivent and we sat on the left side. The air force crew chief stood at the front of the plane with a microphone in his hand, giving us instructions. The men's bathroom was a funnel with a long tube that disappeared beneath the floor. There was a closet for solid waste. . . . The crew chief's voice became harder to hear, and I ended up reading lips near the end. That was because the rear ramp was being raised. The engines were still revving. Guys were yelling, clapping, and high-fiving with excitement.

In my breast pocket I had my Olympus camera, which was flat and copper in color. I liked the way it fit in my pocket, but the main reason I brought it was because it was water-, dust-, and shockproof. I pulled it out now and snapped off a few pictures: the guys grouped in full battle dress, some with stoic faces, some with huge smiles.

Minutes after takeoff the Ambien kicked in and I slept all the way to Germany, where during the layover we got to watch the Giants win the Super Bowl.

8

FIRST MISSIONS

IN IRAQ WE RECEIVED A RUDE WELCOME. The frustrations of logistical planning and coordination with the US military were no surprise, but I learned immediately that things were worse than all that. Once in the Green Zone, the coalition's occupied seat of control in central Baghdad, I realized the army guys viewed us as greedy, overpaid contractors. A lot of them didn't think we should be there in the first place. They certainly didn't think we should be given a role in their ongoing operations. So we didn't get any jobs right away.

I had plenty of time to wander around and get to know our forward operating base, which was located a twenty-five-minute drive outside the Green Zone, just south of Baghdad. FOB Falcon covered a square mile and was rectangular in shape. It had a great chow hall, complete with huge salad bar, hot meals, and a dessert bar complete with cheesecakes and Baskin-Robbins ice cream. It was no wonder there were so many fat Joes. The gym had more, and in some cases better, equipment than my own back home, including a separate cardio room with treadmills, elliptical machines, and stationary bikes.

There was a PX with all the basic needs: clothing, toiletries, snacks, and plentiful quantities of protein mix that usually sold out on their first day on the shelves. There was a Haji market, staffed with local nationals (LNs) who sold bootleg DVDs. (Ironically, in New York the sale of bootleg movies had a direct link to the funding of international terrorism, but for some reason on an Iraq military base, its questionable legality was overlooked.)

The laundry facility was run by the general contractor KBR and staffed by third country nationals (TCNs), Bangladeshis and Sri Lankans who always had a smile and a courteous greeting. I would occasionally buy them a carton of cigarettes, as they were ravenous smokers.

The detention facility housed approximately fifty prisoners at a time. The medical unit could provide basic treatment, emergency triage with a surgical staff, and a medevac helicopter that was all too often needed for the more serious injuries.

The base housed a brigade headquarters, which was responsible for the more than thirty-five hundred men and women soldiers. There was a chapel for religious services and the "Velvet Camel," a clubhouse that for one night a week, thanks to *First Sergeant Soloway*, celebrated Latin Night, replete with thumping music, red Solo cups filled with the liquor of your choice, and grinding dances. There was also a barbershop, a Pizza Hut, an Internet café, and a phone trailer for calls back home.

The place, however, where I spent most of my time, and would for as long as I was there, was the Green Bean, the friendly neighborhood coffee shop that became my refuge. It was like the coffee shop on the TV show *Friends*. It was where one went to shoot the shit, where guys paid off bets by buying coffee for everyone. It was where the baristas, Magish and Ganish, quickly memorized who you were and how you liked it, and had it steaming and ready for you in a flash.

My living quarters were in a structure called a CHU, a containerized housing unit. It was a shipping container approximately fifteen feet wide by twelve feet deep, bisected by a wall locker to give some measure of privacy from your roommate. My room had a single bunk bed and a handmade desk built out of plywood, big enough for my computer and some personal items.

After weeks of waiting around, wondering if we'd ever see the outside of our base, at the beginning of March 2008 I heard those magical words: "Up and at 'em, boys. We've got a mission . . ."

The objective was to support an army infantry unit called 1-28, which was based on Joint Security Station Jihad. JSS Jihad was located about eight miles north of our home at FOB Falcon. Our job was to clear a mostly abandoned residential neighborhood of Baghdad that was previously occupied by insurgents.

J.R. gave us our pre-mission briefing, including convoy configuration, billeting, and an estimated time of mission start and completion. I assembled my gear and packed an extra day's clothes and supplies—just in case. The mission wasn't much, but I didn't care. We were going outside the wire for the first time.

As I got dressed I thought about the different interrogation styles that might come up. Would it be Straight Interview style, very polite, as if I were an entertainment reporter asking a star about his latest movie? Or would it be In Your Face Fear Up style, in which I essentially worked around five primary questions:

Where are the weapons?
Who are your associates?
Where are your associates?
What's your communication plan?
What is the next target?

The idea was to enhance the psychological effect of "capture shock"— that is, the extreme fear and disorientation a subject feels during the first five to ten minutes of captivity. Capture is a traumatic event, especially if your front door has just been shotgunned off its hinges while you were fast asleep. The idea is to get as much out of the subject as possible during the period of disorientation.

We suited up in camo uniforms and checked out our gear and weapons. I put on my vest of two steel plates, seven thirty-round magazines of 5.56 mm ammunition, three fifteen-round magazines of 9 mm

A whole row of new detainees experiencing "capture shock."

ammunition, a radio, first aid kit, video camera system, helmet, M4 rifle, and 9 mm Sig Sauer pistol—more than seventy pounds of stuff. Standing up from a kneeling or prone position, or any movement for a prolonged period, was physically taxing. Temperatures were in the eighties, so heat was a factor. Dehydration is a silent killer on the battlefield. We were reminded to do a buddy check and make sure that you and your partner were well watered.

We gathered in front of our shop, bundles of anxiety and nervous energy. I was surrounded by retired Army Special Forces, Rangers, and Navy SEALs. We were a serious force to be reckoned with. Age was not an issue; maturity and battlefield experience would be the deciding factor. Many of these folks had experienced combat several times during Gulf Wars 1 and 2 and in Panama, Africa, and Europe.

For a photo op we stood in front of our MRAP (mine resistant ambush protected carrier), some climbing on top of the front bumper and roof. J.R. took photos with several cameras. It was symbolic and a way to memorialize the moment. Nobody joked after the last picture was taken.

There was an awkward moment as we shook the hands of those remaining behind. We loaded into our vehicles, signaled with a thumbs-up, and, using the vehicle's hydraulic piston, closed the 450-pound rear hatch. It was advisable to keep limbs clear of the closing hatch. The force could easily shear off an extremity. The engine roared and we commenced the twenty-minute ride to JSS Jihad.

"Lock and load," came the order. We loaded and chambered ammunition into our weapons.

The sound of rifle and pistol bolts slamming home was disconcerting. The gunner in the turret above loaded his .50-caliber machine gun. The driver, the TC (tactical commander, right front seat), and the gunner spoke to each other through microphones and headsets. I felt tightness in my stomach as I squeezed my M4. It was dark and I saw the face of my comrades only when we passed a streetlight.

At our destination we unloaded our weapons into a barrel for safety reasons. With our rucksacks on our shoulders, we were shown to our quarters, then assembled in the tactical operations center (TOC) for a briefing on the following morning's mission. Captain McClennon, our ground commander, pointed out sites of previous engagements of sniper fire and weapons cache seizures.

He told us of a prior mission during which a hundred homemade explosives were discovered in a house. The material was too volatile to move, so it was "blown in place" (BIP, or "bipping"), creating a huge blast that leveled the building, and—pause for comedic effect—rendered the lieutenant's Humvee inoperable. The blast's shockwave blew out all the tires. This same officer, Lieutenant Hutchinson, was to accompany us on our mission tomorrow and was given specific instructions on where to park his vehicle should a similar situation occur. We all had a good laugh.

"Any questions?" the captain asked.

We all shook our heads. "No, sir."

Exhausted and back at our sleeping quarters I bunked next to a K-9 team, retired air force staff sergeant Gary Martens and his dog Falco. For our mission we had two Belgian Malinois dogs with human tracking and explosive detection capabilities. Falco was two years old and mischievous, at one point jumping partially up on my cot trying to follow Gary to the bathroom.

"*Nee! Af!*" Gary commanded. Trained in Holland, Falco understood Dutch.

In an instant, Falco got off my cot and lay down on the floor. That's the last thing I remember. In seconds, I was fast asleep.

———————

Breakfast was potato chips and Gatorade. We only received one hot meal per day. Our indoor plumbing was for "water waste" only. Number two was reserved for the porta-johns outside. I found a sergeant willing to give me a hot cup of coffee from the TOC.

Our convoy consisted of two M-1 Abrams tanks, two Bradley Fighting Vehicles, two MRAPs, and two Humvees. I was assigned to a Bradley. One of the seats was broken, so I sat on a plastic cooler containing twenty one-liter water bottles. Nerves up, I had to take a last leak before we pulled out, and bellied up to a wall.

The driver stuck his head through the rear compartment opening and said, "I apologize in advance for the rough ride ahead." But he didn't sound that sorry.

The gunner announced, "Closing gate." As with the MRAP, the hydraulic rear hatch closed with a mechanical thud, followed by the clatter of a heavy steel latch. With a lurch and a roar that reminded me of a jet engine, we were on our way. The fifteen-minute ride was like driving over the metal grate on the Williamsburg Bridge in a Radio Flyer wagon.

Once we arrived at the mission site, down went the hatch and we took up a defensive posture. Iraqi civilians stared. Zack Conte assembled his team: two tracking dogs with handlers and four human trackers. US and Iraqi troops established perimeter security.

It was understood that there would be no element of surprise. Prior to taking any military action in a residential neighborhood, an officer known as the battlespace commander (a.k.a. the "landowner") would meet with local sheiks, mayors, and Iraqi Army officials to announce the impending operation. The Iraqi Army contained informants, holdovers from Saddam Hussein's Ba'ath Party, a factor that made it difficult to determine whose side they were actually on. Not that any real vetting was done—loyalty was tenuous at best.

The K-9 trackers went to work. After an hour, Falco sat down in front of an abandoned house, indicating the presence of explosives. I hurried toward the location with my terp (interpreter), Mikhail Greiss. Mikhail—we called him Mike—was an American from Newark, New Jersey, who came to the United States from Egypt as a small boy. Fluent in Arabic and Spanish, he was former US Army, with one tour already completed in Iraq.

After we established a perimeter around the house, Gary and Falco began their sweep. I was standing in the driveway and saw a shadow pass my left shoulder. I heard a thud followed by a yelp. Falco had jumped from the second-story roof, a twenty-five-foot drop. Gary screamed from inside the house.

"Gary, are you all right?" I yelled.

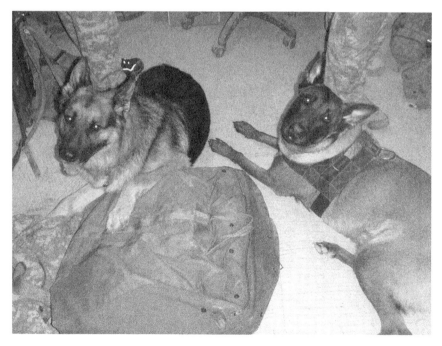

We never entered a vacant building until our K-9 bomb-sniffers had cleared it. Here are Rocky (left) and Bickel (right), ready for their next mission.

"Falco!" Gary cried. The dog was howling in pain with a broken leg.

Gary was distraught. Falco had an impressive pedigree: he was a direct descendant of a five-time Dutch champion. Plus, Gary loved him.

We loaded Gary and Falco into a Humvee and they were transported to the Green Zone for veterinary treatment. The rest of us continued our search of the area. After four hours, we happened upon an unexploded mortar round partially submerged in tons of garbage and the remnants of a bulldozed home.

With a smile on his face, Captain McClennon said, "OK, this time let's establish a perimeter to include not only the safety of personnel but equipment as well," a comment directed at Lieutenant Hutchinson. Everyone, including Hutchinson, laughed.

Moving onward, McClennon was met by a resident, who informed him in English that an unexploded mortar round was on his roof. Could we please remove it for him? After confirming the finding, Captain McClennon relayed the information over the radio, giving his grid coordinate from his portable GPS.

Zack wanted us to return to the house where Falco was hurt. Another K-9 team—Rodney and his ever-playful dog Bickel—arrived, and the dog immediately sat in front of the house. We searched for twenty minutes but came up empty. This didn't mean Bickel was wrong, just that none of the explosive residue left behind was recoverable. After six hours on target, we loaded up and headed back to JSS Jihad.

––––––––––

We debriefed with the captain, analyzing what went right and wrong to enhance future patrols. The report was made into a formal communication and forwarded through the chain of command.

After the debriefing, several soldiers thanked us for our help, which was nice. I would learn that didn't always happen. Many soldiers were jealous of how much we were paid. I would explain that we were older and wiser, that we'd paid our dues, but that explanation didn't always take. Same work, same pay, it seemed to them. But the soldiers and their CO on this day were great, and representative of all that was right about the army.

On the way back to home base there wasn't much conversation. After six hours of trotting around in all that gear I felt every day of my forty-six years.

But there was good news. The veterinarian was able to set Falco's leg, and the pooch was going to be OK. (In fact, when Gary later rotated out of the theater, Falco would return to the States with him, a very happy ending to that story.)

———————

Two days later, a call came in that an EFP had just struck a convoy, seriously injuring five soldiers in a Humvee. The battle commander requested our assistance in investigating the scene. A team was quickly assembled and the MRAPs readied. A call for air space was requested to enable overhead imagery from our drones.

We worked a rotation to enable training for each discipline, so this time I remained behind as the team rolled out, glued to the radio as new info came in regarding the device and the terrain. A teammate named Spike and his crew were on top of an adjoining building running aerial reconnaissance in real time for our guys on the ground. Spike's real name was Jason. He worked for a UAV (unmanned aerial vehicle) company, and only stayed with the program until the summer of 2008.

A medevac helicopter landed directly behind our office, triaging the affected soldiers. The damaged Humvee was towed back to the base. I went to the motor pool to exploit the crime scene. The smell of human blood and torn flesh was still fresh. The guys from the motor pool were washing the interior when I arrived.

I introduced myself as a member of Phoenix. "OK if I take some photographs and measurements?"

"Knock yourself out," the sergeant in charge said.

Teammate Mike Dominique had returned from investigating the scene. He and I took turns pointing out various examples of physical evidence, photographing as we went along. The stench was somewhat thinned by the hosing out of the vehicle's interior.

With a piece of string stretched from the interior through the six-inch round hole that had ripped clean inside, we diagrammed the trajectory of the projectile. Mike and I would need to interview the crewmembers concerned.

I wrestled between my recent training and my experience as a cop. It was a draw. I had to deal with a system that was foreign to me. When a cop was seriously injured or killed, police stayed, flooding the area, bringing in all necessary assets. The army pulled back and left the scene. A CO's main responsibility was to the safety of his men.

It took three hours to process the damaged Humvee. When we got back to the office we transformed into clerks and scribes, creating our work product, a comprehensive crime scene analysis, for the army.

Mike told me that while out in the field, he'd spoken to a man with eight children who said that the night before the explosion a yellow dump truck parked directly in front of his house, while a road crew repaired something in the median. Mike hadn't had an interpreter present, so I suggested that we follow up with the father of eight. "Let's talk to the supposed road crew, too," I said.

I asked the battalion commander to please inquire as to who was the landowner in charge of the road crew. After a few phone calls, I received a big "hands off." Apparently, the captain in charge of the battlespace had finally assembled a crew to do some public works projects and was not willing to let our little investigation ruin his relationship with his workers. He knew about the injured soldiers and was putting them second.

In the NYPD, that captain would be vilified. But I swallowed my fury. This was only a temporary setback. In less than a half hour, someone with authority granted me full access to recanvass the scene and interview potential witnesses.

J.R. said, "Before you talk to the road crew, let's look at Dad and the dump truck."

Another pearl of "wisdom" from a non–law enforcement SF soldier, a guy who thought most cops were stupid. As it turned out, I *never* had an opportunity to interview the road crew. The crew never returned to the road project, nor was I given the ability to contact or locate them through other means. A soldier had lost his legs, almost died, but that incident's importance paled in comparison to completing a captain's urban beautification project.

On March 7, 2008, Phoenix went outside the wire to reinterview the witnesses to the EFP attack. Again, I was not included in this mission, to make sure everyone got trained up. The morning before they left, I spoke with a team member who was going in my place, Lou DeAnda. Lou was a retired sky marshal with fifteen-plus years with the US Customs Service and the Houston Police Department. I gave him my two cents regarding what I would ask if allowed. Lou agreed. As they rolled, I monitored the office radio for any changes from the ground or air.

Two hours later, the team returned and gave an after action report (AAR). Mike reinterviewed the dad, and his story remained the same. Four others had been interviewed, one of whom raised red flags. His body language was bad, and his story stunk. He said he was home during the explosion. Rather than investigate when he heard the big boom, he claimed with a smile, he had sat inside his house and ignored the outside activity.

"You didn't get up?"

"I was watching TV," *Mr. Smiley* said.

If he'd been talking to the NYPD, that response might've earned him a punch in the mouth. No matter; we had his identity and photograph, which would be uploaded into the system.

We learned that two individuals present during the attack were not available for interview, because it was their day off. We were told they would be back on Tuesday. Till then, I was hopeful that Mr. Smiley was somewhere in a database and we could pay him a surprise visit with a set of plastic flex cuffs.

March 14, 2008. Mike Greiss and I were in the middle of moving into new quarters when I got word there was a mission, and this time I was going out.

I arrived late. "Didn't know you guys were having a party," I quipped.

"Hurry the fuck up," J.R. said.

I put on my seventy pounds of equipment as fast as I could.

We received a hasty briefing from our battle commander, Captain McDonough, who earlier that day had received intelligence regarding three subjects being sought for killing US forces. They were preparing to skedaddle, so they'd been arrested. Our job was to exploit their vacated house.

We got to the subjects' street and dismounted. There was the usual peanut gallery of civilians watching, in this case predominantly adult men and small children. Women peeked out of windows but did not venture out.

The K-9 team went in first, and we were given the all clear. While the dog worked, I photographed a concerned man and woman at the scene, who turned out to be the father and wife of one of the subjects. During an informal interview, the dad showed signs of deception, repeatedly proclaiming his son a good boy, acting nervous about the search, and answering repeated calls on a cell phone he kept under his robe.

I was partnered with Lou DeAnda. Our team lead was Tom Powell, a retired Navy SEAL. On the underside of a bedroom nightstand Lou found $4,700 in hundred-dollar bills, sequentially numbered.

In the kitchen was a refrigerator sitting atop a wooden box. With great difficulty we got the fridge off the box, busted the box open, and inside found several rifles. We called in Chuck Delp, a retired navy expert in EOD, explosive ordnance disposal, to see if the weapons were booby-trapped. As we waited for that, I advised Captain McDonough to take away the father's cell phone.

We repeated the search process at another residence two houses down. The wife of one of the arrested men stood outside with children in tow, begging us not to take her money. Inside, it didn't look like a home where a woman and children lived. It was a pigsty, with evidence of male-only habitation, more like a safe house than a residence.

At a third house, I was advised that there were six females inside, and one older man who turned out to be their father. This was a concern, because we'd heard women were being recruited to wear suicide vests to kill Americans. The sun was setting, and the house was without power. Our only light was battery powered. As I began my interrogation, the women demonstrated signs of deception and collaboration, so we separated them and interviewed them individually. Muslim women were not supposed to address or interact with strange men without a male relative being present, so the dad sat in on all the interviews. Predictably, he whispered in their ears and coached their responses. One woman with a small child told us she was a widow, her husband having been killed by terrorists. She wasn't good at providing the details, however, and her crocodile tears were wasted on me. When the interviews were completed, I photographed and videoed all of them.

One of the women, we were told, allegedly threatened to strap on a suicide vest and kill the commanding officer of the Tenth Mountain Division. The source of that info (SOI) was known only to his handler. We asked for a confirmatory identification to establish which woman made the threat. The SOI arrived, face wrapped in a camp scarf, two holes cut for the eyes, wearing sunglasses. The women were paraded for him until he picked the one.

All the women were processed with a system called BATS—the Biometrics Automated Toolset, used to take a retina scan and fingerprint the detainee. That info would then, in theory, be put into a central database for future cross-reference. The problem we were having was that the army was not putting all the gathered scans into the database, so when the same person had contact with US forces for a second or third time, depending on the capturing unit, the information was not shared. Additionally, there was no downward telemetry while out on the "X"—as in X marks the spot, while at the intended target location or in a declared combat zone. Out on the "X," there was no real-time verification like a computer check from a police mobile unit, so in essence, the ability to confirm who was actually in front of you could only be done at a hard site, and even then, only provided that the collected data was saved or accessible. (To me it smelled like the FBI in the JTTF in NYC: taking in all the intelligence collected from the battlespace and keeping it to themselves.)

Whether the BATS would do any good was anyone's guess. We were living in a world where a rich sheik's word was more credible than a photograph of a suspect holding a smoking gun.

Back at Falcon we received a message that a law enforcement professional (LEP) was to conduct a tactical questioning of the three detainees rolled up earlier. I knew what I had to do. I grabbed Mikhail and headed over to battalion headquarters to find a friendly face. I met with Captain Reno, the overnight supervisor, and explained my intention of interviewing the detainees. Reno directed me to a Gunnery Sergeant Casner for clarification.

I could tell by the look on Casner's face that this was going to be a hard sell. As a rule, he said, no one was allowed to interrogate the detainees except guys from HUMINT.

I smiled and said, "Hold on, Sergeant. I turned in my slapper and rubber hose when I retired from NYPD. The word *interrogate* has a negative connotation. I don't interrogate people, I interview people."

"In either case, you'll need a letter from brigade legal to gain access to speak to the detainees," Casner said.

"I'll go over to brigade to get the letter," I said.

I walked into the fusion cell, where all the collected intelligence is analyzed. You need Secret/Top Secret clearance just to set foot in the door. There I met up with the officer on duty, an attractive female captain in her late twenties. As it was 3:00 AM, she'd lost her formal ACUs and was wearing much more flattering black PT shorts and an army tee.

"I'm trying to get an endorsement to gain access to the three detainees that 2-4 rolled up, if that's possible. My services were requested by 2-4, and I have the blessing of Captain Reno at battalion."

She said she'd need to verify the request. I waited. She worked quickly, and in five minutes I was in. I learned the location of the detention facility and began to map out in my head what type of questions I would ask.

We were escorted to the interview room by two soldiers. It was a concrete bunker with a rebar shackle point in the center of the floor for securing prisoners. There was a cot up against the wall and a desk, if you could call it that, with a broken seat.

With a clatter of steel bolt and a squeak of rusted hinge, there in the doorway appeared this large man, his hands flex-cuffed in front of him, wearing a pair of blacked-out ski goggles. A soldier remained in the interview room with us and gently removed the goggles from the prisoner's face, revealing the eyes of a stone-cold killer. He tried to project innocence and was prepared to deny everything he was accused of. Trouble was, he had no idea what he was and wasn't accused of.

I could see the coldness and guilt shining through his weak-sauce facade. I pulled my Olympus from my pocket and instructed the prisoner to stand against the wall where height marks were painted in black. After taking front and both side photos, I motioned for the prisoner to take a seat on the cot. With Mikhail translating, I introduced myself and began with basic questions about his background and work experience. The prisoner answered comfortably.

As the interview progressed, however, his facial expressions changed, and he had trouble making eye contact, obvious signs of deception. When I caught him in lapses of logic, he would recant earlier statements, qualifying his previous response if he could, changing it completely if he couldn't.

I asked if he wished to make a written statement. "You can write anything you want," I said. He said that was unnecessary and gave me a long speech on the virtues of his character and innocence, thereby negating the need for him to write any statement.

In my notes, I wrote, "Refused to make a statement."

I stood up. The prisoner tried to reengage me in conversation. "What am I being charged with? I am innocent," he said.

"All information and evidence will be presented at trial," I replied.

I looked into the eyes of a killer who had been caught and for whom reality was starting to set in. The soldier placed the goggles back on the prisoner's head and led him away.

———————

The second prisoner was brought in and the procedure was repeated. This prisoner was scared to death. He was a friend, not an enemy, he insisted. Surely I could see that. He told me that at one time he'd worked with US forces to interdict terrorists and their activities. I could hear the tension in his voice and knew this guy wanted to talk, and given time, I knew he'd crack.

As it turned out, my time was limited. We were informed that the prisoner transport detail had arrived and was ready to take the prisoners away. I asked for and received an extension of fifteen minutes.

"Care to make a written statement?" I asked.

He nodded, and held up his cuffed wrists.

"Sorry, not possible. You'll have to write with the cuffs on," I said, "but I will allow you to use the desk."

I took more photos of him as he feverishly wrote a statement in Arabic. A rap on the door signaled the end of my fifteen minutes. The prisoner quickly finished his statement. We shook hands. To non-cops, this gesture flew in the face of acceptable behavior, but I understood that this extension of humanity would have benefits for the next person in the interview chain.

———————

The next day, back in the shop, Phoenix was abuzz with activity. We'd hit a home run with this mission. J.R. was feeling pretty good about himself and the results.

"These guys are *done*" was the theme, referring to the terrorists we'd rolled up. We'd made a positive impression and justified our presence. We were, after all, an experiment, so that was important. We envisioned a situation in which our program could be expanded and used throughout the entire theater of war.

It could have gone the other way. Two key administrators from our sister unit had quit, citing "lack of job satisfaction." The reports coming back from Doran and El were painful to listen to. Apparently, the leadership on the other side of the "island" could not even get a sit-down with Big Army, much less be tasked with a mission. They had essentially been grounded, confined to the base, and never left the wire.

9

UNDER ATTACK

MARCH 20, 2008. THE PHONE RANG. An IED had detonated, killing one soldier and wounding another. We rolled to the scene to search for secondary devices. In weekday morning traffic, it took us fifteen minutes to get there.

As a standing order, at intersections the lead vehicle peeled off, holding back traffic for the rest of the convoy. This process repeated itself in leapfrog fashion. When we pulled onto the block where the explosion had hit, the pedestrian traffic was moderate, with most of the children standing close by their elders.

We stationed ourselves in the courtyard of an occupied house. While waiting for EOD to give the "all safe," I spotted a group of men standing beside the gate and decided to conduct interviews.

I learned that the *muhallah* (neighborhood) had been relatively calm for the past seven months, ever since the Sahwa, an Iraqi civilian patrol, had taken over. Prior to that, the area was under constant threat of Al Qaeda violence. The IED we were investigating had claimed the life of one Sahwa and seriously wounded another. A woman and her child had also been hurt.

All the gentlemen claimed to have heard the explosion but not to have witnessed the event prior to detonation. After recording their statements, I photographed the individuals for future reference.

The all-clear signal was given, allowing two of my teammates to move toward the blast site for exploitation. I remained on standby, providing additional security. Working a post-blast scene was the same as working any other crime scene. Rule of thumb: the fewer people involved, the better. With too many cooks in the kitchen, evidence tends to become compromised and degraded. Big Army, though well intentioned, was notorious for stomping on and screwing up crime scenes.

Twenty minutes later, I was called to the scene to help bag and tag evidence. I snapped a few pictures documenting the scene and nodded to my teammates that I was ready to leave whenever they were.

EOD was finished as well and was returning its remote-controlled robot to its JERRV (joint EOD rapid response vehicle). At a looping hand signal, we all returned to our respective vehicles.

Back at the shop, I quickly wrote my report, adding pictures from the scene. The Phoenix Team's report, compiled with contributions from across all disciplines, was completed in less than two hours. We were in a groove.

The power of an insurgent explosive device.

That same night the 1-28 Black Lions spotted an IED and wanted us to exploit it. There was disagreement as to whether the IED was real or fake. Tom ran the three-quarters of a mile from the shop to our hooch to apprise J.R. of the situation. After some consideration, J.R. decided against exploiting it. Intelligence reports later confirmed the IED was real and had been destroyed without incident.

The following afternoon I was invited by Captain Kevin Thomas of the 2-4 to view the results of a recent ISR (intelligence, surveillance, and reconnaissance) mission. Looking over Kevin's shoulder, I watched the video file load up on the computer screen, then an aerial shot taken by a Predator drone. It depicted a residential neighborhood with a vehicle speeding through a driveway between two houses. As the vehicle pulled to a stop, it was swarmed by a half dozen people. The occupants attempted to exit the vehicle when there was an explosion, filling the screen with black smoke and dust. When the smoke cleared the vehicle was essentially gone, as were the humans.

"What was that?" I asked.

"Hellfire missile attack on Iraqi insurgents," Kevin said. "Not just any insurgents—the ones that launched six mortars onto our base two days ago, causing serious injuries to two of our soldiers."

"Excellent. How many KIA?"

"At last count, six. Number should go up."

Poetic justice, I said to myself. I'd heard about the mortar attack on the 2-4 and had been worried when a candy-ass major threatened to retaliate with "sound deprivation." That was a PSYOPS program by which the army would go out and blast audio recordings on a loop from a mobile vehicle. On the recording, a voice would insist it was not nice to direct mortars and bombs at the army. At best, the loudspeakers annoyed the terrorists—and everyone else. The major was an asshole. Soldiers were under attack and he wanted to respond with a stern lecture.

Later that day, I gave Debbie and the kids a call. They were all out shopping at Target. "I just wanted to give you and the kids a quick call since the weekends seem to be so unpred—" I began, but got no further. There was a huge explosion, followed in rapid succession by two more.

"Gotta go," I said.

FOB Falcon was under mortar attack. After clearing the front door, I put my head on a swivel, searching for the source of the attack, but saw nothing. I made my way to the fallout shelter. Eight more mortars fell, emanating from a distance of two hundred meters, just beyond the "T-wall" barrier.

After a minute of silence, I headed toward the shop. Two ambulances screamed by. At the shop, the phone was ringing off the hook. We took roll call and everyone in our shop was OK. I wondered if Debbie had heard the explosions.

Lights were on in front of the base's chapel. Several people had gathered, milling about the entrance, talking in soft tones and smoking cigarettes. In traumatic times, the base chaplain set up grief counseling. That function was necessary on many levels and had a sobering effect on the soldiers as they passed by the chapel, a grim reminder that we were in a war zone and lives could be changed without warning.

I ran into Will, one of our interpreters. His face was white as a ghost. He told me he'd been in the Internet café, a joint run by a thief named *Simon*. While he was on the computer, the front door to the café burst open. Six soldiers came in, cuffed Simon and another man, and took them out. The café was closed and locked.

Apparently the army had been watching Simon for some time. Will said, "He'd been acting as a forward controller, calling in the near misses from the previous mortar attacks via cell phone, redirecting coordinates."

"Bastard," I said.

I called Debbie back.

"Sorry for the interruption" I said.

"Stephanie was concerned. She said, 'I hope Daddy didn't get blown up.'"

The attack killed two soldiers. One died instantly inside his Humvee, the other in the medevac helicopter. I took a look at the damaged

Humvee. The mortar had pierced straight through the hood on the passenger side. We, unfortunately, would have to retaliate under the Congress-approved rules of engagement. I swallowed my fury and went back to work.

By the end of March, I was fighting fatigue. The attacks continued—four more soldiers had been killed by an EFP, incinerated inside their Bradley. Two weeks prior, members of Phoenix had supported a mission with the very same soldiers who were now gone.

We had strict orders to wear our seventy-pound flak vests to and from work. Plus, sleeping at night was sometimes interrupted by the sound of 155 mm rounds launched from one of the base's artillery units. Outgoing fire was easier on the nerves than incoming, but just as apt to cause insomnia.

Stephanie had sent me and the guys Girl Scout cookies, and we posed for a group photo holding a sign that read, THANK YOU ROANOKE GIRL SCOUTS.

I received an e-mail from my son requesting that I call him on the phone.

"Hello," came Christian's voice over the phone.

"Hey, buddy, how are you?"

"*Gooood.*"

"I tried to call you on your cell phone, but I got your voice mail instead."

With that the phone went dead and Debbie came on. "Hey."

"Hey, I tried to call Christian on his phone, but I guess it was off or something."

"He's so funny. He talks about you all the time, then picks up the laptop computer and says 'I'm going to e-mail Daddy.' When he was finished, I decided to check it to make sure it went through and don't you know he did it all by himself. Thankfully he's got your genes in that area."

"I'm gonna make this short, I've got some work I need to finish."

"OK, I love you. Call us over the weekend."

"Not a problem. Love you, too."

———————

That evening I attended the memorial service for the four soldiers we knew who'd been killed by the EFP. The service was at the jam-packed Steel Falcon Chapel. The lights on the base's firefighting vehicles were flashing. An honor guard was posted in the vestibule.

From the side of the chapel I heard a young sergeant command, "Honor guard, attention!"

Seven soldiers snapped to.

"Forward . . . march!"

The honor guard took up a position in front of the chapel.

"Halt! Port arms! Prepare to fire!"

They brought their M4s to their right shoulders.

"Fire!" came the order.

Three times, seven rifles fired in unison—muzzle flash and the smell of gunpowder.

The honor guard saluted as a trumpeter played "Taps."

"Order . . . arms!"

The honor guard positioned their rifles in front of their chests, holding them at a forty-five-degree angle, butt facing downward. The sergeant called out the marching cadence and the guard exited the chapel.

After the service I congratulated the sergeant for doing a terrific job: "You guys looked sharp out there. You were great."

"*Hooah!*" he replied.

Exiting the chapel, I saw one soldier consoling another. One sobbed, the other held it in. A number of guys patted the emotional soldier on the back.

To most people in civilian life, sacrifice was just a word that meant minor inconvenience. The type of sacrifice these soldiers demonstrated was unfathomable. The expectation was you'd "put it behind you" and move on with the mission. Whether the young soldier could move on and put it behind him I will probably never know. I only know how sad he made me feel at that moment—and I wasn't the one who'd lost my best friend.

———————

I'd like to think of myself as a guy who gets along with others, but I am also one who doesn't suffer assholes lightly. Which brings me to this guy *Larry Humphries.*

Larry contributed five-page reports on missions he wasn't on. When others gave one-minute elevator speeches, he went on five times as long. He proclaimed himself an expert on "organized crime."

I suspected from the start that he had been an internal affairs officer stateside, and this turned out to be the case. He'd worked the rat squad for his local police force. I am all in when it comes to weeding out bad cops, but the guys who *prefer* that task are usually of a type: jerks. And that was Larry all over.

I wasn't the only one who found his behavior boorish, but I was the first to speak out. After he delivered one particularly self-serving monologue, I advised him to look up the word *brevity.* Several times I caught him sneaking off when he should have been working.

For a while I covered for him. If someone asked where he was I'd say he was at chow or something, but I got sick of it. After a while I just said, "Who knows?"

———————

Early in April, we went out on a mission during which we discovered a pristine Iranian rocket on a crude launching pad. The incident caused a rift between Phoenix and EOD. We were supposed to work together to catch bad guys, but it didn't work out that way. Anytime we seized enemy weapons, First Sergeant Soloway with ordnance disposal would order us to blow in place, thus destroying all forensic evidence.

The given reason was safety, but it was a slap in the face of the soldiers who were getting killed out there. Soloway could pretty much do what he wanted, because his commanding officer was a milquetoast. The rocket was found in front of an auto shop, but Soloway ordered everyone to return to base before the "mechanics" could return and be questioned.

Our report on the mission pointed out the stifling effect these orders had on our detective work, which might have hauled in terrorists. Those candid comments touched off a firestorm with the brigade commander, *Colonel Buford*.

That night I went to chow with the three Mikes on my team—Sullivent, Dominique, and Greiss—and who showed up but Soloway, who apparently had just gotten chewed out about the mission. He stared at us with a scowl. "Is there something funny here?" Soloway said, standing directly in front of me.

"I have some funny photos of a rocket you might like to see," I said. It wasn't really funny, of course, but the fact that the rocket in front of the auto shop was to remain mysterious stuck in my craw.

He got up and moved toward me, pointing his finger within inches of my face. "You're a piece of shit."

"Get that finger out of my face or I'll break it off and shove it up your ass."

"I'm going to have your job!" he announced for all to hear.

There was a mini-investigation about the mess hall incident. J.R. had my back, and in the end, it was Soloway who was deemed the primary offender.

Which brings me back to Larry Humphries. After my trouble with Soloway, Larry started to buddy up to me and, using his "rat" skills, ask a lot of questions. It was a mismatch, and his attempt to investigate me went nowhere.

―――――――――

April 13, 2008, 1300 hours. The phone rang and we were spun up for a mission. Word was a "high-value individual" (HVI) had been detained and the services of Phoenix were needed for site exploitation. It was a hot and sunny afternoon. The tactical commander made a radio request for a status check on the roads along our route.

Amber meant clear. *Red* meant take another route. *Black* meant impassable and closed. In theory there was also *green*, which meant perfectly safe, but in Iraq there was no such thing, so it was never used.

We got to the *muhallah* in about twenty minutes. As we neared the HVI's house, my services were redirected to the location of the detainee. I grabbed Will, my interpreter, a funny guy originally from the Sudan with an accent that made it especially amusing when he used American slang. We followed the staff sergeant as he led us around the corner to an Iraqi male, rear handcuffed, blindfolded, and sitting on the curb.

The battle captain gave me a quick down and dirty on the detainee. He held a case folder with more than ninety separate detainee interrogation reports (DIRs), some implicating the detainee's involvement in the emplacement of IEDs, causing the death of US coalition forces (USCF).

Looking at the photograph of the subject, we had some discussion as to whether the current detainee was the same guy. A fingerprint check came back "no match."

"I'm far from read on the case. Best I can do is a quick street interview," I said. My more immediate concern was the detainee's house. Phoenix was preparing to search it, and I was concerned it might be booby-trapped.

I approached the detainee and asked the soldier guarding him to please remove his blindfold. I had the detainee stand up and pose for a full-body photograph.

I introduced myself and asked if there were explosives in the house. "Tell the truth," I said. "We'd like to avoid any loss of human life, especially the children in the neighborhood."

He shook his head no.

I asked questions designed to confirm his identity, and he interrupted me to ask why he'd been arrested. "I can't tell you. There will be a formal reading of the charges at a later time in a court of law," I said.

I received a call over the radio, requesting my status. Phoenix was waiting to enter the detainee's residence.

"You learn anything we should know about?"

"No."

Apparently the detainee had left his residence and was apprehended coming out of the adjoining house, which was his sister's. Three adult males and four females had also been detained.

Interviewing Iraqi women was tricky. Under the dictates of Muslim culture, male interviewers were prohibited not only from speaking with female subjects without a male chaperone but also from any physical contact. This presented many problems from a law enforcement perspective. We followed their rules, but our courtesy was exploited.

Our immediate concern was the whereabouts of their cell phones. Inside the residence, there were several chargers plugged into the wall but no phones. When the women were searched by a female soldier, three phones were found under their *abayas*. One of the women was caught trying to discard a SIM card, dropping it to the ground. An observant soldier retrieved the card.

Photographing the women was tricky, too. Nonetheless, I always photographed everyone at crime scenes. If I didn't do it, it was never going to happen—so I made it a standard procedure regardless of hurt feelings.

Because a thorough search left a mess and didn't win us any friends, the decision was made to conduct a limited search of the residence, causing minimal damage. I made my disapproval clear. "You only get one bite at the apple," I said. "Anything we miss is gone forever." It wasn't my call, however, so there was no point in arguing.

I completed my interviews, took my photographs, and awaited the completion of the house search. The search yielded some computer media and text documents in need of translation.

We rallied up and headed back to our MRAPs for the short trip back. On the return trip we discussed the reluctance to tip—that is, thoroughly search—the house and the lack of a fingerprint match on the HVI. Was he the right guy or not? We looked at the photo from the file beside the one inside my digital camera, and the vote was about fifty-fifty. I said no. The photo evidence might have been inconclusive, but the lack of a fingerprint match wasn't.

While I was writing my report, the battle captain from the 2-4 asked for the current picture of the detainee. I e-mailed the photo and finished my report.

Later that evening, we received a copy of that day's storyboard. In the opinion of 2-4, they had in fact captured the correct bad guy. No matter to me either way. I stayed in my lane and avoided further discussion on the topic.

It was an example of how forensic intelligence can be lost or compromised. I mean, it is either a matching fingerprint or it's not.

10

A JOB WITH MEANING

Our next mission was to be in support of 2-2 Stryker Cavalry Regiment, Eagle Troop, in taking down two HVIs and a possible torture house. The mission involved all of Phoenix: UAV, K-9, human trackers, intelligence, EOD, and two LEPs. That included me.

This was a big one, months in the planning stages, but recently gathered intelligence had lent it a new urgency. We were told we might encounter hostile fire from the insurgency. At the briefing I reminded everyone not to touch anything that might be evidence.

We rolled outside the wire at 3:30 AM, my vehicle sixth in line in a massive convoy. The night was pitch black and a slight breeze blew fine dust throughout the base, coating our faces with dirt. Our parade was so loud there would be no element of surprise. They were going to hear us coming. Intimidating, yes. Stealthy, not so much.

I switched on my night vision goggles (NVG) and a green hue replaced the total darkness. The back of our helmets contained a glow stick that was only visible to someone wearing the NVG. We reached the first target at 4:00 AM, but the first HVI had squirted—that is, left in a hurry.

We turned the place over thoroughly and moved on to target #2, which turned out to be a false alarm.

At target #3, the potential torture house, a bad guy got in his car and screamed away, the good guys in pursuit. In his house we found four black ski masks with holes cut out for the eyes. There was also a gun belt complete with holster and magazine pouch, but no gun.

They caught the bad guy and word came down that he was suspected of kidnapping and torturing Sunni Muslims. We found what we believed was the torture house, a shell of a residential home with looped restraining pins cemented into the walls at head height. Narrow strips of torn clothing that resembled blindfolds and pieces of rope were lying on the garbage-strewn floor. On one wall, where the restraining pins were, we saw the vague outline of a human body.

As a camera crew from the army's Psychological Operations filmed the scene, a crowd of children gathered around. The kids were cute as could be, holding out their hands for candy.

I first saw the suspect in the courtyard, cuffed and blindfolded. I told the soldier guarding him that I was there to interview the detainee, and to please remove the blindfold so I could photograph him.

"What is your occupation?" I asked.

"I am a technician."

"What do you do?"

"I repair generators."

I had struck gold with that response. In a previous interview, the detainee from the prisoner detention facility said he also fixed generators for a living. His text messages indicated that the term "generator" was code for IED/EFP. "Generator repairman" was code for bomb-maker.

Ironically, most of the *muhallahs* were powered by a huge Caterpillar diesel generator courtesy of the US government (i.e., you, the taxpayer). That the earlier detainee claimed to be a generator repairman was an obviously rehearsed cover story that almost immediately fell apart.

Now I had a *second* generator repairman.

We knew a great deal about insurgency codes, which ranged from items you might find on a CV to terms of tender endearment. In Al Qaeda, the insurgency spoke in love poems and rhymes to help disguise their text messages, which they rightly believed were being intercepted by USCF. We had this guy's cell phone and he was laying down his cover.

Here I am making sure a detainee understands what's up. Thanks to Lou DeAnda for taking this photo.

In interrogation, the object is to keep the detainee talking. Calling the detainee out on every lie usually results in the subject shutting down. But even in a lie, there's almost always some kernel of truth and certainly valuable intelligence that helps move the investigation forward.

"Where do you work?"

This is where he screwed up. He hesitated. "There is no official name," he said.

"Where is it?"

He gestured vaguely, as if to say *over there.*

"How do people find it?"

"My customers already know where it is."

"Where is it?"

Again, the vague gesture.

"Is there a sign? Has it a name?"

"No sign. No name."

"Replace the blindfold," I said to the guard.

As I assessed the body language and facial affect of the detainee, I noted signs of deception, primarily the breaking of eye contact and continuous swallowing.

Many think there's only one interrogation of a detainee. The reality is that, based on my HUMINT report, the next team of interrogators would have a working roadmap based on my initial contact with the detainee. A behavioral snapshot of his psychology, physiology, and level of compliance all factor in and, more important, give insight into this person sitting in front of you. Responses to questions can now be exploited for inconsistencies, follow-on questions asked, other forensic evidence collected from the scene, and, my favorite, statements from fellow detainees can be gathered that either support or negate a working theory.

As I stepped away from the detainee, I noticed a large blue-metal drill press hooked up to some type of timing device with electrical cord attached, a machine used to form and shape metal. Believing that this machine could possibly be used in the manufacture of EFP liners, I said to Mike Dominique, "You see what I see?"

Mike was astonished. "Dude, that's a fucking EFP press," he said. It was funny—we'd all passed by it, believing it a piece of garden sculpture or trash.

I pulled out my Olympus and scaling ruler and systematically documented the press. My discovery was reported via satellite phone to the company commander, and it brought every Joe in from the courtyard for a peek. I looked to the detainee's wife and her face registered despair, the agonizing realization that her husband wouldn't be coming home.

Out on the street a group of twenty kids were looking at me expectantly. I reached into my pocket, pulled out the candy I kept there, and doled it out one by one. No seconds.

As I did so, out of the corner of my eye, I spied a PSYOPS cameraman taking a photo of me doling out candy. I don't know why he took the photo—potential public relations, maybe, a "We are your friend" pamphlet in Arabic. I didn't care. I knew what that photo was going to

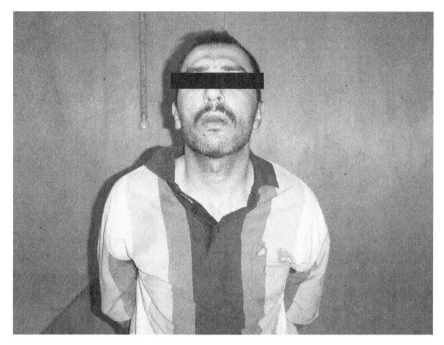

A prisoner tries to look defiant while wondering if he'll ever see his family again.

show: the face of a man whose mind had ever so briefly been transported home to his own kids.

Looking at those innocent, laughing children, I wondered how their parents could without guilt suit them up and use them as suicide bombers—all in the name of Allah. It affronted the sensibilities of any civilized person.

Meanwhile, back home, my son was wearing a suit for his First Communion, another milestone in his life that I wouldn't be a part of. I shook my head and returned to the here and now. The environment was too dangerous for daydreaming.

"Pedro, pose with the kids while I get a pic," I said.

Pedro was a fellow New Yorker and former marine, a reader of written reports, and this was his first time outside the wire. He was getting the full experience.

The kids gathered around me again, pawing for a view through my digital camera. They'd never seen one before.

Back in the courtyard, with much cursing and grunting, I helped drag the five-hundred-pound EFP press then hoist it over the front-edge cage of one of our Stryker combat vehicles.

By the time we returned to FOB Falcon, I'd soaked through my clothes three times over, and it felt great changing into clean clothes before I processed evidence and wrote reports. Once done, I went home, showered, sent a quick e-mail to Debbie, and passed out.

The next day, leadership up at brigade wanted a full briefing on the discovery of the press, with a PowerPoint presentation of the entire mission. It was an undeniable fact that a killer and his ability to create lethal weapons had been removed from the streets, and that was a success we could all share.

I point this out because our achievement that day earned Phoenix much respect, and attitudes changed after that. Soldiers realized we were there to help. You could even feel the shift in the chow hall. Facial expressions softened with newfound friendliness. We had been tested and had demonstrated our capabilities with flying colors. We were a force to be reckoned with, capable of great things.

On a personal level, I was pleased I'd made a difference. My decision to leave my family and do this had *meaning*.

It was nearing the end of April 2008, and the temperature in Baghdad was frequently over one hundred degrees Fahrenheit. No matter how much water you drank, you couldn't overhydrate. I swear I went days without urinating.

I'd just finished a workout and was already lathered with sweat when J.R. told me to get ready for a mission that had just been phoned in. I changed clothes, loaded up my ancillary gear, and inhaled a power bar. Who knew when the next meal would be?

Our target was a residence where two HVIs had been arrested, suspected of building and emplacing improvised explosives. The task was to provide tactical site exploitation (TSE) at the scene and then return to the base for evidence processing.

My team consisted of Will, my interpreter, Steve the tracker, and Chris the medic/tracker. Thumbs-up, and the rear hatch hydraulically closed. As we rolled to our target, the streets were congested with vehicle and pedestrian traffic.

We'd grown increasingly wary of civilians. A troublemaker named Moqtada al-Sadr, a radical cleric, had proclaimed an uprising of all Muslims in Iraq to fight the infidels—that is, *us*. His statements had anti-US sentiment simmering. Al-Sadr had been a wanted man for the past five years after he formed the Jaysh al-Mahdi, or Mahdi Army, and was responsible for bloody riots on the streets of Basra in southeastern Iraq. Two years before my arrival in Iraq, his army shot down a coalition helicopter and killed five British soldiers. That same year, his militia also killed as many as seventy US troops in Najaf, a city to the south of Baghdad. After a failed mission in Sadr City in which many US soldiers were killed, the army declared that no further operations to capture or kill al-Sadr would be authorized. The reason would soon become all too apparent.

Once on target, our K-9 team searched the HVI's house. After the all clear, I entered the house and conducted a systematic search. Searching a room in Baghdad was the same as searching one in Brooklyn. First step: look under the bed. My teammate Brian and I hoisted the bed and found the underside clear.

It was hotter inside than outside and the air was stale, no oxygen. Sweat rolled down my face, burning my eyes. "Bingo," I said.

"Whatcha got?" Brian asked.

"Passport. Some photographs," I said, already getting the evidence bags ready before I dripped sweat on the evidence.

When the search was complete I began the arduous task of interviewing the detainees' six wives. A female soldier searched them, found one husband's cell phone underneath their untouchable Muslim garb. The phone was immediately bagged, secure from contamination and view.

All six women were sitting in a living room, each with a squawking brood of kids in tow. I was not even remotely optimistic about this. I had almost no hope of getting usable intelligence out of this chaos.

One by one, I called them into the kitchen. I photographed each woman, awkward but necessary. I tried to obtain pedigree information—name, address, name of husband, easy questions—but they were all liars. Again with the sad faces. One detainee was escorted past the kitchen just as I was interviewing his wife. She began to sob uncontrollably. She had not been forthcoming to begin with. Now she completely clammed up.

Interviews finished, we were ready to roll. Before leaving, everyone made sure the guy on either side of him was there. Leaving someone behind could be fatal. There was a crackle on the internal radio. I saw Chris's expression change.

"What's up?" I asked.

"SOI is pissed about one of the guys we rolled up."

"Shit."

"They're walking off their posts in protest."

That figures, I thought. SOI stood for the Sons of Iraq, another name for the Sahwa civilian patrol. They were frequently dirty, with direct ties to organized crime and Al Qaeda. The problem, of course, was we felt like sitting ducks as we rolled down the highway.

The battle captain transmitted orders: SOI who didn't return immediately to their post should turn in their weapons and badges. Missing security details should be replaced with US troops.

Ugh. It wasn't how I wanted to end an otherwise uneventful mission.

———————

Back at the shop I wrote my report, included the photos I'd taken, and, with Will's assistance, translated the names. I laid out the property and separated the evidence into groups of like items: cell phones, papers, and identification. Mike D. downloaded the confiscated media. He found some porn, which at first we found pretty funny. These guys prayed five times a day, but they were hypocrites—sinners just like the rest of us. The humor soon stopped. Sadly, some of the porn involved young children, twelve to thirteen years of age by my estimate, homemade and local to our area of operation (AO). That meant the movies, despite their sick nature, had to be watched to look for evidence of either propaganda or insurgency operations.

After nine hours in the shop, I headed home. My walk was interrupted by my good friend Chuck Delp. Chuck and I had stuff in common: raised by grandparents, Italian wife. He worked for a company in direct competition with my employer.

"Hey Chris, what are your plans after this rotation is over?" Chuck asked.

"You offering me a job?"

"Yes," Chuck said.

I told him I was under an at-will contract with MPRI, free to leave my employer at any time. "I'll shoot your boss a résumé," I said.

I was reminded of what Debbie had told me: "God's plan and your plan are not always the same thing."

Less than a week later I was in the office working my first cup of coffee when the phone rang. Lou DeAnda picked up. US patrols had located an EFP site and an associated weapons cache. It was J.R.'s call as to whether we rolled on it. He was contacted by phone and gave the order: "Suit up." Outside temperature 108 degrees.

I boarded my MRAP and we headed toward Phoenix gate. I inserted a thirty-round magazine into my M4 rifle and let the slide run home. With a distinct click, I pushed the forward assist to ensure positive contact with the bolt.

Next, I loaded my 9 mm Sig Sauer pistol with a fifteen-round magazine, repeating the process, ensuring that the bolt had seated and that a round was present inside the chamber. I made a time check, announcing our rollout time to my teammates, documenting it with an ink pen on my wrist for future reference.

We headed north down a familiar stretch of road, infamous for the many soldiers killed and maimed there. As I looked outside through a pane of bulletproof glass, I could see a narrow view of hot spots, traffic, and Iraqi checkpoints manned by corrupt SOI, paid by us and loyal to them.

There was a sudden lurch. "What's going on?" I asked.

The radio crackled. "RTB. Repeat, RTB." Return to base.

"What happened?" I asked.

"Mission canceled. EOD fucked the scene," the sergeant said. "They are leaving the scene now with ordnance in tow."

We shook our heads in disgust.

Back at the shop the battle captain from the 1-22 called to explain that EOD had raised the "safety flag," halting the operation.

"That's bullshit, sir," J.R. said. "Stateside, sir, they'd be arrested for tampering with a crime scene—and this isn't the first time. This incident needs be documented. The EOD has blood on its hands for not allowing us to do the job we were sent here to do under the direction of JIEDDO. Our primary focus is to help save Joe's life, and this pettiness, allowed to fester undeterred, is spinning out of control."

J.R. could be an ass, but this was one of his finer moments.

The biggest loser, of course, was Joe. The system was fucked top to bottom. But what the hell did I know? I was here to do a job. I was under no illusion that I was going to save the world. But my teammates and I were real. Genuine. We were here to help, but at times it was like watching a train wreck.

Late that April, I turned forty-seven years old. I kept it close to the vest. One time Staff Sergeant Babineau let slip it was his birthday, and in the chow hall everyone acted like a waiter at Outback Steakhouse, singing and clapping hands. I got a birthday card from my kids, and I risked exposure by proudly attaching it to my bedroom wall.

It happened just after lunch: 1-22 reported that one of their MRAP crews had been struck by an EFP. Two soldiers were killed instantly. We were told to dress and gear up on the double, and we did so with a combination of anger, sadness, and fear tying our guts into knots.

Crews made sure we had ample ammo. The .50-caliber machine guns were readied. Thumbs-up. Hatch closed. Roll out.

Then the radio: "RTB." The crew and convoy on scene were taking small arms fire from the insurgency. I was sickened to my stomach and angry all at the same time. I wasn't intentionally looking for a gunfight,

Mushy stuff can catch you flak when you're working in a war zone, but I was a dad whose kids loved me and I didn't care who knew it—as you can tell by my wall.

but at this point I was more than willing to give it to someone who legitimately deserved it.

Back at the shop there was no joking. My buddy Chris the tracker/medic asked, "Can we please have a moment of silence for our fellow brothers in arms?"

We all bowed our heads. I'd come to admire Chris greatly. He was a battle-tested war hero, winner of two Purple Hearts, and qualified for more if he bothered to put in for them. No one dared to move until Chris gave the "Amen." With that, we all continued to get undressed and pre-positioned our gear for the next eventual mission. From years of religious training and personal belief, I made the sign of the cross, making a silent prayer to the fallen heroes.

I went to the gym and ran on the treadmill, four miles in twenty-nine minutes, fifty-nine seconds, breaking the half-hour mark on my birthday, a personal goal. I reached Debbie and the kids via Skype and

The inside of a personnel carrier burned to ashes by an IED attack.

they got to say happy birthday, but there were reception problems and the conversation was cut short.

One of my friends grew sad when I received attention from my family. His daughter had been incommunicado since he'd been in Iraq. I realized how lucky I was. He was being overlooked by his family. He was heading home soon, and I assured him that that would fix everything. I promised him that when we were both back, our families would get together. That part of the commitment was easy for me. For him, it was an entirely different story.

During the first week in May, I was having coffee at the Green Bean with Chris and Chuck. Our K-9 handlers Gary and Rodney were walking past, headed toward the PX, when they were approached by a staff sergeant with an EOD patch on his left shoulder. Because of J.R.'s tirade, we said

"Uh-oh." The guy looked familiar to me, but I couldn't place him. He wanted to talk to Chuck specifically.

The staff sergeant introduced himself and said he was looking for a job once he got back stateside. I provided a notepad and pen. Chuck wrote down his company's name, tore off the sheet, and handed it to the soldier.

"Use my name when you talk to HR," Chuck said.

As soon as he had that piece of paper, the soldier turned into an asshole. He said he heard we had a problem with EOD, that we came into his workspace "a little heavy-handed."

I felt the blood rushing to the back of my ears. Then it hit me. I realized where I'd seen him before. There had been a briefing weeks earlier for Phoenix at EOD HQ, an overview of EOD capabilities and procedures, during which this same staff sergeant had said, "I don't see what it is that you guys do that isn't already being done over here."

Recalling this, I reacted to his "heavy-handed" comment: "That's a complete lie!" I explained that he hadn't been on any missions of ours and hadn't read any of our reports, so he was an idiot. For good measure I threw in, "For the record, I'm the guy that told your First Sergeant Soloway that I would break off his finger and stick it up his ass."

I drank my coffee and waited for this creep to leave.

When he did, Chuck said, "You all right?"

"Yeah," I said. "Sorry. I can't stand those guys that don't know what the fuck they're talking about. I'm trying to imagine a moment during the time I was a marine when I'd've had the gall to accuse a civilian of fucking up. And I know in the past contractors have shown their ass and performed poorly under pressure. But I'll tell you one thing: I've learned to trust my gut. When a guy first strikes me as an asshole, damned good chance he's an asshole."

11

THE SOLDIERING PART

THAT MAY WE HAD A MORNING BRIEFING, details of an upcoming three-day mission with the 4-64. OK, but apparently J.R. and Zack the 2IC had a hard-on for working with this particular unit, so much so that we camped outside the shop in sleeping bags for better reaction time. The alternative was to stage at a combat outpost (COP) with three days' worth of gear, no showers, and portable toilets. (We'd tried that. It didn't work out. You ended up with cranky forty-year-olds that smelled like dead animals.)

Truth was, we could be spun up in thirty minutes and be at a scene minutes later. So we were camping out, but close to home. At 1:00 AM the temp dipped to a refreshing ninety-five degrees, but heat continued to radiate from the concrete pad and the surrounding T-wall barriers. Sergeant Beckerman, one of our tactical commanders and team lead of an MRAP crew, drove somewhere and picked up ten folding cots.

"Here, Chris, don't sleep on the ground."

"Thanks, Beck."

The instant I got on the cot I heard an AK-47 firing in the distance. In the sky, tracer rounds hurled through the night like neon string, disappearing into the distance.

Gunfire at night was nothing new to me. I'd heard it regularly riding sector patrol in the Edgemere Houses complex in Queens and as a sergeant in Brooklyn's Red Hook Houses—so frequently we learned to ignore the gunshots that weren't called in.

Sunrise was at 4:50 and, one by one, we started our day. J.R. was in a piss mood. We assumed it was 'roid rage, him being a dedicated anabolic warrior. Someone, doesn't matter who, made a suggestion that we call the 4-64 and ask if they were in need of our services and, if not, shut it down and head back to our hooch for a shower and real sleep.

J.R. went berserk. This was the mission, J.R. said. It was a three-day thing and we were sticking it out for the entire seventy-two hours.

The hue and cry was loud, and J.R. gave in. He tried to call in, but it took time to find someone who was awake. Did they need us? No. OK, and we were released until 2200 hours, when we were to report back for another night outside the shop. Nobody was certain why we couldn't sleep in our own beds and rally for the mission as we had before. J.R. seemed to favor misery for misery's sake. Had to be the 'roids.

That night there was some amusement as I attempted to unfold my cot for the night without assistance, a repeatedly futile effort that I jam-packed with comic timing. With the cot upright and me standing with one foot on the ground and the other atop the bar, I applied downward pressure. The bar slipped out of position, causing the cot and me to fall to the ground.

Because of the roars of laughter, guys who'd been in the shop came out to see what was so funny. Sergeant Beckerman came over and snapped the cot into position in eight seconds. That only added to the comedy. What could I do? I had to laugh at myself.

Sleep wouldn't come. Incoming and outgoing helicopters blew dust onto my face. As I lay awake I developed a more three-dimensional understanding of my job—and there were parts I liked better than others. Loved the cop part: crime scenes, interviewing guys, tipping houses. It was the soldiering part I didn't care for. I hated the part where I'd be on a road and be unable to see clearly what was ahead. I hated the green otherworldliness of the night vision goggles.

When it was all over, I slowly realized we'd slept outside three days for no reason. They had nothing for us to do. They never did. The momentum

I'd felt was gone. We were slowly being uninvited to the dance. For a while there we had been in high demand, with all the battalions asking us for assistance. The tide was shifting. But why?

There had been an incident, and the more I thought about it, the more I suspected it was pertinent. Hammy had altered evidence— the asshole fabricated a story in which he trailed a man from a crime scene to his residence.

Maybe that had nothing to do with our inactivity. Maybe it was because we lacked a technical exploitation operations (TEO) officer. Maybe the army just didn't get it: *Why bring them to the fight? They're just civilian contractors.*

Or maybe it was something bigger than all that. We'd had a meeting at brigade HQ, at which we spoke about Phoenix's capabilities with Colonel Buford and his three JAG lawyers. As a closing remark, J.R.— a.k.a. the fucking bull in the china shop—said, "In addition to all the great things we can do for you in this program to help your soldiers, all my men double as *shooters*."

He meant, of course, that we could kill bad guys if given the opportunity. It was the last thing he should have said in front of a group of lawyers, who are very risk averse. If the legal department was worried about our trigger-happiness, it very well could've led to the team sitting around with no work.

Five days later our world was again shaken when we learned that all of our army crews were being replaced, transferred to northern Iraq. We'd had the same guys for a few months, our teamwork was battlefield proven, and now they were gone, replaced by a question mark.

I went to J.R. "What the fuck is going on?" I asked.

"That's the army, bro," he replied.

"Bullshit. Those are our guys out there. We have a history and a comfort level of safety. They can't just up and take them. In this whole fuckin' army, with over eight hundred thousand troops, they gotta take our crew? I don't believe it, not for a minute."

I would later learn that my suspicions were entirely justified. J.R. had gone to the sergeant major at brigade command and made an arrangement to get us some more work. As part of the deal, he had to fire our original army crews, who were seasoned veterans with multiple tours and combat experience who knew the terrain. They were replaced by administrative soldiers with zero combat experience, guys who weren't familiar with the terrain and looked at a fucking map every seven seconds.

At the time of the transfer, though, I didn't know anything about the deal, just that the situation didn't make any sense. J.R. insisted that I was being paranoid. I agreed that nothing mattered less than what I thought. The army was going to do what the army was going to do.

We had our last meeting with all the old troops. J.R. gave a bullshit speech, hollow at best. Zack the 2IC gave the soldiers each a Gerber utility knife, a nice gesture that I thought came up a little short. I got maudlin and gave a speech about Sergent Beck and how he'd gotten me—gone out on his own and gotten me and some of the other old men in the group—a cot to sleep on during the three-day "mission."

Sergeant Beck interrupted me. "You know, when I got that cot for you, I didn't think you were going to sleep right next to me!" Everyone fell out laughing.

I concluded my speech by addressing them all: "You're not replace-able, regardless of what the army might think."

As we said good-bye, they were just kids to me—I couldn't help but worry about their well-being. Their new assignment put them on route clearance, by far the most dangerous job in theater. And they didn't complain, further testament to their mettle.

At the next team meeting, I told J.R. I thought the transfer of our crew indicated that the primary contractor on this project was in default on ensuring our personal safety.

J.R. just stared at me.

I said God forbid we incur injuries or worse, because the lawsuits will be incredible. I had already contacted a lawyer, and I suggested everyone else do the same. I'd even informed Debbie of the situation; in case I was killed, I wanted her to know she had legal recourse.

Later on, J.R. came to visit me and he advised me that new crews were out practicing with night vision goggles, learning the routes and security protocols out on the "X."

I said that was a good idea.

We ignored the elephant in the room—that both the army and the contractor were assuming a risk without my permission. They had the ability to influence and minimize the risk but chose not to exercise it.

————————

During the six down days that followed, I received a disposable video camera from Debbie and was making filmed vignettes of life on the FOB in Iraq. I filmed K-9 training. We did have a dog that couldn't understand English, but most of them did—and their noses were magical.

I photographed what guys look like at breakfast, that kind of thing. I gave the movie a sarcastic narration, geared toward my son: "Here's what a grown man looks like speaking with his mouth full. Whatcha eating, Bill?"

"Bacon and eggs," he'd say, food falling from his mouth.

"Remember, Christian, don't do this at home. Bill here is a trained professional."

I had four minutes left and was looking for something to fill the space.

————————

It was the third week in May when we went on a surprise mission. We were relaxing in the Green Bean when our K-9 team lead Gary sought us out.

"The 7-10 CAV has stumbled upon a weapons cache during a dismounted patrol," Gary said. "They rolled up some prisoners from the local *muhallah*, not far from the FOB."

After getting ready, I felt inspired and used the remaining time on my video camera to film myself, to show that I was in uniform and prepared to load onto an MRAP for a mission. I figured this might be exciting for Christian. The dogs were fun, but most of the video was of mundane crap. So I gave my son just a taste of action, then went to work, the first mission with new MRAP crews.

The time for complaining was through. It was time to put on my helmet and get to work. We rolled out at twilight and didn't have to go far. When we stopped I spotted a baker's dozen of prisoners, cuffed with hands in front—an NYPD no-no. Why do it that way? So they can do things with their hands? How is that helpful? I couldn't fault the army, but really, was it that difficult to rear flex-cuff these demons?

While Phoenix inspected the weapons cache site, I went to work interrogating the prisoners. Prisoners #1 and #2 were not noteworthy. It was being with prisoner #3 that made my hairs stand on end. He looked like he'd just stepped out of a shower and was wearing a pristine white man-dress and brand-new shoes that were exceptionally clean. Later, I would need to separate him from the others and interview him out of earshot, but for now I asked him the usual questions and moved on to #4.

We actually identified detainees by number, and when there was a chance that they might try to play the old switcheroo with us, we wrote their number in the middle of their forehead. It might be offensive to some, but the numbers were easily washed off. At the time of the interviews, it helped us keep the detainees straight.

Mike Dominique radioed me. An EOD technician was readying to blow the weapons cache. We were to take cover. I told the guard to move the prisoners two hundred feet away from the controlled detonation but to separate #3, whom I wanted to question alone. All thirteen of the prisoners were blindfolded, and once moved, #3 was plucked away and placed in the rear seat of a Humvee.

He professed his innocence.

Through my interpreter Mark, I gently asked, "Are there any other weapons, IEDs I should know about?"

He shook his head. "You found all of it," he said.

"Good," I said with an icy calm. "Let me explain something: if you ever want to get out of this mess, as a sign of good faith, you should tell me about the man who brought this trouble to your *muhallah*."

A detainee, identified as #1 by the number written on his forehead, has been separated from the others and is being questioned by me (right) and my interpreter in the backseat of a Humvee.

After some prodding, the prisoner was like a fountain of information. He gave me the name of the bad guy, his vehicle description, and possible bed-down location.

My snap judgment as to character and probity was baffled. There was a chance he was lying, but I couldn't tell, and we had to start somewhere. There was also a chance that #3 was a hell of a lot worse than the guy he was giving up.

The worst-case scenario for him was that we'd let it be known he'd cooperated and release him. Such men were kidnapped, tortured, and eventually killed, their bodies discarded like trash on the curb, in plain view, conspicuous even, so as to discourage others.

In my written report I suggested the army recanvass the affected *muhallah* for other witnesses. This was a common NYPD practice but foreign to the army's way of thinking.

The next day we linked up with 7-10 and moved toward a target that offended civilized sensibilities. It was like an apocalyptic movie: raw sewage and garbage–strewn mud huts, wild dogs ambling around, boys riding mules. Twenty small children mobbed me for the Jolly Ranchers in my pocket. Some said "Thank you" in heavily accented English. I asked one kid's mom if she knew anything about the recent activity. She said no, clearly terrified by the question.

Moving on to a nearby house, I spoke with a man who said he worked for an American company. "Where is this company?"

"In Baghdad."

"Where in Baghdad?"

"Baghdad International Airport."

"What do you do?"

"I am a laborer. Here, I show you." To prove his point, he displayed for me a photo of the man he claimed to be his boss.

"What do you know about terrorist activity?"

"Nothing, but if I hear something I will share it."

"When is the best time to get in touch with you?"

"In the morning."

I was working well with my terp Mark. He did more than alleviate the language barrier. He had an easy way about him. Mark was a local national; he'd been an accountant under the Saddam Hussein regime. For security purposes, Mark wore a green scarf over his face along with oversized sunglasses.

At twenty-nine, Mark had witnessed much horror. One of his brothers and one cousin were taken away in the middle of the night, never to be seen alive again. His sense of national pride was damaged, but his determination to improve life in Iraq was undeterred. He had a fiancée who worked as a doctor. They hoped one day to move to America. He'd make a great cop, intelligent and personable, with a knack for spotting bullshit.

I've mentioned Hammy, our resident asshole. Unfortunately, I am going to have to mention him again. On this mission his inability to be a human being with a spine again plagued us. I watched as he tried to take a picture of God-only-knows what. A crowd of kids gathered around, thinking he would take their picture. Apparently, that wasn't his intent, and he reached out and slapped an older boy across the face, knocking him down. The other children ran away, frightened. I was in shock and confronted him.

"The kid wouldn't get out of my photo" was Hammy's only defense.

As far as I was concerned, this was the end of the road for Hammy. This guy was more than capable of causing an international incident, and in the current climate, contractors were on the menu for slaughter.

12

A NASTY POTPOURRI

IT WAS NEARING THE END OF MAY when Chris knocked on my door at 1:30 AM and told me we had a mission. He gave us a quick brief on what to expect. The 1-22 had conducted an intelligence-driven raid and discovered a weapons cache containing homemade explosives, mortars, and EFP liners and sleeves.

My new roomie *Sam* wiped sleep from his eyes. Sam had rolled into Phoenix from another team, where he'd outlived his welcome because of a tumultuous on-again, off-again relationship with a woman employee. He was five years Army Special Forces, and now contracted to the corporation at the rate of $900 per day. He was a smart guy, and the move to FOB Falcon was apparently good for all involved. As they say, sometimes a change of scenery does the trick. He was my roomie for only two, three weeks before he was processed out.

But on this day Sam and I rode a Humvee to the office, where we donned camo uniforms and associated gear. For the new MRAP crew this was another milestone: their first *night* mission.

Larry Humphries was also on the mission. I've mentioned him before. A slow mover. A clown. But after a while you noticed that his stunts were always selfish. Now he plopped himself down in a seat and allowed us to pack up the vehicle around him. But Larry was the least of our problems. At least he was there.

We were down one man. Will, my interpreter, was missing. Will may have had an excellent sense of humor, but during his off hours he moved in mysterious ways, and trying to find him in the middle of the night could prove frustrating.

Battling ever-present technical difficulties, I struggled through a communications check. The obsolete radio more closely resembled a brick than a communications device. It was relentlessly in need of recalibration, because the corporation bought them on the cheap.

There was no joking around. The Fourth Infantry Division continued with a big push, cleaning up trouble spots. The phrase used was that we should expect that *intensity would vary*.

We were working in an area heavy with Jaysh al-Mahdhi (JAM) cells loyal to Moqtada al-Sadr. At our objective, the streets were empty. No streetlights. Larry Humphries walked down the ramp first, misjudged his step, caught his toe, and took a complete tumble to the ground, but he was OK. We met up with the 1-22 platoon commander, a young lieutenant with the surname John.

"We had an intelligence-driven raid resulting in the arrest of some local nationals obviously up to no good," Lieutenant John said. "The men blabbed, gave up their neighbor rather quickly."

"How long since you found the cache of weapons?" I asked.

"Approximately ninety minutes." During that time, he explained, EOD had been at it and there was no longer anything resembling a pristine scene.

"I'd like to see the weapons," I said.

"Right this way," Lieutenant John said.

In a room to my right, EOD had with an artistic eye arranged all the confiscated weapons. It was beautiful. I took pictures. What else was there for me to do? My work product was meaningless here. I investigate crime scenes, but there's not much I can do after they've been transformed into something that looks like a display at the convention hall gun show.

Speaking to Lieutenant John on the way out, I said, "In the future, if you could secure the prisoners on-site for a hasty interview, that would be helpful and beneficial to me."

Lieutenant John said he'd bring them back if he could. He said his best success with getting information from difficult detainees was when accompanied by the Iraqi National Police. Apparently, the INP had greater influence over the detainees than Americans did.

"I track you one hundred percent," I said.

At that point Larry Humphries entered the conversation. He told Lieutenant John he'd send him a copy of our report. John went to give him his address, but Larry said no bother. He had an audio file, as he was wired with a voice-activated tape recorder.

A lightbulb went on over my head. With his background in internal affairs, I'd already suspected him of being a rat, and now he was bragging about secretly recording us. He was laying cover. I wasn't concerned that Larry carried a recorder, it was the fact that, for a while at least, he'd kept it secret.

Getting back on base proved complicated. A female captain had accidentally discharged a .50-caliber gun after reporting it cleared. In reaction, the battle commander ordered that *all personnel*—us, officers, enlisted men, everybody—had to wait for the command first sergeant to come out and visually inspect our weapons before we could enter the FOB.

––––––––––

There was no rest for the weary. The following afternoon, I was mid-lunch when Tom Powell came into the chow hall radiating urgency. "We need to roll now."

I grabbed a couple more bites of my sandwich and finished my soda before dumping my tray in the garbage. We gave Will a sarcastic cheer as he graced us with his presence after his no-show the night before.

The mission took us back to the previous night's *muhallah*—same street, in fact. Only now there was a bustling chaos: more than twenty official vehicles, military, Iraqi police, thick pedestrian traffic, our security cordon ineffectual. We learned that a dismounted patrol had taken the initiative to conduct a house search of an abandoned residence. An alert soldier spotted a military vest and smoke grenade. A more intensive search revealed a nasty potpourri of weapons in the interior and on the grounds of the residence.

Everybody and his brother responded to the site. To enhance the circus-like atmosphere, an Iraqi film crew invaded. They had a seemingly limitless sense of eminent domain.

I processed as fast as I could. If I couldn't document pristine evidence, I could at least memorialize it as it was when I conducted my interviews. I sealed paper documents inside plastic bags, marked the find, grid location, time, and type of evidence. I snapped off a couple of photos with my Olympus. Good thing I did. One tidbit of information caught on film would prove useful later on.

The film crew was crawling all over the residence's front yard, setting up. Phoenix rallied up and got the hell out of there. Riding back, Larry Humphries asked me to read his seventeen-page written report for his corporation about the previous night's mission. He wanted to include my name and any input I might have regarding his authorship.

Weapons intended for use against coalition forces, now seized and to be rendered harmless.

"You think that's appropriate?" I asked. "I don't work for them. The report could be construed as a conflict of interest between your employer and mine."

"I hadn't thought of that," Larry said.

Bullshit, I thought.

Back at the office, Will and I donned latex gloves, and piece by piece we went through the confiscated documents. "We have aerial imagery with grid coordinates overlaid," Will said. "Arabic text describing location and activity. Holy shit. Descriptions of US forces' locations and building configurations."

"Get it translated quick," I said.

As I forwarded the information to the S-2 shop of the supported unit—what we called the head-of-intel shop—Larry Humphries asked me if he could be of help. I suggested that in the interest of time he and Will should go to the S-2 shop with the photocopies I'd just made so Military Intelligence could get to work. With Will in tow, Larry left to deliver the information.

Looking at his own photos, Brian noticed the inventory provided by EOD didn't jibe with the photos of the scene. A particular weapon reported on the inventory was notably absent. I checked my photos. I had no evidence of this particular weapon either. J.R. predictably disregarded any input and insisted that Brian include the weapon's presence in his report.

Nonetheless, when it came time to commit words to document, Brian noted the missing weapon. By the following morning we were contacted by Major Dufour, the Canadian green-suiter. "Where the hell is the weapon?" Major Dufour asked.

J.R. said it had to be there since it was on the inventory, that we'd just somehow failed to photograph it. Somewhere, he believed, there was a photo that would establish the weapon's presence in the confiscated cache.

That photo of course never arrived, and J.R.'s credibility took a humongous hit. He reacted without humility by browbeating Brian.

Brian was a relatively quiet man, but he eventually roared back at J.R. He was at that point in the rotation when he would write what he thought was right. I had never seen Brian so upset—and rightfully so.

As May 2008 came to an end, I was thinking about getting a raise. For that to occur, my security clearance needed elevation from Secret to Top Secret / Sensitive Compartmented Information, a process that required a clean background and a formal interview with MPRI's senior security officer. Unfortunately, he was six thousand miles away. I submitted a second set of my fingerprints and a couple of computer checks.

Bingo—I was approved for an interim TS/SCI clearance and a $60,000 raise. But to get the raise I'd have to relocate to another FOB when there was a vacancy. I said I was all in. I had little emotional attachment to Falcon. Chuck would lose his gym buddy, but he'd get over it.

As I waited out my days at Falcon, I sensed that weird itch in some of my teammates, so long in Iraq and still no gunfight, no real action, no shooting and ducking. Why a man would want that is beyond me. If all my days are bullet free, I'm fine with that.

That same itch to be where the action is happened with cops, too. Guys that had never discharged their weapons started feeling like there was something wrong with them or with their experience. They felt as if they'd missed out on something. It was a dangerous mind-set and a tendency that was being overlooked by the current leadership.

I thought about my kids, who didn't want to chat with their dad as they had when I was first away. Debbie was always there, but the kids made excuses and she relayed messages. They were used to being without me. Skype conversations made the kids freak: "Daddy looked like a prisoner." It would take days to calm them down, and it made me a particularly bad type of lonely.

On June 2, my sleep was interrupted by a nightmare involving my mom and my kids. My subconscious was playing a mean trick on me. My relationship with my mother was nonexistent, toxic long before I met Debbie.

At home, Debbie was struggling. School was about to end. How would she keep the kids occupied with Daddy so far away? Debbie's brother was taking his kids to Universal Studios in Orlando, so Debbie and our kids went along. It was Star Wars weekend, and when Christian got back home he posted a stormtrooper bobblehead by his bedroom to protect the family.

As it turned out, MPRI kept moving the goalposts, so I never transferred from FOB Falcon and never got the raise.

J.R. was instructed to have one-on-one sit-downs with his team members to air out difficulties. With Chris joining me to witness, I said I would not be leaving the wire unless Hammy was pulled from the team. The kid-slapping incident a few weeks earlier had been the final straw.

J.R. went beet red. "What the fuck are you talking about?" he asked angrily.

"Hammy's behavior is escalating. He's going to get someone hurt or kill someone out there."

"I can vouch for Hammy. He's well versed in the rules of engagement and would never pull the trigger on an innocent civilian," J.R. said.

"Twice he shot stray dogs in front of kids. A lot of army guys saw him slap that kid. You don't think word is out we've got a dangerous guy with us? What he did constitutes serious misconduct. Ignoring it could prove costly on many levels."

J.R. turned to the other Chris. "Do you consider Hammy a risk?"

Chris responded, "I do, J.R. He makes me nervous with some of his actions."

J.R. responded, "Well, then, it's done, I'll speak to Hammy after I finish with you. Hammy will no longer leave the wire. Chris, let Hammy know that I need to speak to him."

Things got worse. During the first week in June our military intelligence analyst *Cunningham* pissed off leadership at brigade and was told to pack his gear and find a new place to work. I dug deeper into the story. Turned out, Cunningham had been working on a targeting package for an HVI. But the battlespace commander, after hearing Cunningham's case, declined to action the target. Cunningham decided, without conferring with our leadership, to shop the info to another unit in hopes of taking the target out. Cunningham thought it best to go outside his lane, usurping the landowner's authority, a serious mistake that again brought no appropriate response from leadership. Cunningham had been exposed as a selfish and immature individual who lacked any sense of professional decorum. For us, it was another step in the downward spiral of our credibility.

We were persona non grata, and again there was a stretch of no work. During the second week in June, at a morning meeting J.R. tasked Brian with calling the five battalions' S-2 shops and indicating we were ready, willing, and able to assist in the "new push" that was about to kick off.

Later, I spoke to Brian: "You know the reason no one is calling us for missions is because of the two village idiots," I said—referring to Hammy and Cunningham.

He nodded. "I'm going to make the phone calls anyway, but I don't think anything's going to come of it."

But something did.

———————

After a few more days of waiting around like firefighters, we received a late-morning call. A convoy from the 2-4 had been struck by an EFP/IED, and they were requesting our services for a post-blast analysis (PBA).

My rollout crew included Mike D.; Will, my terp; and a K-9 handler, also named Will, with his dog Django, better known as DJ. Nearing the objective, we hit a traffic jam so severe that we crossed the median and drove on the left side of the road.

I smiled inwardly. I remembered Brooklyn, which was the worst when it came to traffic problems. It was in a chronic state of congestion. I remembered I was on my way to a brother officer requesting help only to be stopped by traffic—so I drove down a one-way street the wrong way and up on the sidewalk when I had to, but I reached my target.

My mind snapped back to the here and now as we arrived at the scene, where I saw five cuffed prisoners sitting up against the T-wall barrier. The scene had been secured by the original convoy configuration and was now enhanced with the addition of our crews. I quickly got to work. The scene had been divided into two basic areas. Mike D. was working his TSE magic while I started in on the detainees.

With Will, I took a look at the men I was to interview, and I didn't like what I saw. All but one of the prisoners were in the Iraqi Army or Iraqi National Police. The nearest checkpoint was only four hundred meters from the blast site. A soldier advised me that all five prisoners tested positive for explosive residue following a test that was conducted on-site.

I separated the first prisoner. No soft talk this time. I needed to establish a tone right off the bat: "Will, please explain to this piece of shit what the soldier just said," I said, my ears burning with anger. Will explained that they'd tested positive for explosives and were going down. I added, "You are essentially fucked. You will not be home for dinner."

I could see beads of perspiration pop out along the creases of his forehead. I could smell the sweat coming off him, enough to make you gag.

Will and I had a quick conference. He explained that there was no way to translate the phrase "essentially fucked" without losing some of the pop. The best he could do was "hopeless." I said tone was more important that wording. Not only was his situation hopeless but we were angry with him.

Will nodded and angrily translated my question. The prisoner's eyes went wide with mock innocence. I started again with the "piece of shit" business and Will raised an eyebrow.

He was right. I had to swallow the bile and be a pro. I got on with the questioning, calm and direct. But in the back of my mind I fantasized that this guy was taking a serious beating for bastardizing Islam, a beating that would make his ribs ache for the rest of his life.

Of course, there would be no beating. These American soldiers guarding this terrorist were too proud and professional to compromise a solid arrest with anything approaching abuse. But that didn't mean I had to be polite with the guy. Regardless of tone, my questioning resulted in nothing but frustration. The first three prisoners lied in my face. They weren't good actors, but they refused to drop out of character. It wore me out.

Ah, but #4. He was ready to shit his pants.

My first question to him was "Have you ever heard of the Virgin Mary?"

Will looked at me in amazement. "Chris, I cannot say that."

"Say it with the same tenor as in my voice," I instructed firmly.

Will spoke the question in Arabic and #4 looked puzzled.

"The thing about the Virgin Mary was that she was never touched. You, you've been touched." I held up the explosive residue test. I pointed at his hands. And turned my palms upward. The evidence was so damn strong. "You tested positive for explosives, which means you touched the shit." I said.

I saw his chest heave, expanding and contracting, a bit of hyperventilation. He was shaking in fear. I stayed quiet for a while and gave him a good visual once-over. He had open sores on his right index and middle fingers, a burn with a cylindrical shape across the sides. I photographed the injuries.

"How did you get that injury?" I asked.

There was a hesitation as his mind clicked for a beat. "I burned my fingers while making chai tea," he said.

"Looks more like a welding torch or possibly a soldering iron."

He shrugged.

I pounded him with questions. Who had helped him with the explosive? Who had helped him with the emplacement? But he continued to profess his innocence.

There was no doubt in my mind that I could have gotten #4 to spill had I had an interrogation room and unlimited time. My minutes with him here were precious and few, and I had limited time to develop rapport or work my psychological techniques.

The interviews "complete," I gave *Lieutenant Burns* my assessment. "Number 4 should be removed immediately from the rest of the group and kept segregated indefinitely until a more in-depth interview can be conducted in a controlled environment. Even if he doesn't provide any additional information, the psychological effect of removing him from his group will impact his demons and improve subsequent interviews."

Lieutenant Burns agreed. One of his NCOs removed #4 and placed him on ice.

I took additional photographs at the detonation site for my report. It was time to wrap up, and again time for me to provide free comedic entertainment for my Phoenix teammates.

I couldn't find my MRAP. It wasn't where it had dropped me off. I held up two fingers, signifying MRAP #2, looking for a little help from the respective crews. Everyone had a good laugh, but the similitude of MRAPs in the glare of the hot sun was duly noted.

The mood grew lighter after we heard the soldier injured in the blast was going to be OK, his injuries limited to temporary hearing loss and facial lacerations.

––––––––

Back at the shop, as I readied my report, we were called to view a video of the day's blast, taken from the dashboard mount of a nearby vehicle. The blast was massive and blew all the dust off the front of the camera-man's vehicle. It was chilling. If the point of detonation—what we call the blast seat—had been a foot or two in either direction, the entire crew might have been killed.

When I finished my report, I gave it to my buddy Brian, who was a whiz at digesting and analyzing intelligence. He assembled everyone's report into one Phoenix report and sent it up the chain of command. As he worked, I found myself in the same room with J.R. for what seemed like forever. He was ranting about how shrapnel from the site was copper that had changed color in the blast. He became so obnoxious that someone unbagged a piece of shrapnel to show that it reacted to a magnet and was therefore not copper.

I got out of there.

A few days later I was having dinner when Lieutenant Burns put a hand on my shoulder and said, "Hey Chris, I just want to thank you for your good work the other day."

"The guy I suggested?"

"Yes, #4—the one with the percolating demons. We got *gooood* intelligence."

"You're welcome, boss. Anytime!" I said with a grin.

"That's the good news. You guys did great."

"What's the bad news?"

"As it turned out, EOD never took a soil sample from the scene, and all five of the scumbags were cut loose. Best news, though, is that the soldier that got fragged is going to be OK."

I was growing almost used to the ghastly injustices. Of course they were cut loose. They knew somebody who knew somebody and off they ran. I thought about the good news some more. The primary value of Phoenix was not as some middle-aged Special Forces action outfit, replete with braggart "shooters," but as a gatherer of human intelligence.

In the aftermath of the mission I had many men come over to shake my hand, thank me for a job well done. That was worth more to me than all the money I'd earned. I looked at my remaining six months in Iraq with an increased sense of optimism.

13

FNGS

In mid-June, Phoenix Team was getting ready to turn over the reins to a fresh group of contractors, the FNGs—the Fucking New Guys. I and a few other guys from the original team were staying behind for the second iteration of the program.

I was thrilled at the prospect of fresh blood and, more important, new leadership. I was tired of J.R.'s incompetence, his tantrums, his attempts at intimidation. But my first impression of the FNGs was far from ideal. They filled my day with their eager questions and cluttered up the shop filling out questionnaires and taking tests on a computer. *Stewart*, our administrative guy, was up to his eyebrows processing the newcomers' access to classified and secret information based on their security clearance. It was all a major pain in the ass. The corporation had sent guys with no security clearance, a fact that they hoped we would ignore. Technically, those guys couldn't even be in the shop because of the secretive nature of the work.

On top of that, they thought they were fucking soldiers of fortune. One had a 5.56 mm ammunition drum. He'd written on it This Is for Sadr City. I spoke sharply with several of them, demanding an adherence to protocol at all times. Mr. Sadr City's name was Jerr, short for *Jerry* in a chummy way. He said he was in TEO. His qualifications? The corporation gave him a one-week course.

"You're a TEO, and I'm a Knight of the Round Table," I said.

J.R.'s replacement as team head was a guy named Ricky Peterson, and he got off to a shaky start. Things in Baghdad were not as he expected, and he was slow to adjust to reality. I had to tell him we weren't getting work because of lapses in judgment by a few guys who weren't around anymore.

He was stunned. My suggestion was that he begin his new gig by making the rounds, apologizing to the lieutenant colonels of surrounding units for the sins of the previous administration. I spoke first but others piped in, giving Ricky an itemized list of bad news. Ricky looked boggled. We were turning his world upside down. Everything he'd been told was bullshit.

Sitting next to Ricky was another new guy, Matt Pucino, who could fill a room with his confidence. He was chiseled from rock and locked in. Matt was on leave from Special Forces, where his specialty was as an intelligence/targeting officer. He was replacing Cunningham as our intelligence analyst, and after what his predecessor had done to damage the team's credibility, he had a tough task ahead. Ricky told him, "Matt, you will be performing your intelligence services from the 1 STB [Special Troops Battalion] instead of at brigade."

Matt looked at Ricky's face. "Why?"

We all laughed. "Previous guy got himself kicked out," I explained. "You'll get the details in the chow hall." Then I apologized for coming on so strong, but I thought it essential that everyone know what's wrong. "That way you have the best chance of being able to fix it."

"Appreciate the candor," Ricky said.

In the chow hall we further blew their minds with the promised details: Hammy fixing evidence, shooting dogs, and smacking kids. Cunningham leaving his lane—by a lot!

Replacing Zack Conte was a new second-in-command, *Paul Johnson*. "Things can only get better," he said. "I hope we don't have to wait too long for our first mission. I'd feel better with one under our belt. Guys'll be chomping at the bit."

"I remember the feeling," I said.

It came on the first day of summer—barely, 12:03 AM—the rapid three taps on my door. Heading to the shop with Laurence, our new weapons intelligence team (WIT) lead, we sighed in the coolness of the ninety-five-degree heat and learned that a practice run for the FNGs had been canceled on account of a recently discovered weapons cache.

I loaded onto the truck with my new teammates Adoni, Ryan, and Danny. Adoni Poledicha was a retired Army Special Forces operator with multiple tours in Iraq and Afghanistan, battle-tested and smart. He was so Greek that he spoke English with an accent. Ryan was twenty-two, a wide-eyed reserve first lieutenant national guardsman, his only experience an eight-week boot camp. Danny was a former marine and very quiet—you might say silent.

Muaad Kholi, my new terp, was twenty-four, of Syrian decent, and an air force veteran who had immigrated with his family to the United States as a kid. He sounded like he was from Ohio. I liked Muaad on a personal level and was eager to work with him.

The plan was to link up with EOD before crossing the outer perimeter of security, but they no-showed. Luckily a Blue Force Tracker (that's a GPS on steroids) brought us to our exact X-marks-the-spot destination. We sat until we received orders to move forward to the objective. The weapons cache had been located in a junkyard, giving the site a surreal postapocalyptic feel. I again thought of the movie *Mad Max*.

As others began processing the cache, I said, "Muaad, let's see if we can find the caretaker of this junkyard for a Q&A."

Once located, the caretaker was promptly brought to us. He was calm, comfortable with both the tone of my voice and the location of the interview. I gathered his personal info and asked about the stuff we'd found.

He said that about a month earlier, four masked men in a black automobile approached him with an offer he couldn't refuse. "I stash their explosives or they kidnap my entire family," the caretaker explained. "After they were stashed I relocated my family and notified the local Sahwa."

The interview had not been challenging, but it was productive. We learned about the particular way in which the terrorists used extortion to acquire hiding spots for their evil product.

And there was something else. There had been a smoothness, a rhythm, to Muaad's translations that gave me as an interviewer a power that I hadn't felt since arriving in Baghdad. I had the sense that I was communicating efficiently with the subject, despite the fact that words were being translated. Muaad and I had a professional and a personal rapport, and he noticed it too. I knew right away that he was never going to tell me he couldn't translate "essentially fucked." He would've used a hand gesture if he'd had to, but he wouldn't have broken the rhythm of the interview.

The mission complete, we returned to our vehicles (I had no trouble finding mine) and were warned that a CNN news crew was inside a nearby vehicle. We left as quietly as we could. Fleeing the media because you're top secret gives you a pretty grown-up feeling, but this was quickly sabotaged back at the base when we again had to wait at the gate for a first sergeant to inspect our weapons at the clearing barrels.

Back at the shop, it was 4:30 AM and sleep deprivation was biting at us. Jerr, who hadn't gone out with us, put on a fresh pot of coffee. Muaad gave me his interview transcripts—in Arabic.

"Muaad?"

"Yeah, Chris?"

"I need it in English."

"Fuck," he said. "Give me two minutes."

That was worth a laugh. *You have one job!*

As I wrote my report, I had my own issues with the sandman: meaning one thing and writing another, spelling like I was in third grade. Mike D., who was still with the team as well, lost part of his report when Jerr accidentally unplugged his computer. It was 1500 hours before my head hit the pillow and I fell into a dead sleep.

During the last week in June we got a call from the 4-64, the first time in a long time that they'd requested our services. There'd been a mishap in which one of their soldiers shot up a confiscated Koran for target practice while his bro filmed the most excellent marksmanship. It went viral on YouTube and the president of the United States had to offer a formal apology to the prime minister of Iraq, Nouri al-Maliki himself.

Now the 4-64 was reporting that a member of the Sahwa had found an unexploded IED/EFP and notified the battlespace commander, requesting assistance. The mission, I was thankful to hear, was to be in the daylight. The heat was worse, but the visibility and processing of forensic evidence was so much easier.

Our objective was twenty minutes away. The *muhallah* looked familiar, with the close proximity of all the homes and businesses. We drove down a narrow street in a wide vehicle. Pedestrians pressed to the sides to get out of the way. Some had frightened expressions. Others blinked too rapidly.

Phone service in the village was cut and jammed because of the height of our MRAPs, further riling the residents. In a terrifying moment, our gunner made contact with a low-hanging wire. He could've been electrocuted but got away with "only" a broken nose.

On-site, EOD waited for a half hour and then decided to blow the device with a water charge. The plan was to disable the device while causing minimum damage. I stayed close to the radio, and when called, I came forward to do my piece.

Our intel team lead Laurence briefed me: "Chris, an INP lieutenant was called by local citizenry regarding a found explosive device. Info is sketchy. No one fesses up to making the call."

I set out to fill in the blanks, first approaching a nearby storeowner. "Did you see any of the events pertaining to the explosive?" I asked.

At that moment, two young men standing beside the store entrance bolted and ran down the mall that bisected the street. In NYC, flight implies guilt. Here in Iraq, the motive could just as easily be survival. After all, folks suspected of loyalty to USCF sometimes were found hung by their balls. I didn't take it personally and continued the interview.

"I came into work late," the storeowner said.

"When?"

"Around 10:00 AM. That was when I heard about the discovery."

"What did you hear?"

"Nothing precise. I am unaware of any specifics."

The funny part about his statement was the fact the device was discovered and reported at 11:00 AM. Time in Iraq was basically meaningless, but I noted the fact that the storeowner had tried to alibi out.

Still, I liked him more than I disliked him, and I felt I was approaching a near-pristine level of communication because of Muaad's skills. The subject claimed his store had been burglarized one month prior, with the majority of his inventory stolen. He believed the people responsible were JAM cell members.

Finishing up, I reconnected with Laurence, and together we watched an interesting incident. A group of Iraqi police used a battering ram to knock in the gate to a mosque. It took seven strikes of the ram before the gate flew open with a metallic snapping sound. Five officers charged inside.

"What the hell brought this on?" I asked.

Laurence shrugged, but we paid close attention. "Imagine if a gang of cops broke into a church in Philadelphia," Laurence said. "It's a whole different side of the Earth we're on."

As it turned out, a show was being put on for the entertainment of all who watched. After five minutes, the INP emerged from the apparently deserted mosque with two posters of Moqtada al-Sadr in hand. The posters had been published and placed against the perimeter wall of the mosque for everyone to see, and now the police were confiscating these images of the notorious US foe.

See? they were demonstrating. *See how pro-US we are?* Russ, one of our intelligence officers, snapped photos of the Iraqi cops and the posters.

Laurence decided to play along. "Can I have one of those posters for evidence purposes?" Laurence said. The cop was *thrilled* to accommodate him.

As we loaded up, the convoy attracted the usual swarm of children. Having policed a crowded city, I wasn't stressed out by the kids. I took a few photos of them standing with my teammates. A couple kids had to move before we opened the rear hatch on a vehicle.

Adoni's years of soldiering hadn't prepared him for this. He felt letting kids get too close was a security risk. "We should be more aware of our zone of safety," he said. I thought he was a bit of a worrywart, but he probably had a point.

I gently shooed the kids away.

Back at the shop, new guys *Art Taylor* and *Dan Comstock* noted in their subsequent reports that Muaad, Adoni, and I had allowed the children to get too close. I lost my mind. I told Art he was making a fool of himself, although I didn't like the way it sounded when I said it. Art hung in like a man and lobbed back a couple of verbal salvos. I came away just a tad impressed with his character. Dan shrank away from the argument altogether. After a zesty argument, Art said sorry, I said no problem, I said sorry I called you a fool, he said no problem, and we moved on.

Here in Iraq, the stress of being away from your family coupled with the stress of the job made people make irrational decisions. Me included. I was far from immune to emotional outbursts and mood swings.

That night Laurence, Mike, and I had fun with the confiscated poster of Moqtada al-Sadr. We posed with it in immature ways at the Green Bean. A female soldier in an adjacent chair turned red, partially covering her face while laughing at the same time. Not quite cop humor but funny just the same.

The new crew clicked. And they were more interesting than the old crew. Sure, there were guys I didn't like personally—egos, braggarts—but they did their job. And there were also guys I did like.

Like Matt Pucino. Cunningham had left him with a big mess to clean up, but he had the smarts and the charm to do it. Within a week's time, he had managed to repair the hurt feelings. He quickly charmed his way back into the SCIF at brigade headquarters, and once there, he proved himself a very adept professional. Phoenix was up and running.

And *Duke Thomas*, a retired marine master sergeant. After the service he was a team lead on convoy security out of north Baghdad—250 missions to his credit. He had written and published a book about it, a fact that (obviously) inspired me. Duke had more experience than the rest of the shop put together, but he kept it to himself. Sure, he had a lot of funny stories, but he knew the loss of true friends as well.

Duke said, "Chris, I looked it up. I have been here seven years. Only twice have children been used in an assault against US coalition forces."

"Thanks, Duke." He'd looked it up—that meant a lot to me.

I was also glad that Mike Dominique was still with us. I came into the shop near the end of June and Mike was hooking up satellite TV. He'd made friends with Iraqi nationals and got permission to run the

My friend Matt Pucino (left), me, and interpreter extraordinare Muaad Kholi. We're wearing T-shirts from my friend's restaurant, the Dogwood.

wires. Imagine that. My first TV in half a year. Life was improving. I gave him a hand, helping snake wires to adjoining shops. The picture was perfect.

———————

Our next mission came during the first few days of July. I got changed and loaded my M4 with a full magazine of 5.56 mm ammo. At the vehicle, Mark, our new K-9 handler, directed a rambunctious German shepherd named Rocky into the confined seating area, where Muaad and Adoni were already in place. If the dog got on his hind legs he could look out the window. Rocky had found his spot.

Rocky was another dog who had received his training in the Netherlands. Mark sounded funny with his midwestern accent calling out orders to the dog in an awkward Dutch.

A twenty-minute ride brought us to the al-Dora neighborhood of southern Baghdad. Our well-grounded vehicle was collecting low-hanging wires like party streamers to hinder the town's communication.

We linked up with *Sergeant Bob King*, who gave us the down and dirty: "While on patrol, my driver, Staff Sergeant Schumann, and I spotted an HVI walking down a street."

"What was he wanted for?" I asked.

"The target was responsible for building IED/EFP's for the southwest area of Baghdad. He's on the kill-or-capture list. We stopped our Humvee and snatched him off his feet and placed him under arrest."

"Nice."

"Subject's name is *Omar*. We cuffed him and returned him to his residence and ordered the occupants at gunpoint to remain motionless. Omar has a big family: many adult women, children, his dad, and a possible neighbor as well. We decided best thing to do was call Phoenix for help."

Got to love that attitude.

Mark and Rocky completed their sweep. I photographed the occupants and took down names. As I worked, I recalled meeting Sergeant Schumann months earlier at the Green Bean over coffee. I'd sung Phoenix's praises. Apparently my pitch had worked.

As I made my way through the family members and possibly a neighbor, the suspect's dad wouldn't shut up. His son was a good boy. His son only had love in his heart—love for *Americans*.

"Tell him to shut up," I said to Muaad.

"Give him a reason," Muaad advised.

"Tell him his son is in deep trouble and anything he says could be used against him. Evidence is mounting in favor of the *Americans*."

Muaad spit the words in Arabic at the detainee and he clammed up.

"I couldn't have said it better myself," I said, and Muaad and I flashed each other quick grins.

When I finished with the occupants' pedigrees I alerted Paul J. our 2IC that I was ready for Mr. Omar, the man on the kill-or-capture list. The HVI was responsible for producing and assembling explosive devices that had killed countless people. I was disappointed. He didn't look physically intimidating.

Omar sat with slumped shoulders, a slight man, blindfolded and earplugged on the living room couch. I felt a lump in my stomach. I was sickened by the man's evil. I could feel it radiating off him, pushing me back in a way that I had to power through. But I was getting used to the scent of terrorist flop sweat. It didn't bother me nearly so much anymore.

I ordered his blindfold and earplugs removed and introduced myself. I told him I wasn't army, but I didn't exactly say what I was. I ordered our army specialist to leave the room and to shut the door behind him.

I was deliberate, stern, and kept a low tone. He thought he was clever and liked to answer questions with questions. Why did I think he should do that? Why did I think he would know them? I poked him in the chest with a stiff forefinger. I got my face in his face and whispered, "I'm not in the mood, pal. I ask, you answer." Muaad translated from a few feet away while Omar could still feel my breath.

Pulling aside my vest, I displayed the empty swatch of Velcro—no name, no rank. His face contorted with horror. He didn't know exactly what the absence meant, but I'm sure his imagination ran wild with speculation. I could tell by his quivering lower lip and flaring nostrils as he approached hyperventilation that he was now in the firm belief I was a spook, most likely out of the US alphabet soup. Who knows, possibly a torturer.

He asked again what he was charged with and I pulled the HVI's "hot sheet" from my back pocket. "Wanna see what your backyard looks like from a satellite?" I said with a smile. I wanted him to think we were all-powerful, capable of seeing into his bedroom at night.

"How did you get that?" he asked, his eyes widening.

I told him his death sentence was pretty much guaranteed, but if he didn't cooperate I could see to it that his children would grow up taunted daily by cruel classmates that their father was arrested for "killing Americans." For dramatic effect, I removed my weapon from around my neck

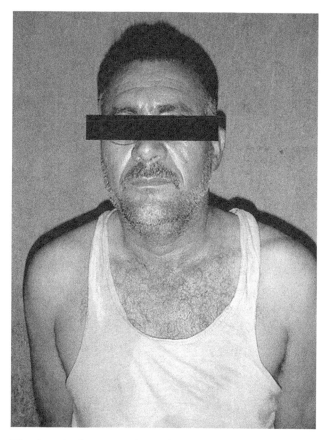

The head of a terrorist cell, under arrest.

and propped it up against the wall. I was jazzed at Muaad's translation, matching my cadence so the interview remained crisp.

"Should I stay or should I go?" I asked.

"Stay," he replied.

"Give me a name, just as a sign of good faith."

He was tempted, but he came up short: "Promise me my family will be protected," he said. And that was as close as he got. But he'd hesitated and contemplated, and he knew I knew it.

Mike D. knocked on the door and apologized for the interruption. "Russ and I found a large cache of electronic components. Look familiar?" Mike held up a clear bag containing bomb parts.

"Ah, same as in our intelligence report!" I showed them to the subject. "Game over, pal—you are seriously fucked."

Omar fell into a silent funk.

"Well, at least I've given you something to think about."

In the next room I explained to Sergeant King that I had the subject considering cooperation. "A change of scenery will do wonders."

The subject was moved to a military vehicle for transport. As we packed up to leave as well, Paul asked how it went.

"I got close, but I didn't break him," I said.

Still, we captured Omar. Word got around this was big—a major investigation.

––––––––––––––

Back at the shop, I changed into civvies and attacked the processing of evidence and preparation of my report with vigor. Over eleven hours I processed thirty separate bags of evidence, enough electronic components to assemble a hundred full-up IED/EFPs. Plus, as Omar cooled his heels in a detention facility, there was a terrorist cell out there that had lost its bomb-maker.

A guy from the army tactical questioning (TQ) unit stopped by the shop and I briefed him on my interview with Omar: "I was very close to an actual confession. Subject stopped short of implicating his pals." The guy from TQ thanked me and promised to keep me posted.

I found Muaad and lauded him for his excellent interpreting. His face was lit up even before I complimented him. He'd felt our two-headed efficiency too. He said we shouldn't spend too much time patting ourselves on the back. I agreed—there was room for growth. It made us yearn for another asshole to interrogate.

14

MR. SUBHUMAN, MR. OSCAR, AND MR. LOVER

AT 10:15 PM ON JULY 5, 2008, there came the telltale knock on my door. We had a trigger-based mission in support of the 7-10 Cavalry. They had an HVI under surveillance and were awaiting a call from their source in order to apprehend the guy. That meant we were on hold, too, all dressed up with no place to go. We had a pool wagering on when the call to action would come. Mike D. was the bookie.

Ryan won with his entry: 12:15 AM. That's when word came that the subject, whom I'll refer to as *Mr. Subhuman*, was being detained.

Moving out, our MRAP became stuck in the mud and had to be pulled out by a truck, a stressful time as the muddy area was in the open, making us particularly vulnerable to sniper activity. You haven't lived until you've scanned rooftops for incoming while hooking up a tow.

It took us an hour to get to the site. Once there, a lieutenant gave me good news and bad news. Good news was, they had a positive ID on the subject. Bad news, the army brought their own TQ guys, not the norm, rendering me potentially redundant. That put a bounce in my step. I read the subject's hot sheet, grabbed Muaad, and entered the house.

They had Mr. Subhuman on a chair in the main room, cuffed, sensory deprived. TQ guys were already there, fuck, and they told me they weren't sure the guy was the right guy.

"What do you know?" I asked.

"He had Mr. Subhuman's phone."

"That's good enough for me," I said.

I observed the detainee and looked at the photo on the hot sheet. There was a facial resemblance, but it wasn't exact. I theorized that

A detainee isolated from the group. As soon as that blindfold came off the questioning began.

Mr. Subhuman might be the target's brother. I had his blindfold and earplugs removed. He blinked at me.

"I am going to ask you some questions. They are going to be repetitive in nature," I said. Muaad fell in seamlessly. "We are going to go about this in a deliberate and systematic manner."

"All right," he said.

I held up my hand. "Remain silent until I actually get to a question." I reached out and shook the subject's head a little bit, gentle but very rude. "I am not army. I am not hindered by army rules. And, I am not here to discuss your past bad deeds. We know what you've done, that it's extensive. Still, I am going to keep my questions to subjects of the here and now. And if you decide to jerk me around, I will throw you back like a bad fish and suggest you be executed."

My words had no apparent effect. That was evidence of guilt. An innocent man barks with indignation. Mr. Subhuman was stoic, committed to his cause.

"The difference between you and me is that, at the end of the day, I get to go home to be hugged by my wife and children. It says here you are married, have a nine-month-old baby boy at home. You want your son to be raised by another man?"

That got him. His face contorted with rage. His guard was down. A door had opened, so I walked right in. I moved within inches of the subject's face.

"I have the power to make your life very uncomfortable, and my patience is wearing thin." I caught the first scent of fear wafting off him like a sour cloud, another indication of his vulnerability. I was getting to him. "Under the law," I continued, "your father, who is currently in handcuffs, is considered equally guilty as you. You want me to release him? Give me a name, someone in your cell."

He choked back words.

"See these soldiers guarding you? They work for me. They can't release your father. Only I can."

I grabbed the subject's sweat-slick shoulder. His breath was labored. I was close. I needed for him to register my sincerity. "All right, look. I know you are scared, and I know you are scared of me."

"I am scared," he replied. "But not of you."

"Do you want me to release your father?" I grabbed him by both shoulders and shook him again.

He nodded.

"Then give me a name."

He opened his mouth but could spit out only unintelligible syllables.

"Give me a name and your father goes free," I said.

"I don't know what to do," he said. "I am a good person. I have never been in trouble before." He gave me the look.

I'd gone as far as I could. Time for me to let up. Besides, we never liked to stay in one place for too long. It was time to move this interrogation to a new and more secure location.

After the interview, Muaad grabbed me and said, "Those bastards."

"Who?" I said.

"Fucking TQ guys. They were smirking during your questioning and distracting Mr. Subhuman."

I fumed. "From now on the only people present at our interrogations will be you and me. Period," I replied.

My interview with Mr. Subhuman showed promise. Other aspects of the investigation were disappointing. Practically no evidence had been found.

It was July 7 and I was doing curls in the weight room when I got word. At the shop, Ricky said the mission was again trigger based. The 2-4 had snatched up an HVI after spotting him in a vehicle.

Along on this mission was *Tim Treu*. We'd gone through orientation training together in Lansdowne. This was his first time accompanying Phoenix, and I was glad to see him. After getting the down and dirty, I found myself with Tim T. and Muaad looking down on a detainee on the ground in blindfold and earplugs.

The first order of business was to locate an empty interior room in which to carry out the interview. A crowd was gathering, and I could hear in their tone that I was about to question a beloved and respected neighbor. He deserved an Academy Award, this guy. I dubbed him *Mr. Oscar*.

Inside the house we took over a living room, rearranged the furniture to maximize the detainee's claustrophobia, and asked the guards to bring him in and place him in the easy chair. His hands were cuffed behind him. Sensory deprivation was removed. I could tell immediately Mr. Oscar was a pro. He showed no reaction to all the attention.

I began with a reality check: "Do you have any idea how much trouble you are in?"

He gave me a sarcastic smile. "I'm not in any trouble at all, because I have done nothing at all."

"Have you ever had someone punch you in the mouth and break your jaw?" I asked.

I offered a sarcastic smile of my own, for effect and not action, but he didn't know that. His attitude did improve. He now offered his lies in a serious tone.

Information from his workup sheet described in detail some of his recent trips to Iran, which was a prominent sponsor of terrorism in the region. Mr. Oscar was a serious dude.

Tim and I had a conference. We decided to send Mr. Oscar back outside with his guard and replace him in the easy chair with passenger #1 from Mr. Oscar's vehicle. I learned that #1 had been a lieutenant colonel in Saddam's army. I pegged him as a guy who knew what Mr. Oscar did but had no direct involvement.

"You know the bad things that Mr. Oscar does, right?"

"I don't . . ."

"Sure you do." Stroking his ego, I said, "You are a man of obvious intelligence. For you to be involved with these terrible things is pointless."

I let that percolate. The effect was more immediate and intense than I'd expected. It was like I'd pulled my finger from the dike. The information began to flow, and it didn't stop. After laying it all out for us, #1 threw in his defense: he'd infiltrated the terrorists because of his connection with the CIA.

The interview was interrupted. Paul J. poked his head in. "Getting ugly outside," he said. "Lot of anger, shouting, clenched fists—we need to collapse and move out right now."

I told him I was getting somewhere with the passenger, so we had Mr. Oscar and #1 moved to the base for additional questioning. The army would get first pick as to what to do: let Muaad and me continue our questioning or do it themselves.

Back at Falcon, Muaad and I had to share the Qs with TQ. I believed the rapport Muaad and I had built was essential to getting more out of this detainee, but I had to settle for briefing TQ on the interrogation so far and suggesting follow-up questions.

It occurred to me that the whole concept of rapport was foreign to the army. In the NYPD world, once a rapport was established with a detainee, the dynamic was rarely changed, as change might create too many variables that often led to failure.

One of the sergeants did the follow-up interview with #1 while I observed. His interviewing technique was very mild, bland. It was like he was imitating an economics professor whose class he'd enjoyed because it was easy to sleep through.

That said, he didn't take shortcuts. His questioning may have been poky and expressionless, but it was thorough. He had me champing at the bit. The passenger continued to dish out info on a silver platter, but it seemed more and more bogus. Still, if only 10 percent was true, he was a gold mine.

Then they let go passenger #1, along with the other passengers. I was disappointed. I wasn't worried about detaining him again if necessary. I was worried about his safety. If he was pegged as an informant, his life was near worthless. Hell, his whole family could disappear.

And he seemed to me to be so promising. He really did have the DNA of a great informant, a guy on the wrong side of the street telling a cop he was only there because he was spying for the company. The idea was already in his head.

Mid-July, midday, Paul J. took a call regarding a new mission. He was still writing down the key info when our incoming siren began to wail. Mortar attacks on the base were not unknown but luckily had been growing less frequent.

Trouble was, the day before there had been a bungled, too-long alarm drill. On this day rather than react with urgency, many just moaned when they heard the alarm. Duke and I paused but then took cover in the concrete bunker just outside our workspace. After ten minutes of silence, we went back to work.

At the shop, Duke checked the rollout roster. He wasn't on it. Duke was a battle-tested marine who had received the Bronze Star with the "V" device. Keeping Duke inside the wire was like putting gas in a Ferrari and leaving it in the garage. The reason was nothing personal, simply risk management. We only brought the personnel we needed, because there was always a chance someone would get killed. This reality was never spoken out loud but was a key component of the Iraq gestalt.

But Duke looked so disappointed. He'd only recently gotten his arming agreement, through which a civilian employee can go on missions armed. Guys that lacked an AA were kept on base.

"Hey Paul, what say Duke accompanies me on the mission? The exposure will give him a real sense of the biometrics on the ground and flow for the work product," I said.

"OK. Suit up, Duke."

Duke's face lit up. He had a shit-eating grin right up until the moment our MRAP broke the wire, when he put his game face on.

We'd been sitting on-site for twenty minutes when Laurence called Duke and me forward. We were in a dirt field, littered with garbage and abandoned vehicles. Laurence pointed to a fuel tanker trailer.

"That tanker trailer has been modified by a JAM cell to disguise and transport Iranian munitions," he explained.

I watched as three soldiers very carefully unloaded the weapons from the hollowed-out fuel tanker. I saw mortars and long arms, by far the largest weapons discovery I'd seen since arriving in Iraq. I snapped a picture. No matter what else happened on-site, we were in for a long night of evidence processing. Circling around, I looked into the tank, where two more soldiers were handing out the matériel. The packaging for the weapons was new, dated 2008. Return addresses were in Iran. The original purchaser would be missing them and in deep trouble for not doing a better job of hiding them.

"We're looking for someone who witnessed the transportation of the weapons to the site," Laurence said.

So I talked to several neighbors, all of whom were terrified of the JAM cell. They were under constant psychological attack. A fifteen-foot-high poster hung outside on a streetlight, a likeness of a JAM terrorist killed by USCF. The poster proclaimed the terrorist's martyrdom.

After twenty minutes of meet-and-greet, orders came to move to a new location. As we walked back to our vehicle, we passed a generator repair shop. I remembered that during earlier missions I had learned that "generator repair" was sometimes a euphemism for bomb-builder.

I asked a grown man if he'd seen any activity regarding the fake tanker trailer. Then an odd thing happened: the man said he knew nothing, but a teenage boy stepped forward and began to speak. But he didn't get very far, as two other teenage boys attacked him and beat the shit out of him, finally sending him fleeing with a kick in the ass. That was our cue to leave.

The team moved to a second location that looked familiar, a neighborhood we'd worked before. In a way that was comforting. The 7-10 had secured the residence of a subject they'd rolled up who was accused of putting the fake tanker in that field. They requested "full exploitation" of the house. I was briefed by a Staff Sergeant Pena. US forces had gotten a positive ID in person from a source.

"Sergeant Pena, please remove all of the curious bystanders," I said. "Neighbors aren't going to help the interview."

Muaad and I climbed into the Humvee with the perp. His blindfold was removed, I photographed him, and the interview began.

"You kill Americans," I said.

"No, I *love* Americans," he replied. He emphasized the word. He went on and on about it. I dubbed him *Mr. Lover* and ended his diatribe by redirecting his attention to the more pressing matter at hand.

"Who are your friends?" I asked.

"My friends are innocent, too."

"Then why would someone say you are an arms smuggler?"

"A week ago, my home was searched by US forces. Perhaps the search made one of my neighbors nervous." Mr. Lover lost control of his emotions. Tears were streaming down his face.

Muaad wrote on his notebook and held it up for me to see. "HE'S LYING," it read.

So I pretended I believed him, and his tears dried up instantly—too fast.

"I would like an opportunity to confront my accuser face to face," he said. That, of course, would be like signing the accuser's death warrant, but I said I'd see what I could do.

I asked Sergeant Pena a key question. How did we get to this point in the investigation? How did we get from the fake tanker to here?

Sergeant Pena explained there were two sources of information, one of them a positive identification.

"What is the second source?"

"That's a close hold."

"From whom did you receive the PID?" I asked.

"An Iraqi police officer. I've got him in the back of a Humvee," Sergeant Pena said, "disguised as US Army—ACU top, shades, and a green scarf to cover his face."

"Let's talk to him," I said.

The location was far from ideal. I asked a Staff Sergeant Rozell, known to all as Rozy, to disperse the crowd before the Humvee's hatch was opened.

It didn't take many questions before I became unhappy with the Iraqi cop's answers—or non-answers. I asked him how he knew about the fake tanker and how he knew the man he'd accused of putting it there. He told me of his many virtues and his deep knowledge of terrorist activity in the neighborhood. He told me he was a personal bodyguard of a local sheik. I felt like slapping the guy, but instead I called the interview and returned to Sergeant Pena, who reiterated that he couldn't tell me about the other source. I respected that.

"Where did you find the Iraqi cop?" I asked.

"Found him by accident during a canvassing."

"What info did you get from your secret source?"

"Location of the weapons cache and the make of Mr. Lover's car—black Mercedes-Benz. While asking around we ran into *Mr. Policeman*. We later received info that the weapons were kept for a time directly across the street from his house, so he knew about the cache five days before he told us about it. He took me to Mr. Lover's workplace and there one more arrest was made."

I thought about the tragedy that had been avoided. Those mortars and long arms were found out in a field where little kids played soccer; their parents were too afraid of JAM to say anything but "Be careful."

I was proud of the sergeant and his men, unsung heroes in a dirty war. Their efforts would never be reported in the *New York Times*. "Great job, Sergeant Pena," I said. "Tomorrow your findings will be reported to the president of the United States during his morning briefing."

"*Hooah!*" he said.

15

MR. BAD GUY

BY THE END OF JULY 2008, Phoenix had become an indispensable asset to the army, grabbing up high-value targets one by one, dismantling their cells, and taking away their safe harbors. A single phone call to Phoenix and we handled everything from the arrest to turning our work product over to the unit in charge within twelve hours. We provided fast, tangible results, delivering the lowlifes, along with meticulously processed evidence. Our reports included sound, detailed, actionable intelligence. It was a prosecutor's dream, and the brigade's JAG attorneys were using us to their full advantage.

Our targets grew more important, until we came to a very big cheese indeed. The brigade's time sensitive targeting (TST) planners called Ricky about a certain *Mr. Bad Guy*, a *leader* of the JAM-affiliated terror network they were about to move on. In conducting their surveillance, they utilized resources provided by the National Security Agency (NSA) and other government agencies (OGA)—code lingo for black ops. These measures included data-mining from cell phones, unmanned aerial drones, and other methods so secret that any dissemination of info about them would be a serious breach of operational security . . . and a one-way ticket home to the States.

Phoenix was briefed the evening before the operation. For all the technological sophistication of the surveillance, our plan was simple:

we were going to snatch the piece of shit out of his bed under cover of darkness and flip his house upside down.

With this mission, we were about to break new ground.

Before rolling out, Ricky called Muaad and me outside for an offline conversation. Grinning like the cat that ate the canary, he walked us across the parking lot and suggested we dress down in civilian clothes and devise a ruse for the prisoner's interrogation. I had told him about flashing the word "Corporation" at a target who didn't read English, and he'd clearly think it meant I was with Central Intelligence. It was against the rules to impersonate a CIA agent, but there was nothing in the playbook that said if a detainee was under the mistaken impression that you were an agent, you had to go out of your way to enlighten him.

Ricky said, "We'll use a vacant workspace for our interview. Set up a few chairs and tables to make it resemble a bona fide interrogator's room."

I knew where he was heading. Ever since CIA and army jackasses crossed the line torturing detainees at Abu Ghraib prison, we've had prohibitively strict rules imposed on the tactical questioning of suspected terrorists. The abuses of a few gave the entire system a disgusting black eye, and the consequential restrictions sometimes handcuffed us.

But now wasn't the time for that. We were closing in on the top men in the insurgents' leadership hierarchy and didn't want to blow our chance.

Ricky said, "If Mr. Bad Guy gets confused about who you are . . ." He let it hang, but I filled in the blank: *Oh well.* That would be on him, not us. "This is a dicey proposition," Ricky continued. "We'd be pushing the limits of conventional interviews." He looked at me. "It's your ass on the line. Yours and Muaad's. So, I want to hear your thoughts." Basically, he wanted to know if we'd be willing to participate.

I considered his idea for a minute, then told him it made good sense from a law enforcement standpoint. As a former cop, that was the only way I could evaluate it. Meanwhile I could feel that Muaad was getting excited. We'd gotten so tight, it went beyond efficiency—we were inside each other's heads.

"We'll be in a gray area as far as legalities," I told Ricky. He already knew it, of course, and I wasn't looking for approval. I just wanted everything out in the open between us. The rule book could give anyone a headache, and I wanted it known that we weren't going to stringently follow its dogma. I also wanted it known that I understood the consequences. "If we aren't careful, we could find ourselves in the deepest shit imaginable. But I think it's worth the risk," I concluded.

Ricky nodded in agreement. Muaad did the same without hesitation. We were on.

Soon the three of us were in the shop waiting for the phone call from the brigade's TST unit. Everyone had suited up for the capture mission except Muaad and me. We remained in civilian attire. I never expected to have much use for my Levi's business casuals and polo shirts when I packed them back in the States, but it paid to be prepared.

A half hour had passed when the phone rang. The call was put on speaker. "*Touchdown!*" came the code word. Everyone in uniform loaded into their vehicles and headed out into the darkness.

Back at the shop, Muaad and I watched the overhead monitors from a surveillance platform. The classified technology that gave ground commanders the ability to track their troops—as well as the bad guys' movements—was truly amazing. It really was a future-shock moment. I felt like I was on the bridge of the Starship *Enterprise*.

Once on target, the team quickly got to work dismantling Mr. Bad Guy's residence. They gave it a good old-fashioned house-tipping. By the time they were done, you'd need a cleaning crew to put everything back in place.

After almost two hours, the team radioed in: "We are inbound with the prisoners." Mr. Bad Guy and several others had been scooped up.

Muaad and I were busy poring over the prisoner's case folder, along with files on several of his associates who'd been rolled up earlier in the week. Reading the reports, I could see the investigation had been limited to circumstantial evidence and hearsay. Mr. Bad Guy was the number-two person in the food chain. I knew the pressure was on, so I digested the case files for information as fast as I could. I made a mental note of everything I could leverage against him—things like family, employment, personal wealth, and possessions, in addition to the obvious: direct links to terrorist activity.

Meanwhile, Airman Neuman from the brigade's SCIF was briefing me on the basics of their investigation. Beside him was Lieutenant Sanchez, a female officer I'd recently gotten to know. Sanchez had become close friends with Matt at the SCIF. Their professional relationship was essential to Phoenix operations. The rest was their private business, though some of the guys enjoyed speculating about it.

As we conferred, Sanchez gave me a typed list of suggested questions to ask the prisoner. I nodded and jotted down questions of my own, after conferring with Airman Neuman about some highlighted bits of info. These were based on intelligence gathered by closely guarded technology, so I had to be careful. It was always better to let a subject know you knew something without letting them know how you knew it. When law enforcement refuses to release surveillance footage, people think it's because there's something on that footage that law enforcement doesn't want seen, when often the secret that is being kept is the location of the camera. If Mr. Bad Guy got wise to how the info was obtained, it could compromise future arrests and interviews.

Once our ground rules were set, Muaad and I walked back toward our ad hoc interview room. As I mentally prepared for the interview, I arranged the table and seating locations. It was always best to keep the detainee uncomfortable. Face him toward a wall, never toward a window. Keep distractions to a minimum. If possible, keep them nonexistent. With our interviewer room's version of feng shui complete, we waited for rest of the team to return with the prisoner.

We were ready to go.

———

Once Mr. Bad Guy was secured, I spoke briefly to the army sergeants who had picked him up. It was mostly a courtesy, but a Sergeant Glasgow gave us some insight.

"He's a biter," Glasgow said.

"Pardon me?" I replied.

"A biter. He tried to bite some of the guys."

"Oh. Thanks—good to know."

I could commiserate. Nobody likes a biter. On the NYPD, we'd dread hauling biters in for interrogation. Not only is getting bitten painful and gross, it isn't sanitary. Human bites can transmit hepatitis B and C, herpes, tetanus, tuberculosis, even HIV infections. Lowlifes aren't known for their dental hygiene. I'd rather be bitten by a stray mutt.

After hearing about Mr. Bad Guy's nasty habits, I traded glances with Muaad and we agreed it was time. Glasgow and the other sergeant, Christensen, came along for the ride.

In the interrogation room, I saw a blindfolded Iraqi male seated at a folding table, his hands flex-cuffed behind his back. After a second, I motioned for an MP to remove the blindfold. The prisoner acted disoriented, but he lacked the skills of a good actor and I could tell right away it was bullshit. He exaggerated his gestures, deliberately trying to look confused so he could dodge my questions.

Walking around the table, I gave the side of his chair a good, hard kick to establish my dominance. As an interviewer, I needed to assert myself over him psychologically, show him right off who was in control. When I ordered him to stand up, I shouted the words with all the volume my lungs would allow.

Mr. Bad Guy jumped to his feet, startled and nervous.

With my Olympus in hand, I snapped off a couple of photos and told him to sit down again.

"I am Strom, and this is my translator Muaad. Muaad will also be memorializing your answers both with recordings and with written notes."

Mr. Bad Guy was squinting and feigning unsteadiness.

"Before we get started, would you like a drink of cold water?"

He nodded and I give him a bottle. The gesture demonstrated that I was capable of offering an unprompted kindness, which could prove to be important as the interview developed.

My ground rules came next. I advised him to listen without responding until I finished my introduction. "I am aware that you tried to bite some of the soldiers who brought you in. I want you to understand something. Unlike those guys, I am not a soldier. If you try to chomp me I will break your jaw. After breaking your jaw, I will continue the interview. So, choice is yours: answer questions with a broken jaw, or answer them without one."

So much for the formalities. I waited for Mr. Bad Guy to acknowledge my instructions, and he did. He had noticed Muaad and I were not in uniform, and that made him curious and apprehensive. He was wondering if we were CIA. No one else in our theater of operations conducted prisoner interviews in civvies.

I opened a folder on the table. I had placed some incriminating pictures inside, including detailed shots of electronic bomb components taken at his residence. My intelligence indicated he not only was the builder of those IED/EFPs but also placed them in locations designed to cause the deaths of American soldiers. By his own admission, he was an engineer with a formal graduate degree, so I knew he was more than capable of putting together bombs, including sophisticated EFPs with parts imported from his friends in Iran.

Besides these photos, I had a mug shot of his terror cell's number-three man, *Mr. Asshole*. I wanted him to know that Mr. Asshole was also in the custody of US coalition forces . . . and that he had been singing like a bird.

I tapped the photo of Mr. Asshole with an anxious fingertip. "What is your relationship to our other prisoner?" I asked.

He said they were just passing acquaintances. *Right.* My intel indicated they were best buddies.

I shot Muaad a glance. Then I kicked my folding chair out from under me and moved with a quickness that startled him. I was around the end of the table and he had just started to flinch when I grabbed him tightly on the shoulder with my left hand and balled my right hand into a tight fist.

"Remember what I told you about lying," I said. My voice trembled with anger. "I'm done fucking around, understand?"

He nodded, petrified, and I eased off. I shot a glance at Sergeant Glasgow and Sergeant Christensen. My display of temper was all an act to get the prisoner thinking about Abu Ghraib and the ruthlessness of CIA interrogators. The prisoner might be a lousy actor, but not me. My thespian skills are part of the job. Al Pacino has got nothing on me.

With my silent message sent to the sergeants, I allowed the prisoner to settle down and resumed the interview.

"Look," I said, calmer now. "How do you think we were able to find your residence?"

"I don't know."

"A smart guy like you? With your education? Come on. You have to be wondering." My implication was that his pal informed on him, but he just crossed his arms and shrugged in pretend disbelief.

"The other man you arrested does not know where I live," he quickly insisted. Too quickly, in fact—before Muaad even started to interpret my words.

I quickly brought my eyes to his face. "You speak English," I said. It wasn't a question.

He stared at me with fake incomprehension but said nothing.

"You speak English," I repeated, pointing out his blunder. "You claimed you didn't when we started tonight's conversation. But you do."

This time he waited for Muaad before insisting he didn't understand me. But it was too late. His quick initial response was a dead giveaway. He was using a counterinterrogation technique to exploit his interrogator. It was clear that he had received formal resistance training and was trying to match wits.

I proceeded with that in mind. "Your friend gave you up," I declared. "Your situation's a result of him cooperating with me."

That was the truth, as far as it went. We had other intelligence leading in his direction, but the HUMINT I pulled from Mr. Asshole was invaluable. Thanks to him, we knew the number-one guy on the terror ladder was called *Jubar*. But we didn't know if that was his real name or a nickname.

I kept up the pressure, explaining that Mr. Asshole had not enjoyed his interrogation and had broken down in tears after being grilled for about half an hour. "He cried like a baby," I said.

Mr. Bad Guy just stared at me.

"Truthfully, I felt embarrassed for him," I added. "He was a pitiful sight."

He stared some more. I changed tacks, mentioning his education again, laying my praise on thick. Part of it was that I wanted to fluff his ego . . . but I also wanted to get across that I knew he was the brains of the operation.

"You speak several languages. An engineering degree shows that you're very intelligent. Unlike your crybaby friend."

A few seconds passed. I waited. After a full minute, he turned to Muaad. "I need to use the bathroom," he said in Arabic. It was more evidence of his resistance training. He wanted to break my momentum, throw me off stride.

I glanced at Sergeant Glasgow to indicate that he would have to escort our prisoner to the can. Then I cut through his flex cuffs.

"Remember," I said. "Any attempt to escape would be a big mistake."

He left without thanking me for the heads-up, but I didn't take offense. Gratitude wasn't a strong point among terrorist dirtbags.

While Mr. Bad Guy was out of the room, I flashed back to my time as an interrogator of the mob for the NYPD, of breaking down gun and drug dealer Pete Medina during a vigorous questioning. I felt inspiration.

When Mr. Bad Guy returned from his rest stop, I cuffed his hands in front to make him more comfortable, and established that he would have to provide concrete information to further improve his situation. Finally, I give him another look at Mr. Asshole's mug shot.

"If you ever want to see your children again, you'll have to serve up Jubar," I said. My tone was firm but reasonable. "If we capture him without you, you're left with nothing to offer us."

He broke eye contact with me, slouched a little, and gazed down at the table.

These were good signs. Signs of defeat. I was making progress. My mention of his children hit a soft spot. The same as it had with Medina. But the deal wasn't done.

I tossed him a yellow legal pad and placed a pen near his hand. "Draw a map of where Jubar lives," I said.

He picked up the pen, hesitated, and put it back down. He spoke slowly, hesitantly: "The man you want . . . it occurs to me there are many Jubars at the ministry."

"Is that so . . . ?"

"Yes. Very many. It is a common name in my country." He shrugged. "I may recall *a* Jubar, though not necessarily *the* Jubar you seek. Let me return to my office and I'll search the files."

"Uh, yeah. I don't think so."

But I had to hand it to him. Just when I thought I'd heard it all, he came out with a novel line of bullshit. "Our surveillance indicates you've worked with Jubar for two years. In the *same* office," I said.

I paused to look him straight in the eye. "I came halfway around the world to lock up you and your friends, and I'm just getting started. I got four of you guys in less than a week, and I'm not stopping till I get all of you. So get used to seeing prison walls for the rest of your *short* life." The implication being he would wind up on death row after his trial.

Mr. Bad Guy opened his mouth silently, closed it, sank down farther in his chair, and dissolved into racking sobs. Some guys fall apart a little at a time, some go all at once. I let him heave and sob for maybe ten seconds and then, softly, I returned to my main question: "Where is Jubar?"

He insisted he didn't know anything about him.

I looked directly into his eyes. "Is it possible Jubar's only a nickname?"

My ploy was a way of giving him an easy out, a chance to save face, to back off his obvious lie without having to look foolish. He didn't go for it, and once more denied knowing the number-one man. It was time to use my ace in the hole.

I leaned toward Muaad and whispered for him to please retrieve Mr. Bad Guy's confiscated cell phone from the evidence processing room, where it had been under inspection since his capture. When he returned, Muaad scrolled through a list of contacts before stopping at "Jubar." Then he gave me a look and I knew it was game on.

I stood up and went back around to Mr. Bad Guy's side of the table. At the same instant, Muaad shoved the cell phone's viewscreen into his face.

"What's *this?*" Muaad asked.

Mr. Bad Guy was shaking in his seat, coming unglued. His cheeks were shiny with tears and sweat. With Jubar's name and number literally in his face, he knew we held the proverbial smoking gun.

Jubar's location remained a problem. There was no address listed in Mr. Bad Guy's phone.

"Where is Jubar?"

"I don't know. Ask me anything else . . . whatever questions you want," he snorted. "I know I can be of help."

I turned him down flat. In order to maintain dominance over him, I had to end the interview. We really didn't have anything else to discuss until he gave us a hard location for Jubar.

I glanced at Glasgow and Christensen, signaling we were finished. Mr. Bad Guy realized his mistake and shut down on me. I mean, he was catatonic.

"Sergeant, I am through. Make sure this man and the next interviewee are not allowed to have a discussion."

"Roger that, sir," he replied. Mr. Bad Guy was led away, his blindfold back on.

And what was Mr. Bad Guy to think but that I—a sizable and determined American man in a golf shirt—was about to tell all the other prisoners that he'd cried like a baby and spilled the beans?

During the break between prisoners, Muaad said he'd already sent Matt our intelligence analyst the phone number that made Mr. Bad Guy freak. The investigation had a starting point.

Jerr was downloading the address boxes from the confiscated phones. Muaad pored over a mound of papers, scanning names and numbers. There was a confusion with the phones. Which phone belonged to the guy we were about to interview? Why not just call the number with another phone to see which one rings? No, that had the potential of being misconstrued as constructing false evidence. Or, worse, the creation of a new ping, no matter how innocently intended, might compromise the forensic value of the phone's data.

The next detainee was more compliant. He had weighed matters and concluded that his freedom was worth more than his fear of Mr. Jubar. I could tell that his position at the ministry gave him a sense of prestige, respect, and credibility. This resulted in an *I could never be involved in the insurgency* attitude.

Whether this was true or not, I was not about to interrupt him. At least at first, keeping the detainee talking is more important than getting the truth. Verbalize him. Truth blurts more easily amid a steady stream of words.

My leverage became stronger as I was notified of new evidence. Once again, Jubar's phone number was found on the detainee's phone. We also matched the phone number of Mr. Bad Guy. That established, I had true leverage, which I used without giving up how we knew about their calls. Let them think we intercepted them, that we were omniscient—not that much of a stretch considering the sophistication of our electronic surveillance.

After some finely paced interrogation, he admitted that he worked with both Jubar and Mr. Bad Guy, *and* that he knew Jubar's address.

"When is Jubar's next scheduled day of work?"

"Sunday."

"When will he come in?"

"Between nine and ten in the morning."

His eyes were bloodshot, his breathing labored. I told him the interview was finished. "There will be other interviews down the road for you," I explained. "You must always remember to be cooperative with the man on the other side of the table." I offered him one last drink of water, which he gulped thirstily and thanked me for, and sent him off to a waiting Humvee.

I relayed all the key info to Matt and suggested we take our prisoner for a ride—a show-and-tell ride, so he could show us the Jubar residence.

Matt said there were a couple of arguments against that. One was that all the other members of his team were fast asleep, and besides, we'd all been up for twenty-two hours and we needed to consider the fatigue factor.

Matt wanted to know how I got the prisoner to open up, and I explained that I'd learned on the mean streets of Brooklyn to treat prisoners with respect. Some cops were incapable of humbling themselves, thinking it was beneath them to extend some courtesy like the use of a bathroom or a drink. The reality was that a single act of kindness would ease the way for the next person to question the prisoner.

"They don't all lack consciences," I said. "They aren't all sociopaths; they believe it is OK to do evil things for what they see as a just cause. But their consciences gnaw at them. Sometimes I just rub their noses in the bad things they've done and they weep and beg for forgiveness."

"Other times?"

"They are monsters. Missing the part of their psyche that feels remorse."

"How do you get to them?"

"I'm practical. I tell them, 'You're fucked, make it easy on yourself.'"

Matt laughed.

Afterward the sergeants told me our interview was one of the best they'd ever witnessed. I wasn't looking for praise, but it was nice to be appreciated, and I promised them a copy of my report as soon as possible.

Back at the shop, Muaad and I had our arms around each other's shoulders, radiating contentment. We'd completed an exhaustive, and exhausting, interview with undeniably positive results. Ricky and Paul had promised us a bottle of booze, type and brand of our choosing, if we scored a confession. They told us they were only too happy to pay up. (As usual, Ricky was high on praise, short on follow-through. No bottle ever came.)

"Credit goes to Muaad," I said, "the way he found Jubar's number on that phone, cool as a cucumber."

"Check-fucking-mate," Muaad said.

I gave Muaad another bear hug. From now on, we understood, we were an inseparable team.

Things continued to get better. Even as we celebrated, electronic forensic work continued on the confiscated phones. For a time there was a bit of worry, because the key phone number, listed as belonging to Jubar, officially belonged to a guy named *Mohammed*. Then, after a brief time, word came that it was confirmed: Jubar and Mohammed were one and the same. And Mohammed had an address to go along with the rest of his contact info. We had located our man.

Now I was the one who was buzzing with manic energy. Unable to sleep, I decided to get started on my report, and kept working as the sun rose over the giant sandbox outside.

————————

Matt and my new roomie Dave McWhirt heroically made a chow run for Muaad and me, as we were sixteen hours without food. The food was great, but I remained delirious from sleep deprivation. I struggled at the end and asked Muaad to please help put the photos into the report, making sure the correct image went with the correct face. In two minutes he had it done.

It was 10:30 AM when the report was completed. I handed the transfer sheet off to Paul J. for delivery to the detention holding area. Muaad finished his last literal translation of a document so that the corresponding security envelope could be sealed for inclusion with the remaining evidence.

Muaad and I took the Fobbit, a transport vehicle that never left the base, for the half-mile ride back to our hooches. By the time we arrived, it was 12:10 PM. Time of the mission: twenty-four hours and ten minutes. I didn't bother to set my alarm. Even if another mission did come up in the next few hours, Muaad and I were sure to be excluded—and I was OK with that. I reminded myself how much Muaad and I had accomplished as I hit the sack. And not a bite mark to show for it.

I was hoping the results of our interviews would soon bear out. We were getting closer and closer to Jubar. The big question now was whether we could reach him before he slipped out of the country.

We were knee-deep in breaking an IED/EFP cell, with the remaining members on the run. In the NYPD, in a case as big as this, the last thing we would have done was to let an important SOI out of our sight for an instant. We would keep him in jail if appropriate, but certainly slap a tail on him if not. It is called *conventional wisdom*—not Big Army's strong point. In fact, it found this concept completely foreign.

We were into the dog days of August when we revisited a bad guy's residence hoping to capture an elusive weapons cache. The original arrest location turned out to be the target's aunt's house, but the army failed to write down the aunt's name. The mistake would prove to have serious consequences. The SOI was never compelled to verify additional information with either a drive-by or publication of other tangible facts. Muaad and I had done our part, but we were dealing with a mobile and stealthy enemy. The remaining elements of this demonic tribe were forty-eight hours ahead of us and had gone black—zero communication or signals intelligence (SIGINT, e.g., electronic or cell phone surveillance or drone platforms).

Further complicating the situation was an arrogant JAG officer named *Captain Wyman*, who proclaimed the four detained cell members ready for release. He was a pinhead, one I'd already encountered unpleasantly. Wyman had once questioned me regarding "probable cause," claiming that the American-killing terrorist we'd rolled up should not have been arrested in the first place.

An army investigation had apparently determined that I provided the factual basis for that arrest. I explained to the JAG bastard that, as a contractor, I had no legal authority to direct anyone to make an arrest—I was an adviser only, and a damned good one, with more than three hundred personal arrests. I was well-versed in "probable cause."

"My NYPD success rate was 99.3 percent," I said.

In the inky night we pulled down an Iraqi block in tight formation. The brigade's TST team stacked at opposite corners and provided a security cordon from all sides. TST requested overhead surveillance, and this was promptly provided courtesy of the US Air Force.

In tactical—that is, swift—fashion, the army reached the house's entrance in five seconds flat. With the thunderous clang of the battering ram, the front gate and front door were unhinged and left flapping. Standing beside a cinder block wall, I caught the glimmer of flashlights moving from room to room and heard muted voices shouting "Clear."

The signal came over the radio: "Dry hole." That was code for vacant house. Mood dropped. The army had learned a very hard lesson: never let go of your source until you verify the facts. I was disappointed on a personal level, having invested so much time and effort into the case.

I searched the house. The former occupants had left in a hurry. The main parts of the residence had been stripped, with only the heavy furniture left in place. Looking inside the closets, I found some clothes still on hangers, the remainder heaped at the bottom.

This was not an army search, as had been conducted the first time at that location. Phoenix was about to give a lesson in "thorough." I took the master bedroom. Remembering my tradecraft, I began by looking under the bed. Satisfied, I lowered it, pulling it away from the wall. On that bed I meticulously stacked articles of clothing and personal effects. When I was halfway through, the room looked like an explosion had hit it, with a mountain in the center heaped five feet tall.

Mike D. finished his room and gave me a hand. After several minutes, he said, "Chris, come take a look at this." He'd pulled an entertainment console away from the wall, revealing a three-by-two-foot hole in the floor two feet deep. The hole, missed during the army's initial search, was now empty. I snapped off a couple of pictures, hoping to include them for leverage in follow-up interviews.

Back at the shop, Ricky had already erected the table for the eventual evidence processing. I showed Ricky the picture of the hole in the floor and managed a smile. "So close," I said.

"We're going in the right direction," Ricky said. "We're just a little behind the curve."

Mike D. pulled an entertainment console away from the wall, revealing this hole.

"It's a minor setback, but not fatal," I said. "We just have to stay focused and pick up the ball again."

As Muaad and I helped process evidence, we learned that documents had been seized that further indicated that this was a case with far-reaching implications involving the complicity of the Iraqi government.

We needed to reignite the investigation, sustain the momentum.

———————

I couldn't be specific with Debbie, of course, but I did indicate that things were going very well—not perfectly, but progressing in a way that was clearly meaningful.

She was quick to say she missed me, but never that my absence was a hardship, unless it was in the form of a joke. She'd say things like "It's funny, no offense, but men are sometimes more of a problem when they are around than when they aren't. Only kidding, I really miss you on Tuesdays when I have to haul the garbage down the 690-foot driveway."

Her dad was a businessman and worked a lot. Her mom had her own tool belt. So all of this seemed kind of normal to her. When we were first married I worked nights, she worked days. It was good, because we were both divorced and used to me-time. It was during our brief stint as a nine-to-five family that we had a hard time.

She understood that I had found my niche, that this is what I'm good at and this is what completes me.

The next day I was e-mailing my buddy Chuck about the job he'd offered me a few months back when Paul J. knocked and said we had a mission. The briefing was in the brigade conference room.

Our job was to locate the remaining members of the JAM cell. Muaad and I had acquired the key piece of evidence: Jubar's name, tentative address, and place of employment. According to recent intelligence, he'd fled to Iran. The names of the other fugitive members were placed on a big board in order of value and realistic chance of apprehension. It was going to be a long mission, and I noticed Duke was not to be included. Muaad and I psyched ourselves up, saying "*Ju! Bar!*" as we bumped fists.

Our convoy rumbled to the scene where we hoped to apprehend the first target. We stacked around the corner waiting for the signal to advance. As contractors, we were under rigid guidelines with respect to taking offensive action. That was why we only moved forward when so instructed. The army could shoot first and ask questions later. We were allowed to shoot only "In Self-Defense and Imminent Threat to Third Parties." Overlooking that could prove costly to a contractor's thoroughly *ca-ching* career and personal freedom.

I heard glass shattering.

"Get down!" a commanding voice called out.

The army breached the front doorway of the target residence in their usual dynamic fashion. After a brief cacophony, there was quiet, during which all I could hear were the whimpering cries of a small child.

A Sergeant Huston called Phoenix forward and gave us the intelligence dump: "The house is occupied by a husband and wife with one small boy approximately four years in age and in shock. The intended target was not present. Information from the male occupant was that he was an Iraqi police officer working as a personal bodyguard of some official."

"Ever notice that no one ever does any menial jobs in the Iraqi police department like patrol or post on a checkpoint?"

Sergeant Huston laughed.

"Could we clear a room for the eventual interviews to be conducted by my crew?" I asked.

Sergeant Huston said he'd get right on that.

Matt and I methodically searched the adjoining sitting room. We pulled the furniture away from the wall. Matt took out a pocketknife and cut a big X in all seat cushions. In more than twenty years of police work, I had only fantasized about destroying property in that way. I could only remember one bust that necessitated the destruction of property. I broke out the window of a perp's car, physically extricated him, and placed him on the ground for arrest.

I continued my search and discovered several important-looking documents in Arabic. The wife of the house said she knew the folks we were looking for, and that a close family member of one of them lived next door. And so Sergeant Huston directed his forces to the next house, taking the same precautions as before.

It was like an oven inside the house next door. The air was still. You could feel yourself baking. The residents were sleeping on the roof to escape the oppressive heat.

Members of the QRF (quick reaction force) secured a female occupant, who was a cousin of a terrorist presently in US custody. After they showed her some pictures, it became apparent that in addition to being related by blood the cousins shared a penchant for lying. The occupant was placed in flex cuffs, and her memory improved. Info flowed with her crocodile tears. I thought she seemed sincere, but I was nonetheless pleased when the names she gave us jibed with those confirmed in our own intelligence analysis.

"I shouldn't need to point this out, but this woman is a hold," I said. In other words, *Don't let her go!* The cuffed woman was led out. "Bring in the husband," I said.

The first thing I noticed about the husband was that he was much older than his wife—at least twenty years older. The husband and wife passed but said nothing. They barely acknowledged one another. He was a tough old bastard with leathery skin and a slight, wiry build.

We had to get on the question-go-round for a while, but eventually he got to giving me the locations of his in-laws. "I want you to understand that this is, I know, where they live, but I have never visited them there," he said.

He felt the distinction important, which I thought lent credibility to the location. We might find something there, and he didn't want to have anything to do with it.

"We'll make a note of that," I said.

Muaad, for show, jotted something in his notebook.

The husband said he thought his father-in-law might be a somebody. He didn't know anything a hundred percent positive, but you could feel vibes coming off the man that he was up to something. "Possibly something big, I couldn't say," the husband concluded.

"What is the address?" I asked.

"I do not know the street address, but I could give you directions as to how to get there."

After flex-cuffing the husband, I suggested to Sergeant Huston that we had the momentum and should continue. "If we stop now," I said, "the phones will be ringing off the hook alerting the scumbags."

Sergeant Huston agreed and radioed the information to the on-scene commander (OSC), Lieutenant Park.

I thought about the case practically. Info from both the husband and wife was sketchy, making it difficult for the army to relay it. There was hesitancy, because a new target in another battlespace commander's area meant permission would need to be given, but only after the specific intent of the mission was stated. That kind of shit drove me nuts. In New York City, the NYPD was the law. Having to ask permission to have a mission was in itself debasing. The only time NYPD made notification was if we were serving a warrant or effecting an arrest. Revealing too much information was considered an operational security breach that could prove costly if it compromised an ongoing investigation.

I realized that it was like a ball club playing at home or on the road. NYC was home. These stone Iraqi streets would always, for me, be away.

Still, there was a sense of excitement as we moved to the new location. That charged-up feeling dwindled with the slow realization that we were circling and meandering. Something was up. Word came down that all was not hunky-dory with the husband and wife. Our increasingly vague navigators were stalling. Maybe it was left at this street, maybe right. No, maybe it was the next block. Uh-oh.

Everyone within many blocks could hear the heavy-metal convoy as we went up this way and down that way for a half hour. We finally stopped at a house just like the one the man and woman had described.

I had to laugh. We'd gone past it at least twice before. Against all odds, we somehow maintained the element of surprise. They found the father-in-law sleeping in his apartment. These terrorist bastards are heavy sleepers, possibly because of alcohol. The rest of his family was on the roof praying to Allah for a helicopter rescue.

Sergeant Morales of QRF called Muaad and me up to the apartment. "We have the father-in-law in the living room," he said.

The guy turned out to be an enthusiastic liar—fabricating with gusto. He denied that the woman in the other room was his daughter. Her husband? Never saw him before.

"Stop with this nonsense," I said. I proceeded to show him photos I'd taken with my Olympus, all of them of a relative of his or someone he knew. I told him who they were. I knew their names and their relationship to him. "You see, I have had contact with each of them," I said.

Muaad was at his best, getting the translations quickly and precisely, so rapid-fire that the interview moved forward almost aerodynamically.

The father-in-law tightened with concern. It wasn't much of a crack, but I kept picking at it, enlarging it.

"Our whole purpose is to find the remaining family members. We're not going to be happy until we talk to them all."

He remained unmoved.

I added, "Oh, and your lack of cooperation will lead to your arrest."
That moved him. "I will show you where my nephews live," he said.

As it turned out, he was a much better navigator than his daughter
and her husband. The residences were in a development that was under
guard by either British or Iraqi forces—a tenuous situation, to be sure.

There was a lot of discussion. It was determined that we were outside the Fourth ID's area of operation. There was a pause as we called
the brigade commander and asked for permission.

I used the downtime to palm the father-in-law's cell phone, to see
what I could learn. In my old world of civilian law enforcement, this act
was illegal, contravening the Fourth Amendment. Here in Iraq I couldn't
care less; I was a self-starter when it came to engaging in black ops.

Sergeant Huston excitedly announced that permission to move in
had been granted.

As the convoy noisily got underway, our surroundings changed. We moved
into an area with indications of affluence: the houses got bigger and now
had ornamental iron-and-glass facades. We came to a halt in front of a particularly upscale gate, one that apparently came with its own guard, a normally inactive fellow suddenly distressed by our overwhelming presence.

Paul J. and the OSC went to speak with him. The guard, it turned
out, worked for a British-owned security company, the equivalent of
Blackwater in the States. The sovereign-nation and diplomatic-immunity
rules were not applicable in this case.

But there was a glitch in communication, apparently, when Lieutenant Park radioed in the info. Brigade had the idea that we were about
to raid a British-owned compound. The compound *employed* a British
firm, it didn't *belong to* a British firm, something brigade misunderstood.

And so it was no dice. Do not enter. Trying to keep the excursion
from being a complete waste of time, we gave the guard, as well as a
few of his teammates on the perimeter of the compound, a list of names.

"These are the people we are after," we said. "Please detain them if
they attempt to enter."

They nodded grimly. "You got it, mate," they said.

"This guy here we are looking for really hard. His name is *Falis*. He is not just a terrorist, he is a leader of terrorists."

"We'll keep an eye out," they said.

I doubted their tenacity. This was a long shot at best.

We didn't know about brigade's misunderstanding at the time and were furious and disgusted. Suspicion was that, given the choice between helping Joe or preserving some idealized political mirage, they had chosen the latter.

Colonels were concerned over the feelings of a few over their own soldiers. I felt a heart of darkness descending upon me, the disorientation of being in a war in which a manifested insanity called the shots.

It was quiet on the ride back as guys tried to bite back their anger. Ricky was mad at OSC. I said HQ was the real culprit. They made the call to stand down.

Back at the shop, the phone rang and Ricky answered. I saw his countenance metamorphose, his scowl twisting magically into a shit-eating grin.

"Ready for this?" Ricky said. "The subject Falis showed up and the Brits detained him. Division is sending a convoy to go pick him up for transport to FOB Prosperity for detention."

The shop erupted in joy. I should never have doubted the British guards. Turned out, they were good guys, and on the ball, too. One more cell member detained. We were crushing these demons.

16

CRUSHING DEMONS

SECOND WEEK IN AUGUST, 2130 hours, just as I'd settled my mind for a quiet evening, a knock came at the door, and by now we all knew what that meant. I was running on fumes, working on three hours' sleep in the last twenty-four, evening duty, then something about helicopters landing and taking off all fucking night.

Paul J. said, "Sorry, Chris, I know you need a day off."

"Don't worry about it, I understand," I said. Muaad and I high-fived. We got it. We'd become essential in the task order. Our hit potential had the attention of division headquarters. We were a valued asset with proven results. Ricky had taken to calling us the "Chris and Muaad Show." The rhythm of our interrogations created some buzz—and more than one suggestion that we should make a rap record. Not going to happen.

As for this mission, Ricky said we were still awaiting the positive ID on the target, an associate of the fugitive Jubar named *Abat*, but all indications were that he was genuine. The ID came, subject was rolled up, and we moved out.

Pulling into the *muhallah*, I recognized some of the streets from past missions, pretty amazing considering I was in the dark and viewing the world from the backseat of an RG-33. The RG-33 was a mine-resistant light-armored vehicle. It cost $300,000 and ran on a 400 I6 diesel engine with an Allison 3200 transmission. It had six wheels, one axle in front, two axles in back, all-wheel drive. It was similar to the MRAP in terms of protection, but approximately eight feet longer and able to accommodate approximately fourteen troops and gear, not counting the driver, the TC, and the crew that served the vehicle's .50-caliber gun turret. An internal headset communications system enabled us to listen in on the ground unit's radio chatter, as well as the internal communications between the TC and crew.

There was no one out on the streets. A curfew was underway; anyone driving after 11:00 at night was subject to being stopped and questioned.

Arriving at the target, we disembarked and performed our tactical search. Brigade TST were on the scene and would conduct their interview first. That was OK. They were the capturing unit and deserved first dibs.

I heard the thunderous metallic slam of the seventy-pound battering ram strike the front door, then the shrieks of voices from within. Muaad and I smiled. Occupants. Most likely bad people.

The residents were secured and the signal came for the TSE team to move in. In most cases, TSE was involved in looking for bomb-making materials, documents, and propaganda regarding the insurgency.

I found Matt. "Target is secured in the kitchen," he said cheerfully. "The rest of the house is ready to be searched."

I was methodically searching the living room when the stifling hot air began to get to me. For all my suffering over the past months because of the heat, the weather hadn't affected my performance. But this time it got to me a little bit. I felt myself gulping air. It was only ninety-five degrees, too.

I removed my helmet, leaned my M4 against the far wall, took a couple of deep breaths, and got on with the task at hand. Fifteen minutes into the search, with sweat covering me like a coat, the power to the house was cut, leaving us all momentarily in the dark.

After the room was searched, I heard Sergeants Morales and Christensen call for Muaad and me.

"How's it going in there?" I asked.

"Target is a liar and piece of shit," I was advised. "You guys want to give it a crack?"

"I believe we do," Muaad said.

The target was seated on the kitchen floor, in front of the sink. Kneeling down, I said, "I'm Strom. This is Muaad. I already know who you are, Mr. Abat. And I already know who your friends are, too," I said.

He took me through his various denials, so I showed him photos. "For the stubborn we have visual aids. These are all your friends, Mr. Abat. And they are all in US custody. They are in my camera because I interviewed them while in custody."

He barely raised an eyebrow, feigning confusion. This confirmed my suspicion that he'd received formal resistance training.

Muaad and I increased the cadence of our questioning, and then abruptly slowed our pace, catching Abat answering a question before it had been translated.

"Ah, an English speaker," I said. "Good. I showed you those pictures because they are all people who work for you, and each and every one of them gave you up as their superior."

He jerked and shuddered a bit. Good, finally a physical response. I leaned on him now: "You are more than just their supervisor, you are the head of their cell," I said. "Tell me about Jubar."

"I know no Jubar. I am on the side of the Americans."

I got in his face and yelled, "*Liar!*" I started to show him the photos again, but he begged me to stop.

He'd broken. "I know them," he said. He told me things about one of our detainees, a guy named *Mathem*. "I know he is bad and I reported him at work. I was visited by Mathem's father. He threatened me with physical harm for reporting his son's involvement with US deaths."

I amped up the intensity. His nerves were betraying him. He squirmed. I told him I had a problem with that. Two weeks earlier, Mathem was already under arrest. No report about him had been received.

"I have identification cards from all of these detainees. I know they work in the same office as you." He cowered and I moved forward, invading his personal space.

"I do know them. I know them from my work," he said.

"What is your relationship to Jubar?"

"I know him. I know a Jubar. I do not know if it is the one you are interested in."

"Don't worry about which Jubar," I yelled. "When was the last time you saw him?"

"I met with him today."

"Where?"

"At his office in the IZ," he said, referring to the International Zone.

"When?"

"Eleven o'clock this morning. I called him first on his cell phone to confirm my appointment before I left for his office."

"How did you get there?"

"It was within walking distance."

"Muaad, take a look at Mr. Abat's cell phone, please."

"Sure thing," my terp said. Then, after a brief pause, "Yes, he has Jubar's number in his call directory."

I glared at Abat. We suspected that he knew Jubar had fled to Iran. I asked him a series of questions about Jubar's whereabouts, not so much for his answers but to watch the expression on his face.

"What is your relationship to Jubar?"

"It is purely professional. Not personal. Not personal."

"Look, Abat, I'm here to do a job. The fact that I've rounded up some of your coconspirators is an indication, you must admit, that I am good at my job. There is one other thing you should know: if you think you are protected because you have a position in the ministry, I assure you that you are not."

The weight of it all was really hitting home now. His eyes were wild, those of a horse fleeing a burning barn.

I continued: "I have the full cooperation of the Iraqi government. I have full access to any and all resources to root this plague from the system."

Abat sat in silence, in defeat. He was weighing his options behind doomed eyes. Then I saw a new resolve—a new commitment to his nefarious cause. He was willing to die for Islam. His breath was uneven with a burgeoning anger, a venomous hatred.

I didn't let up. "Who will care for your wife and children when you are imprisoned and later hung for your crimes?"

Abat shrugged. He broke eye contact. He attempted to answer with body language alone.

"Where are the explosives, Mr. Abat?"

"What explosives?"

"Mr. Abat, I am a man of honor. I will release you immediately if you agree to lead us to the explosives."

"I know nothing of explosives."

"I'm not army, Mr. Abat. I can do things they can't do. I snap my fingers, you walk."

"I wish to be cooperative with you, sincerely, but I know nothing about any explosives."

I looked to Sergeants Christensen and Morales and signaled that I had completed the interview. They thanked Muaad and me for the help (a big change in attitude from a time only a few months before, when the Joes thought of us as no more than overpaid civilians). The sergeants took physical custody of Abat and transported him to the main detention facility.

"That got intense," Muaad said with wide, excited eyes.

"I think it was a success," I said. "We learned some things. Plus, we planted a seed in Abat's head."

"His head is spinning," Muaad said with a grin. "He is wondering how, one by one, we are rolling up all of his scumbag friends."

"The psychological effect will make him more compliant with the next fellow down the line who interviews him," I said. "That's when we'll learn how effective we were."

"Icing on the cake," Muaad said. "Physical evidence seized at Abat's home will seal his fate."

"I think we are closer than ever to collapsing the cell and rolling up the remaining demons at large. But I'm left with one burning question: Where are the explosives?"

"Copy that," Muaad said.

During the third week in August, Phoenix's military supervision was enduring its own changing of the guard. Our new program manager was Lieutenant Colonel Walters, a man I first saw sitting inconspicuously at one of our desks working a laptop. He was about forty, and I figured out who he was by the black oak leaves attached to his army ACUs. He was the guy who communicated directly with JIEDDO back in Washington, DC. I told him I was Phoenix's LEP subject matter expert. His handshake was firm and warm. I felt his strong character.

After the meet-and-greet, we had a multimedia briefing for Walters. A screen and projector—we called it a one-eye—were set up. The presentation showed off Phoenix's capabilities and gave highlights of our success stories. Matt gave a PowerPoint talk; Ricky had put together a slide show for him. Everyone cheered when Matt showed on the screen the "money shot": photos of evidence seized during our missions. Written on the slide were the words "You've Just Been Jacked by *The Chris and Muaad Show!*"

That got a laugh, and it felt great. Muaad and I high-fived.

"When it comes to tactical questioning, Chris and Muaad are the best," Ricky said.

I piped in: "Muaad's ability to mirror my questions in tone, emotion, and inflection is the greatest ever." I put my arm around my interpreter. "Love you, man."

Duke said it—"Why don't you two get a room?"—and everyone cracked up.

Muaad whipped out his Borat impression, saying, "I just like to say, working with Chris, is very nice." The laughs got even louder.

When the presentation was over, Ricky told us we might have a mission that evening. "Don't wander too far. Be ready for the call," he said.

The mission on deck was twofold. The targets were a *Mr. Scribe*, a journalist of dubious allegiance, and the front building of one of the Iraqi ministries.

Muaad and I had interrogated Mr. Scribe once before, and to be honest we hadn't been overly convinced of his guilt. But there was new info making Mr. Scribe more interesting than ever. Evidence recovered from Mr. Scribe's residence included a GPS with suspicious waypoints in its memory. In a previous interview, Mr. Scribe had revealed that one of the waypoints in his GPS was our target building.

The IED/EFP cell we'd been tracking seemed to operate a lot like a crime family in New York. They shared ethnic ties and funded larger operations through extortion, on both a large and a small scale. At our target building, cell goons would drop off the money that terrorized members of the community had paid them to prevent bad things from happening to their businesses, property, or loved ones. If not paid, the goons gleefully dished out punishment in the form of kidnapping, rape, and murder. So when the goons came to collect, everyone paid—all under the nose of the Iraqi government.

Mr. Scribe was said to be such a goon. He supposedly removed arrest warrant files from the Ministry of National Security Affairs (MNSA), the Iraqi equivalent of the FBI, and then used them as templates to fabricate new warrants. He visited prospective arrestees and extorted them to remain silent. The victims were Sunni, the goons Shia. If anyone cried foul, the complaints would be dismissed as tribal retaliation and left essentially unaddressed.

Ricky put down the phone. "It's a go." We started getting ready. "Colonel Walters and I will be accompanying you," Ricky added.

As we pulled down the street, I recalled the markings on the front gates of neighboring residences. Initial contact was made with Mr. Scribe, and Sergeant Huston called for Phoenix to move up and perform the TSE.

Muaad and I went into the home just to the right of Mr. Scribe's. It had been vacated fairly recently, with just a thin layer of dust on the flat surfaces. Fresh electrical tape capped the ends of recently cut wires.

"Hey, Russ," I said. "Do you have wire cutters so I can bag and tag the wires with the tape intact?"

Russ handed me a tool. "The Leatherman," he said somewhat lasciviously. It was multifunctional like a Swiss army knife.

"That'll work," I said, cutting and bagging each wire individually, marking the time and date.

Searching the rest of the house, I found a metal box, twice the size of a shoebox, with a hasp and eye-hook. At the top was a slot like that on a ballot box. Surmising that the box was used to collect the day's "tribute" money, I bagged and tagged it in hopes that a lab might find prints or DNA.

At a house on the other side of Mr. Scribe's, we found occupants, and after the OK, Muaad and I were called in to interview them. We were led into a kitchen where a family—a husband, wife, and four kids—huddled fretfully.

I addressed the husband, explaining who I was and that I was not out to get them, that we were interested rather in his neighbors next door.

He said, "I know little about the occupants. I am too consumed with work and family to even notice my neighbors' daily comings and goings."

"In that case, sir, would you mind if I asked your wife a few questions?" It was risky to ask permission. He could say no, and then I'd have to be rude to continue—but I thought showing respect in this way might be a help in the long run.

"I do not mind," he said.

"Lead her into the living room, and keep the others in the kitchen," I instructed.

We sat her on the couch and I sat beside her, determined to be as nonthreatening as possible. I explained that I was going to show her some photos from my camera, and I wanted her to tell me if she'd seen anyone before, perhaps going into her neighbor's house. She said she understood, and we went through the photos.

"No. No. No. No. Yes, him! Several times."

She had identified a known terrorist named *Hani*. I sensed a presence behind me, and it was Ricky with a shit-eating grin on his face. If Hani was in and out of Mr. Scribe's house, we'd just confirmed that it was in fact the cover location for the extortion operation.

Ricky gave me fifty dollars. "Give it to the lady as a sign of our appreciation," Ricky said.

I was familiar with the concept of "flash money." It was a technique used in NYC all the time. Hell, without flash money many cases would run cold. I thought the fifty dollars was generous, though. I gave it to her and told her to get something nice for her kids.

"Who else should we talk to?" I asked her.

She gave the names of neighbors she thought might be able to provide additional info.

I placed my right hand over my heart and thanked her for the information. I did not offer to shake hands, as even that level of physical contact between a man and a Muslim woman was never allowed, especially if the woman was married.

We went to the house that the woman had recommended and knocked politely on the door. It was answered by a man in his sixties wiping the sleep from his eyes. Once the house was searched for weapons and bombs, Muaad and I were called in to interview the occupants. We began with the head of the household, and the guy had a bad attitude. He wanted me to understand that he did not care very much about our stupid little investigation.

I cut it short with the man and moved on to a fourteen-year-old boy. I showed him the photos on my phone and he picked out Hani.

"I saw this man on a nearby street nine months ago," the boy said. "But I never saw him in my neighbor's house."

I knew the boy was lying, but the confirmation was in some small measure relevant to the investigation. The real question was why he insisted that he hadn't seen Hani either nearby or recently.

Colonel Walters observed all our interviews that day. I usually would have banned him as nonessential personnel and a distraction, but I understood that the colonel needed to know what Muaad and I did to evaluate our effectiveness. Over the course of the day he saw the entire Chris and Muaad Show. We were kind, polite, respectful, harsh, insistent, and frightening—sometimes all of these during the same interview.

"Colonel Walters, I'm sorry the interview process took so long," I said when we were through.

"No problem," he said. "It was like watching art."

"Wow, thanks," Muaad and I said, more or less in sync.

Lieutenant Colonel Walters was a man of great character and it was my honor to take him along on a mission. He said watching the Chris and Muaad Show was like watching art.

Back at the shop I processed the day's evidence and had time to get home for a shower and some sleep before the 1800 hours briefing. At that time, Colonel Walters gave a five-minute speech, thanking us for the ride-along and complimenting each of the team's facets, calling Muaad and me the wind beneath Phoenix's wings.

During the last week of August, Phoenix was assigned to round up bad guys and deliver them to other units, mainly Delta Force, the SEALs, and Task Force Troy. The process was essentially the same: drive to the target's bed-down location, arrest the individual, and TSE the shit out of the residence. The rule was, let Phoenix do it.

Once finished, we'd meet the other unit at a prearranged spot and dish off the prisoner. The NYPD would've called us the Warrant Squad.

Good-to-go fugitives would be divvied up among the boroughs and processed for arrests.

For one such mission, Ricky handed me the intelligence package. "One page?" I said.

"Target package is a little sparse," he said.

"Maybe even scarce." My eyes scanned with concern. "It's lacking things like history and, uh, details."

"There are no photographs, either," Ricky said.

The package also didn't detail his propensity for violence, his access to weapons or explosives, or the extent of his geographical domain—all genuine concerns. About all I knew was that Special Forces guys wanted him but were either too lazy or too busy to pick him up themselves. I liked the thrill of the hunt, don't get me wrong, but I didn't appreciate being handed a bag of shit—sloppy fucking seconds—by the unit responsible for the arrest in the first place.

And maybe I wasn't in the best mood because, although I hadn't thought it possible, the weather became even more unbearable. Suddenly there was humidity, a sandy sauna—and we were all coated in an adrenaline-spiked froth. Heat affected distant light, giving the world a surreal shimmer. Beyond our heavy-metal convoy, below the moonlit horizon, I saw the craggy shoreline of the Tigris River looping in and out beside the road.

As I stepped down from my RG-33, the sweltering night air stroked my face and neck like a fine mist from a light but scalding rain. Inside the target residence, conditions were *almost* bearable. Guys who normally bit the bullet were bellyaching about the heat and lack of breathable air. Some said it was like breathing sandpaper. Others compared it to huffing a bag of chalk dust.

The good news was that the house was only three rooms, including the bathroom. I cleared the living room and was called to interview the detainee. The guy was well educated and spoke fluent English. Nonetheless, Muaad and I went into our routine. We always cast a wide net, in case the guy had connections we didn't know about. This time it paid off. Despite the fact that we knew next to nothing about the guy, we rather efficiently got him to admit that a known suspect was his direct superior. This revelation came as a complete surprise: I'd thrown some darts into the darkness and hit a bull's-eye.

Then, realizing perhaps that he'd already said too much, and seemed very honest when he did so, he zipped his lip.

My enthusiasm subsided. Maybe we had solid info, but I still needed to identify this person by name and establish that he was the target SF was looking for. In this I was hindered by the skimpy intel package. My guess was that we were purposefully being kept out of the loop. Special Forces really didn't want us to know who this person was or what he meant to them. SF was like the FBI—those guys kept their cards close to the vest.

Although he said some incriminating things, my overall impression was that he was a good person. For all I knew, he was a paid source and my job was to arrest him to maintain his cover. The SF guys could've called him in advance and told him to cooperate once we got on-site.

I advised Sergeant Huston of what I'd gotten and he ordered the man to be arrested. I had a bad feeling in the pit of my stomach. He might be innocent. That's how I felt. But not my call.

The prearranged location to meet up with the other unit and turn over the prisoner was just outside the main entrance to Baghdad International Airport. We found them at dawn on a stretch of dirt highway median. The sun pressed over the horizon and the desert dust took on an orange glow. The transaction took less than two minutes. With the prisoner dished in an incident-free manner, we headed back to base.

Back at the shop I said I didn't want to talk about Warrant Squad. I wanted to get back on the cell case that had been our focus now for more than a month. Ricky said that we were on hold because the JAG office was deeply involved now, making excuses why certain bad guys should not be taken down. JAG was giving the commanding officer an earful of legal advice all the time. And we knew Captain Wyman and how his motivations sometimes strayed far from what was best for Joe.

I said, "Ricky, you and Matt should schedule a meeting with the CO and make the case for pursuing these ministry scumbags in the presence of that pinhead Wyman. That guy is lazy and won't test the fire."

(Spoiler alert: Matt's intimate knowledge of the case eventually exposed Wyman for what he was: a house mouse relentlessly covering his own ass, more interested in meting out punishment to Joe for drinking alcohol or having sex in another soldier's quarters.)

Of course, we all realized that we were attempting to expose a corrupt Iraqi national agency, and that the Iraqi government really, really didn't want us to. In the path of that political wind, no one bothered to count the number of US lives lost because these bomb-makers were not picked up. I was sickened by the scenario and decided to think outside the box.

"Let's leak a story to the press," I said. "An exposé that will force the spineless Congress's hand . . ."

"Chris," Ricky replied patiently, "there's a political process at the State Department level. It's un-fuck-with-able."

"But *American lives.* Blood of soldiers worth less than the feelings of a corrupt government."

"I hear you, Chris." Ricky had lost men in combat. "But any attempt to circumvent might prove detrimental to US foreign policy."

These politics-over-guilt cases were making me crazy. Because of the madness, the next few months were largely a waste of time. We spent our days thinking about a single target who'd captured our imaginations, a suspected supervillain cell asset named *Dr. Z.* This guy was a genuine physician working at an MNSA site. We spent a month planning a raid on him, but it was canceled. Dr. Z was eventually detained and made some incriminating statements. Now there was a meathead named Bob assigned to the Combat Operations Intelligence Center who wanted to release Z because, Bob figured, only an innocent man would have admitted the things that Z admitted.

Same old story: detainee knows a landowner who knows a mayor whom the United States wants to stay friendly with. The clock was ticking, and the further we got from actioning the remaining scumbags, the more likely it was that they'd flee to a harboring nation, destroying incriminating evidence along the way.

My mind counted off the days until I'd earned a trip home to visit Debbie and the kids.

17

"DADDY, WHY ARE YOU GOING BACK?"

AFTER STONEWALLING ME ON A TRANSFER and a raise for more than three months, MPRI added insult to injury when my new contract came out: it included a 6.5 percent reduction in pay. With that I submitted my resignation. Ricky P. asked if I'd be willing to re-sign with another contractor in the program, NEK. I said sure, if the price was right. After speaking with Rob Lambert, who was running things back stateside, I negotiated a $1,000-per-day salary. But in order to make the switch, I would have to leave the country, re-sign in DC, and fly back to Iraq.

The timing was fortuitous. September 11, 2008, was approaching and I was thinking about Stephanie, who'd be celebrating her eleventh birthday in Virginia. I had not received a response from my soon-to-be-ex-employer regarding my resignation letter, so after several more unanswered e-mails, I booked a forty-five-minute flight from Baghdad to Kuwait. After a six-hour layover in Kuwait, I booked business class to Washington Dulles International Airport. In DC, I rented a car and drove home.

During my time back with the family, I reassured myself that I was as close to my daughter as ever. We fell quickly into old, fun patterns. The best part of the trip home was bonding with Christian. I did whatever he asked: We shot BB guns, watched movies. When we got to the end of our driveway I let him drive the rest of the way to the house. I remembered my father doing the same with me, teaching me how to drive with a three-speed shifter in the steering column. Christian sat on my lap and steered our way up the hill, and when we got there Debbie was waiting with a camera to capture the moment.

During my absence there'd been an ice storm and they'd lost power for three days, but our neighbors John and Karen took Debbie and the kids in, so my visit gave me an opportunity to invite them over for a barbecue and thank them for their kindness. Near the end of my stay John's dog had to be put down, and the kids and I built and painted a casket for the dog's burial.

And, of course, it was Christian who asked the inevitable question: "Daddy, why are you going back?"

The easy answer was that I had to in order to maintain the house and pay the bills. The more complicated issue for me was my personal *why*. I could come back to Virginia and have a great job waiting for me. But I had to get back to Phoenix. They were my team. I had to finish what I started.

Just before my departure, I promised Stephanie and Christian that the next time I came home I'd take them to Disney World. At the end of our driveway I said good-bye to the kids, hugging and kissing them before putting them on the school bus. Debbie, Juneau, and I made the long, steep trek back up the driveway. After a quick shower and shave, I got dressed and loaded my rental car for the four-hour trip to Dulles. I said a quick good-bye with a hug and kiss to Debbie and got on the road.

———————

It was mid-November 2008. I'd been back in Iraq for about a month, and certain military antics were starting to get on my nerves.

One example involved one of the new guys on the team, Dan Comstock, a former Marine Recon and a weapons expert. Dan was a quiet guy who'd joined the marines to escape California gang life. He was on his way back from the gym one day when an army captain anxious to assert authority picked on him, demanding ID and dressing him down for his lack of subservience. Dan, who hadn't uttered five syllables in the previous week, told the captain that he'd enjoy meeting the captain at the dump so they could settle this like men. When the captain began looking around for backup, Dan walked away and didn't look back. Before Dan got to his room, the captain had "launched an investigation." Ricky tried to intervene: Both parties could admit to some fault, right? The captain not only said no but interrupted our evening briefing.

"I need to get a visual on someone," the captain said, staring at Dan. "Are you the person I spoke to earlier today?"

"I don't know, you tell me," Dan said, and we all fell down laughing.

The captain turned his back to leave.

Everyone heard it: "[*Cough*]—asshole—[*cough*]."

The captain wheeled around. "Did someone have something to say?"

Duke had something to say: "Captain, you're acting like an eighteen-year-old private, showing none of us any respect whatsoever. How do you get off demanding respect?" That was just the start. He used the most vulgar terminology in truly inventive permutations and assassinated the captain's character in a wide variety of politically incorrect ways. The captain left in a huff, leaving us all stunned.

"Sorry, I lost my head there," Duke said. But we all agreed the captain had it coming. Ricky wasn't that happy. There was going to be a formal investigation that was bound to put Phoenix in a poor light.

I helped Dan write his statement for the hearing, emphasizing that we weren't questioning the captain's right to make spot corrections but asking, *Why pick on a contractor when there were plenty of soldiers he could've focused on?* When all was said and done, Dan was separated from Phoenix and shipped over to Camp Liberty for two weeks, which satisfied the base commander that justice had been served. Then, quietly, Dan was returned to us for a hero's welcome.

———————————

By the end of 2008, every fucking thing got on my nerves. There was an influx of air force airmen at the base, like the boys from the country club had arrived. They acted like it was field day, never actively engaged in the fact that there was a war going on. They were selfish individually, but especially in groups. They snuck over in the middle of the night and shut off our hot water so they'd be sure to have hot showers when returning from tour in the wee hours of the morning. They were also womanizers and pigs in the toilet. In the gym, they walked away from their treadmills without bothering to turn them off. They thought they had a butler following them around straightening up. How did these guys make it through boot camp?

The rainy season came, and I got a knock on my door from a soldier in physical training garb asking me where I got the rug at the steps of my CHU. I told him I bought it. He said it looked like his, which had been stolen, probably because of the rain. "I promise you, bro, I didn't take your damn rug," I said. We all bought the same rugs from the same PX. They all looked alike. But he thought I had his. Asshole. He left brusquely. Now I couldn't get back to sleep because someone thought I stole his rug.

It seemed like the weeks after my return from my visit home were all like that. There was always something irritating me, some injustice, just enough to keep me from sleeping comfortably, and insomnia gave me plenty of extra time to dwell on all the things that were bothering me.

One of the army's peccadilloes is its acceptance and encouragement of internal informants, the slimy practice of ratting guys out. One soldier snitching on another was widespread, common practice, and so ingrained in the fabric of the service that the rat and the guy he ratted on might be seen later that day sitting across from one another in the chow hall. Backstabbing and throwing one's friend under the bus were also the norm. This made my skin crawl. In the NYPD, ratting out a fellow officer was the ultimate betrayal.

One night I was headed to chow when a young specialist told me I shouldn't be wearing my sunglasses on top of my head. I told him I liked them where they were, and he repeated his instruction again and again until I put the sunglasses over my eyes. In the chow hall I watched him patrolling up and down the tables, looking for violations. I thought to myself, *Where do they get these people?*

18

MADAME DEATH

We had just finished our nightly meeting and Ricky was on the phone with the "CHOPS"—the chief of operations, sometimes just called Boss—getting the lowdown on the night's missions. For the past two nights, we'd waited on standby for the signal to suit up and arrest a female subject—a woman I'll call *Madame Death*.

In the world of radical Islamic terrorism, women played a silent role for the most part. In this particular situation, however, this woman not only facilitated the flow of money and explosives but also had developed a reputation as the on-duty whore, servicing JAM cell members with sexual favors.

The thought process behind her arrest was to gain intelligence on the remaining at-large JAM cell members. Perhaps, like many women of ill repute, she kept a list of clients.

"Change of plans," Ricky said.

"What now?" I asked.

"We go to her house and give her a good scare."

In the NYPD, this was known as "tickling the wire"—a way of creating chatter for electronic and physical surveillance. I lost it. I told Ricky, for the record, that I strongly disagreed with the mission objective.

"Tell you what," he said, "call CHOPS and express your point of view."

"I'm not in a position to tell the army what the fuck to do," I said. "But how is scaring Madame Death better than arresting her? She's a killer in a nest of killers."

Ricky was annoyed.

My background as a cop told me we'd only have one shot at bringing the woman in. If we left her home without her, she'd flee to the farthest corner of the Earth. But the mission seemed to have shifted away from its original objective. Were we shutting down a terrorist cell or not?

Ricky was unhappy with my remarks because of my reasoning. He was former Special Forces, and outside criticisms weren't welcomed in the world of SF ring-knockers.

I walked over to Muaad. "What do you think?" I asked.

"I'm concerned," he said. "I don't like the new mission parameters."

"It's bullshit," I agreed. "We'll just be errand boys."

Overhearing me, Ricky chimed in from behind his desk. "So you don't support the mission?"

That made my blood boil. "I never said that," I answered. Now we'd both raised our voices. "I said the mission is stupid as it stands. We should be arresting Madame Death, not *scaring* her."

"So you're saying you don't support the mission." This time it wasn't a question.

"We've had the target on deck for the past two days," I said. "Suddenly we're going out to scare her. And potentially never see her again." I paused. "But what do I know? I only have twenty-two years' worth of experience as a cop. You have twenty-plus in the army."

Ricky didn't like my tone. In front of everyone, he instructed his 2IC to erase my name from the board. I was off the mission.

I sat there for a minute without blinking, stunned at what had just transpired. Muaad had this look of disbelief on his face. I stowed away my gear and left the office. On the project we were currently involved in, not being able to recognize a differing point of view was narrow and dangerous thinking.

That night I talked to Debbie and told her about the problems between Ricky and me.

"I don't think your little fight had anything to do with the mission or strategy. It had to do with fatigue. You were both overtired, and you're homesick," she said. "Here's what you do: you go to the Green Bean and you buy Ricky a latte with two dollops of whipped cream and hand it to him. You don't even have to say anything."

Debbie always knew best.

"You all right?" Ricky asked.

"I'm fine. You OK?"

"I'm good," he said.

That led to small talk, then to jokes and laughter, and life went on.

Failing to capture Madame Death turned out to be a big mistake. The intelligence obtained from her residence turned out to be less than anticipated. Matt told me that Madame Death's boyfriend—one of our prime targets, murderer of Americans—had fled to Iran.

Again, I sensed JAG's presence. Lawyers were filling only slightly pliant military heads with fearful notions that somehow, some way, rolling up murderers was on a regular basis a detriment to the big picture. JAG advised Colonel Buford, who didn't have to take their advice but almost always did—in my opinion because that was the fast track to career advancement. (Don't get me wrong, he was an aggressive commanding officer, but like many colonels, I think, he was chasing the elusive star, a key to the Generals' Club.) In this case, there was another problem: gender. The army was very concerned about feelings and political correctness.

We were also handcuffed by an Iraqi government we knew to be corrupt. Largely, I suspected, because of our successes, the rules were changing: the Iraqi government, we were informed, would decide which Iraqi citizens would be prosecuted over wrongdoing alleged by US contractors. That might've been partially palatable if all the victims were Iraqis, but that wasn't the case. The Iraqis wanted to tell us which killers of US soldiers we could and couldn't prosecute. Totally unacceptable. But that was the new reality we had to work with.

Ricky asked me if I was interested in attending the meeting discussing the new rules. I said, "No, it's up to the deballed army to unfuck this goat." There was a serious message there, of course, but it came out funnier than I expected.

It occurred to me that Colonel Buford and his troops were scheduled to leave Iraq in March, and perhaps the hope was to wait it out and dump the situation in the lap of the incoming brigade. I found myself reciting a mantra that had been common among thinking men since the days of Vietnam: let's win or go home.

November 24, 2008. The call came in and it sounded like a goat rope from the start. Sergeant Huston and his team had already been on-site for five hours, looking for an EFP/IED that was supposedly buried in a palm grove. The brigade commander requested help, so Ricky assembled Phoenix and off we went to assist Sergeant Huston and his boys.

From a tactical perspective, the call for help made perfect sense. We had bomb-sniffing dogs and electronic equipment capable of making short work of finding any potential explosives. Our presence minimized the risk to personnel.

On-site, an exhausted Sergeant Huston gave us a quick intelligence dump and directed us to the first of two detainees. I realized almost immediately that the bust was good. The detainee was a liar, and most deceptive when I asked questions about the movement of explosives. Muaad and I were trying to get the guy to give up the one outstanding accomplice when he shut down.

I'll be honest, I fought back the urge to beat the shit out of the guy. Instead, I ended the interview. Maybe we'd have better luck with the second detainee. Word was, the second guy was the first's brother.

The brother was a kid, a teenager, maybe fifteen, no more. He spoke a fair amount of English, and I could tell there was at least part of him that enjoyed the attention he was receiving. When I asked him questions, he smirked at me. I ignored his attitude and concentrated on keeping him talking, in hopes that something important might slip out. And talk he did. He told us that his entire family was involved in terrorism, even his cousin who lived in an adjoining apartment in the same building.

"After we finish with this guy, we should venture out and investigate," Muaad said.

"Tell you what, why don't you pass on the info we just got from the kid to [our teammates] Artie and Russ. I'd like to finish the interview in the back of an MRAP—might wipe that expression off his face."

So Muaad left, leaving me alone with the squirrelly kid. We were standing out in the open—dangerously in the open. There was an open field on one side of the lot. In my time in Iraq, this was by far the most vulnerable I had felt.

Twenty minutes passed. Where was Muaad?

So, with the kid in tow, I went looking for him, and moved into shadowy areas where I didn't feel so conspicuous. Instead of Muaad, I ran into Russ and Ryan, who told me Artie wanted me to come to his location. Muaad was already there, and I was to join him. The frustrations of poor planning began to eat at me. Still dragging the kid along, I followed Russ and Ryan to an apartment building two hundred meters away. Russ sensed my annoyance and made small talk in an attempt to keep it light. Artie, as it turned out, was mad because I wasn't there with him, and he'd instructed Muaad to commence interviewing detainees without me.

When I arrived, Artie said, "Where the hell have you been?"

"I was standing in the dark with this asshole," I said, gesturing at the teenager.

"Why weren't you in the truck as instructed?" he asked.

Again, I gestured boldly at my youthful detainee, who looked at me and then at them. I think even he was on my side. "Something came up," I said. "We're going to have an after-action report on this, Artie," I said.

There was hostility in our voices now that got the attention of bystanders. This made me feel ridiculous, but Artie, emboldened, puffed out his chest and belittled me.

"Not in front of everyone," I said. "We'll talk about this back at the shop."

"You need to interview anyone else?" he asked Muaad, a dig, a reference to the interviews Muaad had been asked to do in my absence.

Back at the shop, Artie ran to be the first one to speak with Ricky, explaining why he did what he did. I changed out of my gear at a deliberate pace, and when I went to speak with Ricky, I took Artie, Muaad, and Russ with me. I entered the room last and shut the door softly behind me.

"I was standing outside with this kid for twenty minutes before Russ came and got me to join the rest of the team. Artie had Muaad, who I thought would return to me after delivering a message, conducting interviews without my presence. I think it's a good idea that my presence at interviews be mandatory as I am the person ultimately writing the report."

Ricky nodded.

"And I shouldn't have to say this out loud, but from a safety standpoint, standing alone with a detainee in the open near a field is totally unacceptable."

I walked out. I didn't care to hear what they were going to say about me in there. I kept thinking about Artie hanging me out to dry the way he did. If this were the NYPD, Artie would have been dismissed for "failure to supervise."

But what happened was Artie came up to me the next day. "Sorry, man," he said.

"No problem," I replied.

It was the end of November, and the newest target package involved a plethora of information to digest. While some missions came with skimpy intelligence, this package looked like a phone book.

The target was *Haydar*, one of fifteen or so associates of bloodthirsty JAM cell members. On multiple occasions, Haydar was responsible for direct attacks that killed Americans. One of Haydar's associates was *Qasim*, a leader of the group that carried out the IED/EFP attacks. Qasim was Haydar's boss, and there was only vague HUMINT regarding where Haydar and Qasim slept.

For Haydar, at least, we had a few locations where he was known to hang; we call them "pattern of life" locations. We lacked their phone information, so there was no electronic surveillance to narrow the search.

These guys might not ping, but we weren't in the dark. We did have informants in the know who were fully cooperating. The 1-22's TST unit, responding to an informant's info, took to driving in circles within Haydar and Qasim's *muhallah* in hopes of finding Haydar walking the streets.

And sure enough, he popped up. Flick on the lights, maybe you catch a roach before he scatters. The search was under an hour old when we got word that Haydar was rolled up.

Phoenix pulled up to the scene, I dismounted, and Sergeant Dave Peluso gave us the rundown. Sergeant Peluso was loud and crass, and he'd turn out to be one of my favorite people in my Iraqi adventure. "Tighten your shit up!" Peluso would say as we drove to the target. Once on target, it would be "Hurry the fuck up!" and "Get the fuck over that wall, where's the goddamn ladder four?" Dave Peluso—the best sergeant first class ever to grace a battlefield.

Listening to Dave on the headset, we'd be crying tears of laughter. Don't get me wrong—he was funny, but he orchestrated the movements of his men and women with precision. During the summer of 2008 his crew had survived a horrific gun battle under his command. In an unprovoked attack, RPGs were exploding before and after his unit's position, yet Dave managed to call in an ISR pinpointing the area of attack for an air strike. Advancing, Dave beat back the enemy, killing many while suffering only minor injuries to his men and damage to equipment. Afterward, Dave recommended some of his troops for well-deserved Army Commendation Medals. Dave was both a mega-warrior and a good friend.

Right now he was eager to clear up some confusion: "Ignore first message. Haydar has *not* been found."

"What happened?" I asked.

"Just a house said to belong to his father was secured by force."

"Big difference."

"I don't know what happened."

"The dad in here?" I asked.

"He's ready for you."

"Lead the way."

Haydar's dad was very unhappy. He didn't like the fact that his son was under investigation, and he didn't like army boots stomping around his house. We were making a mess. The search was thorough.

During the Q&A with the dad, I got the impression he was proud of his son's work. I offered him a deal: "Lead me to a location where one of your son's criminal friends lives, and we'll release you."

"It's a deal. I will show you."

So, we moved to the residence of a friend of the detainee's son. Sergeant Peluso and his men breached the entryway and secured the occupants. Muaad and I were presented with a new detainee, a fresh-faced young man who had "I want to cooperate" written all over him.

"I can show you another neighbor's house where Haydar was just hours ago," he said.

"Thanks," I said as I flex-cuffed him.

When I passed this info on to Sergeant Peluso, we had to laugh. The evening was playing out like a comedy. We were going house to house collecting detainees. The new locale was just down the block.

We walked, and I got to see Sergeant Peluso invade the house as horrified neighbors watched. I felt I was watching brave men running into harm's way, but I'm pretty sure those neighbors were thinking something else. Five times we heard someone shout "Clear!"

And we were invited in. Muaad and I set up the kitchen as our interview headquarters. I began the first interview.

"What is your name, sir?"

"I am Qasim."

We almost shit. Hiding our excitement, we paused and Muaad and I exchanged written notes to make sure we were on the same page. We then continued the interview, asking, "Who are your friends?"

"I am good friends with one of your confidential informants and good friends with a US Army captain."

"What are their names?"

"I don't remember."

I detected an arrogance, a sense of invincibility in Qasim, that seemed out of sync with his dilemma. He acted like a man with a get-out-of-jail-free card, and by this time I was smart enough to know there were plenty of them out there.

When I informed Sergeant Peluso of the size of the fish we'd caught, his face lit up into a brilliant smile, and I heard excitement in his voice when he radioed the news to his command.

I helped Ryan with the photographing and fingerprinting of the remaining occupants of the building. I was still at this when I heard Sergeant Peluso muttering with disgust.

"Let him go!" he said, meaning Qasim.

What the fuck?

Back at the shop, I learned that Ricky had been told only that the mission had come up empty. I had to tell him that we'd had Qasim and had been ordered with no given reason to release him.

I saw Ricky's expression go from inquisitiveness to exasperation. Ricky may have understood what happened, but when he opened his mouth he said orders are orders and the army is going to do whatever it wants.

I eventually had a discussion with an intelligence officer at 1-22 TST. After intimating that Muaad and I were torturers, the lieutenant said the army rejected our suggestion to arrest Qasim because he was a valuable informant, part of another unit's investigation.

A known terrorist was being used as a source. Think about that. In my years as a cop it would've been unthinkable. We were all put in harm's way for nothing. Only by the grace of God had no one been killed or injured on this mission.

19

THE BOY AND
THE POLICE STATION

IT WAS THE FIRST WEEK IN DECEMBER. Temperature-wise, it could have been an autumn day in Brooklyn, around forty degrees. We'd been riding round in the back of our RG-33 for what seemed like an eternity, but the air conditioning was nice. Word came over the radio: "Move forward."

We'd learned that our target Haydar had a brother named *Murad*, and one was just as bad as the other. We had them under electronic surveillance now, but the brothers confounded it with mobility. They were, as we called it, dynamic.

Then we heard on the radio: "Got him. Believe the subject is Haydar."

Muaad and I looked at each other excitedly.

Sergeant Peluso gave us the dump: "Subject was located during a dismounted patrol. Subject was apparently in a big hurry to leave the area. During initial questioning he told us his name. We asked for proof of identity and he said he left it in his house, but he pointed us to a neighbor's house, and that's where we have him now." They had the house secured but were certain the occupants were innocent bystanders caught up in Haydar's failing alibi.

So, that was where I began. I told Haydar to cut out the games, to take me to his house and show me his ID. He complied. His residence was only a few steps away. Sergeant Peluso and his men quickly secured the new location.

Bingo! In the house was Haydar's brother Murad. After clearing the main floor, Muaad and I set up in the kitchen. The lights went out.

"Those bastards. Not again," Muaad said. Lately, when we came to the *muhallah* to do our thing, the asshole in charge of the generator that provided everybody's power liked to flick the switch so we'd have to do our interviews in the dark. It was annoying, but if that was their most effective form of harassment, we were OK with it.

I didn't let Haydar know we thought him special. Muaad and I went through our standard routine, taking notes as the man gave us a biography and pedigree.

"When was the last time you were visiting Iran? When was the last time you were in Sadr City?"

"I have never been to these places," he said.

"Bullshit." It was like I was asking a guy from Brooklyn the last time he'd been in Manhattan. "Let's not waste our time with this guy. Let's talk to his brother."

We switched out Haydar for Murad and the interview continued.

"When did you last travel to Iran and Sadr City?"

"I was in Sadr six months ago," he said. "I walked there with my brother."

The statement seemed altered to appear more distant and insignificant than it was, but I felt, because he included his brother, that there was an admission of some sort there. The part where he claimed to have been on foot was insulting to my intelligence.

When I was done I had Murad brought back to the courtyard, where his brother and others were waiting to be photographed and fingerprinted by Ryan.

In the courtyard I kept my eye on the women and the children. There was a young boy who was doing a great deal of fidgeting and was making hesitant eye contact with me.

Muaad and I approached the boy, maybe thirteen, and spoke to him in Arabic. We decided to take the boy into the kitchen for questioning, but his mother became terrified and clutched at the boy's arm.

I have to admit, I felt bad for the woman. Of course we had no intention of hurting or mistreating the child in any way—we planned on being more gentle than gentle—but she didn't know that. Who knows what she thought of us? She may have been listening for years, indeed for her entire life, to the brainwashing of zealots until she couldn't tell the good guys from the bad guys.

We did our best to reassure her that her son was going to be fine, but nonetheless, we took him into the kitchen and questioned him. We learned he was Murad and Haydar's little brother, and a most observant teen.

"Have a seat up on that propane tank," I said, and he hitched himself up there. Our eyes were at the same level. During initial questioning, I found the boy almost overwhelmingly compliant. He had no filter, so I moved the questioning to the meat of the matter. He had a brother that did bad things, right?

The boy became a fountain of information, with remarkable appreciation for the importance of facts and details for a kid his age. He gave me the lowdown on his brothers and the roles they played in JAM cell activity, specific crimes they had been involved in. If I were a prosecutor I could've had this kid talk to my jury confident in knowing that in the end his brothers were going down.

"Do you know the current location of any explosives?"

"Yes."

"Can you take us to it?"

"Yes."

We hurriedly told Sergeant Peluso to prepare to redirect to a new location, a possible weapons cache. Five minutes later, Muaad relayed a message to me. We were going to action the new target, with baby brother in tow.

Things were going so well, and then the kid said the explosives were in a building that resembled a mosque. My heart sank. There were special rules regarding places of worship—which is why terrorists so frequently used the mosques to meet and plan and store their implements of death.

The signal came on the radio. Move forward. Like ducks in a row, we moved steadily through the filthy market, littered with garbage and rotting food, me holding firmly to the shoulder of the boy. There was a police vehicle standing in front of the door to our target building—which had been recently converted to an Iraqi police station but still resembled a mosque, a very important point from a public relations point of view.

With a bright flash and deafening explosion, the breach team shot-gunned the metal doors, ruining the locks and slapping the entrance open. Pushing the doors aside, the team tossed in a concussion grenade that was even louder than the shotgun blast.

If there were occupants, they would be in shock and a little deaf. I heard a woman scream.

"Lie down!" a man yelled in English.

The radio sputtered: "Move forward."

Walking inside with the boy, I saw more than twenty Iraqi men in various stages of undress. They'd been sleeping and were in their bed-clothes. We separated the men and methodically searched their clothes for weapons.

The boy was secreted into the kitchen, where Muaad and Sergeant Peluso kept him talking. The array of men in the other room had been quickly photographed, and the boy now looked at the impromptu por-traits, several of which caught his attention.

One by one, the boy pointed to certain individuals, indicating their involvement with JAM cell activity. All the while, Ryan was busy with the BATS system, taking fingerprints and retina scans, then entering them into the system super-rush.

We still hadn't found the explosives, and the kid's fountain of information was beginning to dry up. Earlier he'd boasted of know-ing where they kept the bombs. Now there was a horrified expression on his face.

It was more than he'd expected, all of these adult men in just their drawers, army guys stomping in big boots—and he was respon-sible, a fact that, if made public, would shrink his life expectancy to minuscule.

So Sergeant Peluso and I got the kid out of there. Outside a crowd had gathered that included Iraqi police and US Army soldiers. We pulled the kid's shirt up over his head to cover his face. Fully realizing his dilemma, the kid shivered violently with terror.

It was just about then that the sergeant realized all was not as it seemed. He was instructed to see an army major, who in turn told Peluso what an idiot he was. The building we'd just raided was an official Iraqi police station. The commanding officer was unhappy with our visit.

Tough shit, I thought to myself. They were nothing but a bunch of corrupt individuals, being paid with American dollars to protect their own people and doing a lousy job of it.

I took charge of the boy and we trotted together away from all the people, maybe a half mile until we were in seclusion.

"Where are the explosives?" I asked, one more time.

The boy pointed to a piece of roadway that was covered over with concrete and blacktop, insisting that this was the location, that the explosives were directly beneath. We tried to refocus his attention a couple of times, but he stuck to his ridiculous story, so we cut him loose.

Back at the shop I learned that Peluso was in deep shit and the army once more planned on siding with political correctness over Joe.

Later, salt was rubbed in Peluso's wound when an Iraqi police commander convinced an army sergeant major to conduct an unannounced search of Peluso's men in hopes of locating five million Iraqi dinars allegedly stolen during our raid. Incredible but not surprising. I later learned the army paid the Iraqi police commander $43,000 to make the complaint go away.

———————————

It was my first Christmas away from home, and with all the political changes going on with the rules of engagement, I was frustrated and homesick. I'd told Debbie to get the kids whatever they wanted for Christmas, hoping to fill the void of me being away—although I now realize it was my own void I was trying to fill. I called home and Debbie told me it took the kids a good half hour to open all their presents, and they were very happy. I felt a lot better knowing the kids were fine.

For Christmas we got Muaad a gag gift, a leash for an invisible dog.

On the third day of 2009, I was rearranging my personal effects. At that evening's briefing we had learned of an arming agreement signed by the US secretary of defense. I was wondering if this would affect our workload when there was a thunderous explosion that shook my entire CHU on its foundation. I awaited an all-clear message over the PA, but it didn't come.

I thought maybe it was just a controlled detonation. That happened all the time, but there was supposed to be a PA warning. The system was flawed, however, with failures to communicate and absentee announcers.

I was back to straightening my stuff as if nothing had happened when there was a knock at my door. It was Muaad.

"We have a mission."

I quickly got dressed and jumped in the back of the pickup truck that would bounce us to the shop.

During the ride I got the lowdown on the big boom. There had been an IED attack on an Iraqi police unit very close to the base. In the shop, Ricky was working the phone and talking a mile a minute. Adoni's hand was a blur as he scribbled the order of march and vehicle assignments on the big board.

News came in. Two Iraqi cops dead. Chaotic scene out there. Ricky briefed us: our own EOD was already on-site, along with Iraqi EOD. This had *too many cooks in the kitchen* written all over it.

"It is a clusterfuck," Muaad said in his Borat voice.

Our nocturnal convoy rumbled us toward COP 820, a former military outpost recently turned over to the Iraqi police. Scanning the dark horizon, I saw five military vehicles silhouetted by the flashing blue lights of the Iraqi cop cars beyond our contact point.

Getting out of our vehicles, we learned that US EOD had refused to move forward because they didn't trust the safety standards of Iraqi EOD. The story went that an Iraqi EOD guy had recently kicked a bomb as one might a used-car tire, causing his immediate obliteration.

So there was a delay as US EOD made certain their own safety standards were met. Eventually we were allowed to move forward and scan the scene for evidence. It didn't take me long to find some, and it was the kind *no* lawman likes to discover. I had only moved forward fifteen meters or so when I almost stepped on what looked like the fragments of human bone with flesh and blood partially attached.

"Human remains," I called out, and photographed it.

As I did that, off to my right Mike D. examined the blast seat. Mike could inform everyone of information he was gathering and talk to himself simultaneously. He surmised that the cops who were hit had dismounted their vehicles to investigate a strip of crush wire typically used in the detonation of IED/EFP devices.

"The question now is how was the device armed?" he said. Looking further, Mike recovered the remnants of a cell phone control panel and a nickel cadmium rechargeable battery. "Aha," he said. "Question now is where were the cell phone components recovered in relation to the explosive device."

Having bagged and labeled the human remains, I looked up and saw an Iraqi policeman escorting an Iraqi national in handcuffs. "Why was this man arrested?" I asked.

"He was trespassing in an abandoned house and had once prior been told to leave the area," the cop said.

"Where did the arrest take place?"

He pointed to a nearby row of houses, some two stories high, many with windows that faced the event site. I politely asked for and was given permission to interview the detainee, so Muaad and I went to work.

"Did the house you were arrested in have a view of the explosion?" I asked.

"I do not know. I was asleep and was woken by the explosion." Which, of course, had nothing to do with the view from the windows.

"Were you sleeping upstairs or downstairs?"

"Upstairs."

"If you had been sleeping upright could you have watched the explosion from the window?"

"No. The room I was in did not face that direction."

"Was there a room on the second floor with windows overlooking the blast scene?"

"I do not know. If there was I was never in such a room," he said, looking at the ground as he spoke.

Wrapping up the scene, Phoenix headed back to its original dismount position. The ground force commander was still holding the security cordon. True to form, EOD had already left the site.

We heard the scuttlebutt from one of the 1-505's squad sergeants. He said he'd heard that the Iraqi police unit residing in COP 820 had targeted an individual for arrest by warrant. The target was, strangely enough, an Iraqi police commander who was corrupt and abusive.

Hearing he was about to be arrested, he planted an explosive device as a way of saying, *Don't fuck with me.*

Back at the shop, Mike gave Ricky the gory details as well as the technical explanation of the event. I related the story that the blast was intentionally directed at the Iraqi police.

Ricky dismissed the story as "hearsay, at best."

"I still think it should be included in our report," I said. "We'll note the source and that it is unsupported, but we should also call it completely plausible."

Adoni was on my side. "I think we should say the attack appeared to be retaliatory." And that was how it went into the report.

The next day a Captain Able called Ricky and thanked him for the great report. Our assessment was spot on. HUMINT supported the story I'd been told. Ricky thanked the captain, gave me a thumbs-up, and we ignored the fact that he'd originally been against including the "hearsay, at best."

———————

There was more frustration in the middle of January, this time just bad luck, typical Murphy's Law crap. Our crews had driven to Camp Liberty to exchange our old RG-33 vehicles for new ones. As luck would have it, a target of opportunity presented itself, the 505 asked for our help, and we were caught dead in the water. It especially sucked because it was the second time we'd been called by the 505 and were unable to accommodate the request. The 505 went ahead without us.

The mission was a warrant-based target in another area of operation. Target was responsible for sniper attacks, kidnappings, and murders. Ricky thought that maybe, just maybe, if we could switch off the RG-33s efficiently we could still aid 505.

Of course, there was nothing efficient about the vehicle exchange. It was hurry up and wait. As we waited we kept tabs on 505's progress, which wasn't good. They couldn't get a positive ID on the target.

Staff Sergeant Rozell, a.k.a. Rozy, signaled his ETA with the new trucks. Just as we were reequipped and ready to roll, word came that the target had been located—and, oh joy, he was an Iraqi policeman holed up in an Iraqi police station. When we got that news, the air hung heavy. Everyone was glum.

Got to give Ricky credit. Knowing that the feckless leadership from brigade headquarters had just handed over $43K to a lying Iraqi police commander, Ricky understood that things would probably go poorly again and another of his men would be accused of stealing something or other. But he decided to go ahead with the mission anyway—anything in support of the ground assault force (GAF) commander, the officer with tactical control.

When the new trucks arrived, drivers were advised to leave motors running and prepare for the upcoming mission. I briefed Muaad and handed him the target package. Leafing through the pages, Muaad said, "It's all electronic surveillance. No HUMINT."

"And no photo," I said.

"Now I see why 505 was having trouble getting a positive ID."

One of our new RG-33s.

As we headed toward the target, there was an amped-up tension. The day before an IED had detonated, narrowly missing the rear MRAP of a military convoy. The convoy hightailed it out of there, leaving the crime scene behind without giving it a thought.

We pulled up to the Iraqi police station and were given the info dump. There was frustration regarding the investigation. The Iraqi police commander had not welcomed the Americans with open arms as had been hoped. In fact, the commander acted like a street thug.

Muaad and I looked at one another, a silent reminder that we needed to be on our very best behavior. That look was code for *Be nice to the asshole*. My first job as I entered the station was to hide my distaste.

I should have been used to it, but I wasn't. Iraqi police stations had a patina of filth. Not that precinct houses in Brooklyn are always lemony fresh, but this was disgusting. Climbing, I noticed the steps were at different heights and slopes, some cracked, all covered with cigarette butts and rotting food.

Ryan found the target and gave him the BATS treatment, scanning his iris and taking his fingerprints. Muaad and I sought out the Iraqi police commander and were led by a Joe down a dark hallway, passing through an open mezzanine area.

Entering an office, Muaad and I were greeted by a man with a toothy grin and slender wrists in civilian clothes, a denim fashion outfit. I shook his clammy hand and introduced myself, trying not to stare at the thick layer of white cream that covered his face. I don't think I'm going out on a limb saying that the commander was a strange bird.

"Muaad, please ask him what's on his face."

"It is, in fact, massage cream," the commander replied, with an elaborate gesture. I creeped myself out wondering about the cream.

The interview with the creamy commander went smoothly until I asked about the man we were arresting, whom I'll call *Mr. Happy*.

"What's his full name?"

"I don't know."

"Where's he live?"

"I don't know."

"What are his duties?"

"I don't recall."

"He has worked for you for over two years and you know nothing about him?" It occurred to me that the cream could be a disguise, that there was a reason the commander didn't want me to know how he looked when he wasn't getting a face massage.

"All of the personal info regarding my men is in another facility," he said.

"I suggest you send one of your men to retrieve the information so I may continue my investigation."

He seemed stunned by this suggestion. "No one is in the office at this time," he said.

"How can that be if it is a police facility?" I asked.

He was silent.

I called him a liar in Arabic. He angrily answered back, looking away from me and speaking directly to Muaad. "Here is the truth: I am not going to give you any information regarding Mr. Happy."

At this point, I instructed the accompanying 505 staff sergeant and his specialist to leave *Commander Creamy*'s office. Now he was alone with Muaad and me.

I said, "Listen to me closely—I'm here to conduct an official investigation regarding Mr. Happy, acting on behalf of an Iraqi court-issued warrant, and you're intentionally withholding vital information. If I do not get your full cooperation immediately, I will recommend to the GAF commander that he place you in handcuffs and bring you before an Iraqi judge who will compel your assistance."

To drive the point home, I opened the door to the office and instructed the staff sergeant and his specialist to have Lieutenant Burns and a sergeant come and detain Commander Creamy, who quickly pulled out his cell phone and made a scribbling motion with his free hand.

"Have a pencil? Be ready to copy down the information," Commander Creamy said to Muaad.

Burns and the sergeant arrived.

"Never mind," I said. "My interviewee has had a change of heart."

Muaad wrote down Mr. Happy's address and phone number.

I pulled out my Olympus to photograph the Creamster, who held up his hand, saying he didn't wish to be photographed.

"Not with the cream on my face," he said.

"Don't worry," I said. "I'm only going to show it to the men under your command and your mother." You can take the cop out of Brooklyn but, well, you know.

Muaad cracked up at my sarcasm and explained that he was going to leave the comment about Creamy's mother out of the translation. I agreed with a chuckle that that was probably for the best.

———————

Next up for me was Mr. Happy, who was in an airless room that stank of sweat and stale cigarette smoke. There were a couple of ashtrays I could see that had apparently never been emptied, filled and overflowing with filterless cigarette butts. Mr. Happy was sitting cross-legged on a blanket on the floor. I had him stand so I could photograph him, and Muaad and I began the questioning.

He began by denying everything, even things that were demonstrably true. He denied that the cell phone found in his pocket was his, for example. I told him to cut it out. Commander Creamy, I said, had already given us the lowdown on him, so he might as well spill. That news upset him. He began to breathe heavily, gulping air.

I suggested to Lieutenant Burns that we toss Mr. Happy's residence immediately, before anything had an opportunity to disappear. Burns radioed in the info to CHOPS.

At that point we were told to return to base, and to bring Mr. Happy with us.

———————

Back at the shop, Muaad went over to the detention facility to extract the vital piece of electronic forensics needed to keep Mr. Happy incarcerated. Ricky was not convinced that we had the right guy, so he and I made a gentlemen's bet. We waited to hear back from the SCIF, and then the phone rang.

I was working on my written report, only vaguely aware of a phone ringing nearby. Tony V., who had replaced Matt Pucino as our intelligence/targeting guy, answered. I glanced up and watched as a huge smile came over his face.

"Thanks," he said and hung up the phone. He sat and grinned at us.

"Well?" the Team said in unison.

"It's him," Tony said.

Cheers erupted.

I looked at Ricky and said, "You owe me a case of beer!"

After a brief celebration, it was back to work. I continued my report, smiling inwardly. Another victory for Phoenix. Another terrorist behind bars. I loved my job. With my family on the other side of the world, all I had was the adrenaline of the mission to look forward to. Luckily for me, hunting bad guys never got old.

Our elation was cruelly truncated the next day when Mike D. took a call from Lieutenant Burns. Of course, there'd been a complaint about our behavior at the police station: "Improper treatment and unprofessional conduct." It was a pain in the ass, because we had to have our shit together when the inevitable JAG investigation came snooping around.

As a cop, I'd dealt with many civilian complaints over the years. It was part of the Job. Difference was, in the NYPD the brass was generally on your side. Here, there were treaties being signed that had the enemy smelling victory, and Colonel Buford, thoroughly covering his own ass, would kowtow to any allegation.

We didn't have to wait long. At that night's evening meeting, we were told to expect a Major Orden, who had questions for everybody regarding the mission of January 19. "Stand by for sworn statements," we were told. A source told us the allegations had something to do with excessive force and that "the Iraqi police were determined to get their pound of flesh."

"It's a fucking harassment complaint," I said.

A half hour later, Major Orden arrived and asked for all people who were in the presence of the Iraqi police commander during the interview. It was established that the people in the room were Muaad and me; Ryan, who came in briefly, took a photograph, and left; and last, I think, Sharif Morsi, our other interpreter, who asked a few questions while I was in another part of the building interviewing Mr. Happy.

We were given blank sworn statement forms to fill out. There were pedigree questions followed by questions asking about the use of force and the witnessing of excessive force, both by Americans, specific affiliation unclear.

When Major Orden was out of the room, I said, "If a question can be answered yes or no, do so. No need to elaborate to help this witch hunt."

While we wrote, Orden interviewed us one at a time in another room. I went last. I knew Orden could not have been looking forward to interviewing me. It was a reversal of roles that couldn't possibly serve him well—the questioner was about to be questioned.

There was a slight bulge in his right sleeve, a digital recorder.

I said, "Look, we handled the guy with kid gloves. We had discussions before we went in that we needed to be on our best behavior, and we were."

When he was through, Orden shook each of our hands and thanked us for our cooperation. But he was back the next day. Just a few more questions, he said, to complete his investigation.

We had another form to fill out. There were again questions about excessive force, but now there were additional queries about "insulting language." I knew it—we were going to go down for hurting Commander Creamy's feelings.

"Captain Wyman is behind all of this, isn't he?" I said to Orden upon his return.

"I don't know," he said.

"You know that a second sworn statement negates the first, right?" I said.

"I think we'll just take the better of the two," he said with a laugh.

Later that same evening, Lieutenant Burns called Ricky and requested photographs of his team. JAG was contemplating this insanity. It was reckless. Knowing what I did about the Iraqis, the prospect of being targeted in retaliation was very real. As it turned out, they were only interested in three photos: Muaad, Sharif, and me.

Ricky told them he would be unable to supply those photos, and hung up. Five minutes later, the phone rang again.

Ricky answered it and I saw his face fall. "Well, there you have it— we're shut down till further notice," Ricky said. "Blanket e-mail went out. We are not to be utilized."

For two days we sat around idly, going through the motions of keeping our chins up while doing busywork and training. Ricky at one point hit a low spot and became emotional during one of our nightly meetings. He'd seen Sergeant Dave Peluso and learned of a mission that would've been perfect for our support. Ricky choked up and we all hung our heads so as not to watch.

Going into midnight chow, Mike D. arrived noisily at the dinner table, slapping a newspaper down and saying, "You see *this*?"

We hadn't.

"Some fucking *Captain Cash*, a coward who never left the FOB, has written a letter to the editor. Doesn't mention us by name, but he's slamming Phoenix. Here," he said. He opened the paper to the spot: "He says contractors have ruined the rapport the military has worked so hard to build with their coalition partners."

He also called us war profiteers and mercenaries. I took these as allusions to our recent Iraqi police station incidents, and I found the accusations dangerous. With the cooperation of the Internet, a letter like this could serve as PSYOPS ammunition for a media-savvy enemy.

Mike D. was so angry, he wrote a rebuttal letter to the editor. Bobby V. wrote a letter that was like a work of art, addressing it directly to Captain Cash. Sergeant Peluso, an aggressive man by nature, hand-delivered Bobby V.'s letter and got in Cash's face.

"Cash was taken aback by my forwardness," Peluso later reported with a twinkle in his eye.

And so here's my final fuck-you to Cash, a coward of a man who, based on hearsay alone, criticized men who'd spilled blood on the American battlefield. He was compelled to take pen to paper and complain about these "contractors" who had so grossly offended his mantle of self-anointed righteousness. Give me a break. Fuck you.

20

WHY I MISSED CHOW

Just when stir-craziness was setting in, the grounding of Phoenix Team was lifted and Sergeant Dave Peluso had us back in the saddle working with his troops.

It was January 25, 2009, and word was the 1-22 TST had tentatively located an HVI. We were told to stand by as they fine-tuned the exact location. We launched just before evening chow, so we went without. It was to be a doubleheader. That night we had a second, more complicated target that involved an arrest warrant—now required by the new security agreement hammered out between the USCF and Iraqis. The first mission was a false alarm. The second was more promising, conducted in a joint venture with the Iraqi National Police, another complicating factor.

"We're going to miss both chow and the gym," my roomie Dave McWhirt said sadly.

A fellow named Jack called out to me: "Hey, Goober." Goober was a term of endearment, I think—like Skillet. He seemed pleasant when he said it. "Target package has no photos—again." Jack was a retired ATF agent with a Tennessee twang to his speech. He was like me: he could never quite get used to how bad the army was at HUMINT. We agreed we shouldn't bellyache too much, as that was why they needed us.

For good reasons we were suspicious of the new warrant system, though—fearful that warrants would come with crippling limitations on what could and could not be done that would cramp Phoenix's style. Plus, we would be placed in a position, after we rolled the guy up, in which we'd be expected to explain the rationale behind the arrest. Hard to do without exposing methods and sources to the Iraqis.

We were to go to the police station to join up with the INP forces, and proceed from there to the target. We'd had our fill of Major Orden and being the subject of a concocted investigation. Now we again had to be in the vicinity of an Iraqi police station. This time, though, the visit was without incident.

We made it to the target area and waited two and a half hours for the exact location. The information never came. The decision was made to make a cruder attempt at locating the target.

What followed was one of the most surreal moments of my life, rolling at pedestrian speed down this village street while wearing NVG. Someone was expecting us, as there were obstacles that needed to be cleared. Barbed wire stretched across the street. Was it booby-trapped? A concrete barrier was in place that hadn't been there the day before, formidable enough to make us go the long way around.

Eventually an exact location was determined, but getting there from here was a challenge. All traffic was disconcerting. In Iraq, the terrorist insurgency would frequently create traffic jams, sometimes gridlock, which would cause soldiers to dismount and travel on foot. This tactic was known as funneling, directing the enemy's flow into the kill zone. So every traffic jam we encountered could potentially be designed to draw us into an ambush—IED attack, firefight, or both.

We arrived at the site and parked our vehicles in a line formation. We were playing a strange form of hide-and-seek, careful to stay outside the target's view but so loud—the RG-33s alone—that people stuck their heads out of windows to see what was going on. Again we waited, and there was much speculation that the night was a bust and we were going to come away empty-handed. Then the radio squawked. We were to move to a new location and stand by.

There had already been much standing by, and we were antsy for action. Out my window I saw a dozen Joes running into a courtyard from two directions. I heard a sledgehammer slam steel doors. On the third solid blow the doors flew open and the Joes barged right in, delivering orders in phonetic Arabic for everyone to get the fuck down or their heads would be blown off. The Joes coming from the other side had more trouble with their door and ended up blasting it open with a 12-gauge shotgun, the report of which made someone inside the structure scream. That always made me smile.

Only minutes later Phoenix got word to move forward and be briefed. Info was sparse. Only one individual had been identified, and that identification was tentative. But it was enough for Sharif and me to have a starting point. (The Chris and Muaad Show was over, my old terp having rotated out. Sharif was my guy now, and he was also great.)

I entered the courtyard and saw three male subjects, wrists cuffed behind their back. Rocky the bomb dog was sniffing them. After the K-9 team cleared the detainees, we moved in. We were still trying to get their names straight when one of them said something to Sharif.

"Detainee #3 here says he has a weapon," Sharif said. The interpreter moved like a cat and removed a loaded 9 mm Walther semiautomatic pistol from the detainee's right jacket pocket. Sharif handed it to me to unload.

"Is anyone else armed?" I asked.

They shook their heads no. We searched them anyway. I have been to too many funerals because of the lax searching of prisoners. We cleared the room, and Sharif and I got down to business.

Detainee #1 was named *Alawayi*, which was also the name on the photo-free target package. The name was tough to say, so I'll call him Mr. Always. Mr. Always was just answering our preliminary questions when there was a commotion.

"Landslide!" Mike D. called out from somewhere outside, code for discovery of an explosive device.

I instinctively grabbed hold of the prisoner's hair and shoved his head with a thud into the concrete floor. I whispered into his ear, "*Ibn sharmuta*"—Arabic for "son of a whore."

Mike was yelling very loud, "Everyone out. Everyone get the fuck out!"

I pulled Mr. Always to his feet by his hair and led him across the street, where we took over a complete stranger's home and continued the interview. The expression on Always's face was priceless. His head hurt *and* he knew he was in a whole heap of trouble.

We were just getting started again when Mike came into the room and said, "Italian land mine, with blasting cap and ready to blow."

"Good job, Mike," I said. Then I asked, "Mr. Always, how is it that you have an Italian land mine in your house?"

"A burglar must have placed it there without my knowledge," came his weak-sauce reply.

Ordinarily, I might've had a crisp reply, but given the current environment, with the INP about, I limited my incredulity to a puzzled shake of my head. We danced around the subject of confession for a few minutes, and I could tell he wasn't ready. I told him I had enough info to establish he was a liar.

I switched to the other two detainees, who turned out to be Always's brother and associate. I interviewed them one at a time, and their stories didn't match. The associate said he'd just been passing by and was invited in for tea. "So you see? This is all just one big misunderstanding," he said with wide eyes.

"Do you always stop in for tea with a 9 mm in your pocket?" I inquired.

He had nothing to say. Without a government permit, possession of a handgun was a crime. When he did begin to talk, he babbled about how much he loved Americans and how he was working to help rid the neighborhood of the JAM cell members.

"Your good friend Mr. Always was just arrested for possession of explosives. How do you explain that?" I queried.

He stammered a bit then concluded, "I have the right to remain silent. I have nothing further to say." Even here in Iraq most of the shows on TV are American, including *Law & Order* and other crime dramas with regular courtroom scenes. Because of this, many Iraqis know more about the American legal system, especially Miranda law, than they do about their own.

I was content that, because of the evidence found across the street, it didn't matter what these guys told me. They were on their way to an Iraqi court and, at best, eventual long-term incarceration.

Back at the shop there was an intense five hours of report-writing and evidence-processing. Lieutenant DeWall from DOMEX, the unit devoted to document and media exploitation, came into the shop holding a plastic bag containing a cell phone.

"This has to go to the feds. There's a call on it to the US." We had the capabilities to exploit the phone ourselves, but the worry was we'd step on the toes of a more sensitive operation.

"Chris, could you deliver the phone to your buddy Jack at brigade?"

"Only too happy," I said.

Walking into Jack's office, I heard "Hey, Goober. Whatcha doing?" I handed him the cell phone from DOMEX and explained its significance.

"You're next in the chain of evidence," I said happily.

"Do you have a storyboard to go with it?" he asked.

I pulled up the report on Jack's computer screen. He asked me to sit and updated me on the INP station raid and subsequent investigation. He had spoken both to Colonel Buford and to his counterpart in the police station's AO, and he'd learned details regarding the allegations. We were accused of having used excessive force with INP guys, and we were said to have ransacked Commander Creamy's desk.

"Colonel Buford has apologized to the INP commander," Jack told me. "He has promised that the wrongdoers will be punished."

"Dramatic?"

"High drama. Colonel Buford pulled off his Fourth ID patch from his sleeve and applied it to the INP commander's sleeve—as a sign of his word."

"Did the colonel ask your opinion?"

"I told him I would get everyone's side before coming to a conclusion. Wait I second, I wrote down a quote . . ." Jack pulled out a green notebook and flipped through its pages. "He said he had three concerns: one, GAF commander's lack of supervision; two, the abusive nature of the interpreter, allegation that a white-haired interpreter had laid hands on INP; three, Ricky's loss of control of Phoenix."

"What are his plans?"

"I don't think he's going to be satisfied with removing Phoenix from FOB Falcon. I think he wants to remove it completely from theater."

"Did you come to our defense?"

"I did. I reminded Buford of what a valuable asset Phoenix had been, and I reminded him that the facts in this case were not complete."

"You know this sickens me . . ."

"I know, Chris . . ."

"Everything we've accomplished out the window because of the corrupt INP—with the help of a colonel who only cares about being made general. But I thank you, Jack. Thanks for defending us."

"Just calling them the way I see them," he said with a sad smile. He was pretty sure we were toast.

Back at the shop, Ricky was interested in anything I might've learned.

"Do you want to hear the facts, or do you want to sleep tonight?" I asked.

"I can take it," Ricky said. Adoni joined us, all ears.

I gave them the bad news, including allegations that Ricky had lost Phoenix. Our team head looked so sad. Adoni reminded us that he'd said it from the start: we were just contractors and the army wasn't going to hesitate to serve us up if they felt that was the easiest way to overcome a problem.

I complained that no one would consider the special interests of the sources. Adoni said, "Remember, Buford is upwardly mobile and well connected. Unfuckwithable."

Ricky pointed out that by going directly to the INP commander, Buford cut out the primary source of the allegations, the station commander, Mr. Creamy.

The only shining light, we agreed, was that the Fourth ID was leaving in five weeks and taking its slimeball leadership with it. Who knew where we would be by then?

"But that fucking Buford," Ricky said.

Adoni and I spoke in unison: "Fuck him!"

"Bottom line," I said. "When we got here Joe was getting blown up daily by IED/EFPs, and now he isn't. That's the only fucking stat that matters."

On January 30, we received excellent news. Colonel Buford asked the battalion combat teams to write testimonials on the subject of Phoenix and the INP incident. This was seen as a tremendous positive, as the testimonials were bound to be favorable.

Buford had apparently learned that throwing us out of theater on the first thing smoking wasn't going to work—we were way too valuable!—and now he needed paperwork to cover his face as he ate his words.

That night at chow I heard that Colonel Buford had arranged for a volleyball game to be played between wolf-faced members of the INP and handpicked representatives of the base's women. Word was that a lady lieutenant from DOMEX and a by-all-accounts cute captain at the detainee holding area were roped into this exercise in sexism, along with many women who had less say when given an order. I felt bad for them.

If a younger male officer had proposed the game, someone in the officer corps might've had second thoughts. But the fact that it was Buford's suggestion made the idea completely palatable to the other officers. So the colonel was going to exploit his female officers and soldiers to build rapport with the Iraqi cops. The women must've felt helpless against the great big male army, and yet none of them would file a complaint with the Equal Employment Opportunity Office.

Amid all of the political decisions Big Army had made that adversely affected my life and job in Iraq, I had undervalued what I'd observed about how the men in charge dealt with women. I'd seen some of them paw women, wolf moves to make an observer wince. I recalled one occasion in particular. A high-ranking officer was strutting down the hall with a lady anthropologist assigned to the Human Terrain Team. She was attractive, looked like Angelina Jolie playing Lara Croft, and was a solid thirty years younger than the officer. With his face twisted with lasciviousness, he gripped insistently at her arm and massaged her shoulders, causing her much tension and near alarm.

Another officer was writing love letters to a female Iraqi interpreter. The guy—married, by the way—thought he was just getting his doorknob polished, but it turned out he was passing on intelligence to a chain that led to American-killing terrorists. Please, sir, just keep it in your pants. The officer and the interpreter, it was discovered, continued their affair once back stateside. If the officer had been a private, he would have been taken into custody and prosecuted for treason.

I wondered if these men's powerful positions in life had caused them to lose touch with reality. Maybe their little heads did all the thinking. Or, and I liked this theory better, the same unquenchable drive that made them pursue a general's star also made them hunger for pleasures of the flesh. Maybe it was all just one big case of relentless gratification, feeding their egos like a glutton.

Truth is, there was a lot of hanky-panky at FOB Falcon—so much tippy-toeing in the middle of the night that it looked like a British sex comedy. I had caught two JAG officers sneaking around in the early morning hours with junior soldiers. And those were the guys who gave Colonel Buford his legal advice.

I'm not the morality police. Just an observer. And I've observed that guys who cheat always cheat, no matter what the subject or category. I'd wager these guys were cheating on their taxes, too. They cheated on their wives. They cheated when playing Candy Land with their kids. They were cheaters.

So there was to be a volleyball game, and we were all expected to come out and watch. I went to monitor the INP and make sure they did or said nothing to offend our women soldiers. The game had just started and there was an announcement over the PA system inviting everyone to come watch the "INP Spikers" take on "Buford's Beauties."

Buford took a position of power right alongside the net and received a steady pounding of high fives from junior officers who wanted to kiss his powerful ass. The JAG guys filed by and thanked the colonel for the—*heh, heh, heh*—volleyball game. Wink, wink. I asked my buddy Dave McWhirt to take photos of Buford and the game to memorialize the event.

It didn't help that the Americans were losing badly. In the end the INP won five of the six games played. Buford had had a big gold trophy made and now presented it to an Iraqi general. Big smiles all around.

Iraqi men versus American women in a volleyball game to entertain our base. Thanks to Dave M. for taking this photo.

Then, at Buford's insistence, there were a series of photo ops in which the American women posed with the Iraqi men, who began to paw and squeeze, while the women tried to figure out how to get the hell away from the situation without causing an international incident. The women were then ordered to attend a ceremonial postgame dinner.

The lady lieutenant spoke to me later, showed me photos of Iraqi cops touching her breasts. But it was the good ol' boy network, she said. They had no fear of backlash. None.

———————

It was the final day of January 2009 when the next mission came along. The timing couldn't have been worse. My head had just hit the pillow at the end of a long day when Adoni knocked.

"Mission, guys."

"What's up?" I asked.

"The 7-10 rolled up a bad guy, a *Mr. Zayid*. They're looking for assistance."

Dave M. and I quickly got dressed, trying to shake off the fugue state, that twilight world between wake and sleep.

"I hope 7-10 has their shit together," I said.

On previous missions with the 7-10, we'd experienced confusion and lack of order while approaching and on the target. They'd once crashed into a home only to realize it was 1) the wrong place, and 2) a place where they'd been trying to develop a source. They had a way of smashing rapport and replacing it with hurt feelings—something I normally didn't mind, as long as you shotgunned the correct door off its hinges.

The sun was coming up and the sounds of cars honking outside the wire indicated the day was already in full swing in Baghdad. It was the second day of provincial elections and we were forbidden to conduct any offensive operation, lest we be accused of trying to disrupt the relative calm at that crucial time.

Boarding our RG-33, Dave M. and I snapped pictures of each other along with the fresh batch of FNGs. The target was less than

Dave McWhirt (left), Lou DeAnda, and me—all geared up and ready for action.

three miles away. As the convoy approached the *muhallah*, a Sergeant Wazz—which was short for something—was navigating in the lead vehicle—no easy task, as certain streets were closed for the election. We should've been there in fifteen minutes. Instead, we drove up one street and down another for an hour. It was the old adage: you can't get there from here.

"Every fucking street is closed," Wazz said into his microphone. We were starting to feel anxious. Safety depended on limiting exposure, and we'd now hung it out for all to see for an hour. Our movements were becoming predictable, raising the prospect of swift-moving terrorists pulling the old "drop and pop"—that is, hastily preparing and placing an IED/EFP in a spot where they knew we would soon be.

On the BFT video screen, I could easily make out the 7-10 elements' positioning. As it turned out, I was an impatient man even in that cluster of totally impatient men. "What the fuck!" I said.

The navigator heard me and snapped back, "What do you want me to do, drive right down the street and kill these fucking people? The streets are all blocked!"

"Pick one and let's get moving. Wazz, it's already been an hour and they're holding the cordon for us."

There was this tense stretch in which we went slowly and people got out of the way. It was surreal—pedestrians dealing with wide combat vehicles—but we eventually arrived at the target without creating any Iraqi street pizza.

Adoni got the dump from the 7-10 GAF commander. "We got an Iraqi judge to sign over a warrant," the commander said.

"What grounds?" Adoni asked.

"Mr. Zayid is a serious dude—and the risk associated with leaving him on the street is unacceptable. Didn't hurt that the judge was Sunni and the target Shia," the commander said with a laugh.

"You guys use this judge before?" Adoni asked.

"We have a Sunni judge and a Shia judge and whatever the target is, we go to the other."

"Genius," Adoni said with a toothy grin.

What we all understood—now that our dreams were destroyed, replaced with a bitter, jaded cynicism—was that little of this mattered. If the target was a friend of a friend of a sheik, he was out of jail as soon as we put him in there. It was a revolving door kind of justice: no justice at all.

Sharif and I walked into the residence. The prisoner was in the living room, in an armchair, blindfolded. His hands, I was stunned to see, were not cuffed, so he was comfortably smoking a cigarette.

Soldiers occupied the other chairs and the couch. Some were standing, leaning against the walls. They were young and had expectant expressions on their eager faces. It looked like the boys had gathered together to watch the big game.

"Why is this man not flex-cuffed?" I asked.

"He's got diabetes, sir," one of the junior soldiers said.

"Do the flex cuffs aggravate his diabetes? I'm just asking." I waited for five seconds of loud silence before adding, "Somebody flex-cuff this asshole right now or I'm leaving."

The man was cuffed.

"I'll interview him in the bathroom, and we don't want company," I said, leading the prisoner into the john by the scruff of his neck. I removed some buckets that were on the floor of the shower stall and had the prisoner stand in there. I removed his blindfold. All he could see was Sharif and me. The shower stall enhanced his trauma, adding an airless claustrophobia to the mix. He must've felt like he was being buried alive.

"Hello, Mr. Zayid," I said. "I've read a lot about you. I'm going to take a couple photographs of you now, one in front and one looking to the side." He was compliant, and the mugs were shot.

We searched him for weapons and contraband—I couldn't imagine those peach-fuzz baby-faces outside being sufficiently thorough when they initially searched him. Then we acquired his pedigree.

I pulled out my knife and placed it near the prisoner's shoulder. Of course, he instantly became horrified, and perhaps I let that moment linger before reassuring him. "My intent is not to scare you," I said. "I merely need to cut away your shirt so I can check you for tattoos and scars," I said. I was telling the truth. Here in Iraq, terrorists were always inking their bodies with tribal nonsense that made them readily identifiable.

I tried to use a comforting tone, but he didn't relax much. Of course, I kept the knife always where he could see it, could watch me cut at the cloth of his shirt, helpless to stop me.

Sharif and I had not quite succeeded in getting a private moment with the prisoner. Also in the bathroom but outside the shower stall was an INP officer, there to take custody of the prisoner when we were through with him.

I kept the interview quiet in hopes that the guard would not hear much of what was being said. Zayid became preoccupied by the presence of the INP man. I could tell that he was far more worried about the treatment he would receive from the Iraqi police than about anything I might do.

He tried to lie to me, of course, and I made a habit of moving so he could better see the guard each time I thought his response was particularly outlandish. Once I allowed my eyes to veer back in the guard's direction. He got the idea: if he told me the truth, maybe things would go better for him when I passed him along.

It worked beautifully, straight out of the pages of Pavlov's experiment. I modified Zayid's behavior, metamorphosing him from a liar to a truth-blurter. He told us who his friends were, becoming a fountain of names and addresses. He told us where the explosives were kept, and expressed a strong urge to leave this bathroom and its INP guard and show us the location of the cache.

And we knew it was all good, because a percentage of the names cross-checked with previous intelligence. He said he wanted unconditional freedom in exchange for the information. I told him no dice. An old cop adage says, "Never make promises you can't keep." If you lose your credibility with a prisoner, no more information will be forthcoming. But I did tell Zayid that his cooperation, including leading us to the hidden weapons, would be considered heavily when an Iraqi court decided what to do with him.

The interview was continuing to be highly productive when there was a knock at the door and a red-faced lieutenant stormed in, holding a black Italian Uzi in his hands. "I thought you said there were no more weapons in the house, what the fuck is this?" he said, shoving the sub-machine gun in Zayid's face.

Zayid said, "It must have been left by the previous resident who rented the rooftop from my father."

The door to the bathroom now open, I heard Mike D. announce that he'd found three SIM cards hidden in teacups in a china closet—further indication that the youthful soldiers that gave the residence its original once-over were inept.

Bizarrely, it was the 7-10 guys who began to grumble. We were making them look bad. We were going to take all the credit. I bit my lip, but I wanted to tell them we were not allowed to take credit for anything ever, not officially. We always worked in a support role. The credit was all theirs. They captured a bad guy and he confessed.

Zayid wanted to take us to the residence of someone we knew was a real bad guy because of previous intelligence, a man named *Zanjari*. It was a big day for Z names. But the 7-10 decided to pass on visiting Zanjari on this night, because the residence was in another AO and they didn't want to go through the rigmarole of obtaining permission to operate there. I felt then, as I do now, that passing on Zanjari that night was an error on 7-10's part, a damaging loss of momentum.

Soon after the lieutenant interrupted, I wrapped up the shower stall interview of Zayid. I ordered the blindfold be put back on. He began weeping, begging to kiss his eight-month-old daughter good-bye. I thought allowing this courtesy was a good way of harmlessly rewarding a cooperative subject, but the army scoffed at this notion of kindness.

Back at the shop, I told Adoni there was good news and bad news. We'd gotten the location of many of Zayid's friends and a cache of weapons, but one particularly important subject was not being pursued by the 7-10 because it involved too much politics.

"We did all we could," he said—which was sadly true. In a different world we could have done so much more.

The GAF commander told Phoenix they were taking custody of all the evidence. This ignored what was perhaps Phoenix's most out-standing skill: the ability to turn evidence into a viable work product within hours. Whatever happened with Zayid was certain to come back to haunt the 7-10 guys.

In fact, things began to go sour almost right away. The evidence they stubbornly held on to was processed by their LEP, *Gregory Better*, a retired New Jersey state trooper who spent his entire twenty-year career writing tickets to people who were trying to get to work on time. He botched the processing to the point that much of the work had to be redone and all the evidence reinventoried. Better went into ass-covering mode: He didn't process anything wrong, he said. He just used a different system, a perfectly good one that he'd learned at Camp Cropper, the army detention facility near Baghdad International Airport.

Lieutenant Lacy DeWall questioned Better: "You said you were the lead DOMEX supervisor at Cropper?" DeWall then demonstrated that it wasn't true. Better was exposed as a fraud and a liar.

At the evening briefing, we learned that a weapons cache containing sixteen mortar rounds and eight hand grenades had been recovered in the area revealed by Zayid. His information, it was now confirmed, was good. That made it all the more frustrating that the army didn't want to pick up Zanjari.

At midnight chow, I sat with Dave M. and discussed the wisdom of doing further business with the 7-10, as they fucked everything up all the time.

———

So Zanjari roamed the streets of Baghdad free from any harm. The best the army could do now was eavesdrop on his conversations while he was safely tucked away in Sadr City. In some insane agreement, the USCF refused to enter Sadr unless authorized by the Multi-National Division Baghdad, the top of the food chain in the coalition's approval process. Once again, the bad guys were using our own rules to their advantage.

21

THE BOMB
IN THE MARKET

IT WAS THE MIDDLE OF THE AFTERNOON, sometime during the second week of February, when Adoni burst into my room: "Up and at 'em, we have a mission."

"What's up?" I asked, rubbing the sleep out of my eyes and getting in a quick stretch before swinging my feet to the floor.

"VBIED," he replied. That meant vehicle-borne improvised explosive device. "Didn't you hear the explosion?"

"No, must've slept right through it," I said as I pulled on my shoes.

"Looks like we've got the graveyard shift again," Dave M. complained about the time of the call.

In the shop, Ricky was reviewing the available imagery of the target location. A color-printed photograph clearly showed a common market bisected by a huge parking lot that doubled as a transfer station for buses. First info was sketchy, with conflicting casualty reports.

Baghdad Hawk, the Iraqis' EOD unit, was already processing the scene. Members from the FOB Falcon EOD and WIT had already rolled. We'd been assigned to provide tactical site exploitation, which amounted to reconstructing the event based on evidence at the site.

As we rode in an RG-33, my question was why we were assigned the mission to begin with. Wouldn't we be redundant? The place was swarming with Americans. And if our reports disagreed with Big Army's official version, there could be hurt feelings.

Though the site was only five miles away, traffic was brutal, tied up by a religious pilgrimage called Arbaeen that closed down the southbound lane of Route Jackson. It took fifty minutes to get there.

"Move out," Adoni ordered.

As we approached the site on foot, the air became rich with the sickening smell of burnt fuel and human blood. Moving toward the site and looking on the ground, I recognized shards of car parts blown over three hundred yards.

Closer to the focal point, sitting on a concrete island in the middle of the road, were four young Iraqi males rear flex-cuffed and guarded by the Iraqi police. The market parking lot was strewn with shoes and sandals. It reminded me of the scene at Ground Zero on 9/11, when women abandoned their high heels so they could better flee the collapsing towers. In this case, however, I suspected the shoes in the parking lot were all that were left after their occupants were blown to smithereens.

A K-9 team pauses at a crater in the road caused by an IED blast.

Pools of blood and body parts were spread out at our feet in a circumferential shape. Charred and torn Iraqi dinars lay flat on the ground, secured in place by the water used by firefighters to extinguish burning vehicles. I walked up to the yellow tape and saw an Iraqi general talking to a sergeant from the US Air Force's WIT element.

We made our presence known and were told to split up to cover more ground and to avoid each other's lanes. As I passed through an opening in a cinder block wall, the smell of pulverized flesh mixed with burnt fruit and vegetables created a sour stench that stuck to my clothes and the lining of my nose.

The bomb crater was thirty by seventy-five feet and had backfilled with water. (The water table was only four feet below the road surface.) Our crime scene was a pond, making the recovery of forensic evidence near impossible.

Smoke still rose from several of the cars haphazardly parked about the market area. Walking around the site, I could tell by the folded-over effect of merchant carts and the debris field that it had been a unidirectional blast.

One car in particular was completely unrecognizable except for a frame rail. Mike D. deduced that this was the VBIED.

"How can you tell?" I asked.

"Absence of any attached vehicle parts, including the engine—all signs of the carrier vehicle," Mike explained.

I pulled my Olympus from my breast pocket and photographed the frame rail.

"How much you want to bet someone is going to disagree?" I said.

"Doesn't make us wrong," he said.

Walking back toward the yellow tape, Mike explained that the vehicles that had caught fire in the parking lot were ignited by a flying car thrown from the blast site as a huge fireball.

"That's over two hundred feet," I said.

"No shit, dude."

Passing the entranceway, Sharif stopped and spoke to a local merchant, a gentleman still in shock. We asked basic questions.

"You seem pretty shook," I said.

The carnage at the market. That thing on the right used to be a car.

"I am. My brother . . ."

"What about your brother?"

"He was injured in the blast."

"Where is he now?"

"He was taken to the hospital."

"Did you see or hear anything unusual before the explosion?"

"Yes. A young boy drove up in a red Volvo, abandoned it in the aisleway, got out, and fled the scene, never looking back. The explosion was only moments later."

The blast was not just placed for maximum damage, he noted, but timed for that purpose as well, going off at precisely 3:00 PM, when after-work shoppers filled the market.

During the first part of the war, he said, the market was encircled by huge concrete barriers that prevented motor vehicles from getting into the shopping area, barriers that could only be moved with heavy equipment. Two weeks earlier, however, the barriers had been removed.

"And now a vehicle blows up in the market," he said, putting two and two together.

We thanked the man for his assistance and returned to the taped-off area. I was approached by a worried captain, who said: "I need to speak with someone from Phoenix."

"You can talk to me."

"Do not look around immediately, but . . . there is a reporter with a camera from the *New York Times* just beyond the outer cordon about to take photographs of the devastation."

"Thank you, Captain," I said. I got on the radio and forwarded the information to Adoni, who gave the team a heads-up so we'd become especially tight-lipped and camera shy.

Commingling with a nosy *Times* reporter was a serious liability. Anonymity had to be safeguarded at all costs, since exposure would both damage Phoenix's ability to do its job and hinder US foreign policy. We routinely learned things that we did not share with anyone representing the Iraqi government, a practice that indicated a firmly entrenched lack of trust. There was distrust everywhere you looked, in fact, but in diplomacy appearance was everything. Shaking hands convincingly with the enemy was a reptilian skill the army had down to a science. It ranked right up there with humiliating the junior enlisted soldiers for minor infractions.

I scanned the crowd. In detective work, investigators look for bystanders who are too curious. We always question the guy with his belly button pressed against the police tape. It's similar in counterterrorism. You look for those who don't appear appropriately horrified. In this case I noticed an Iraqi man in a tan suit, walking the scene as if he were somewhat pleased.

"Sharif, find out who that guy is," I said. "Ask one of the INPs."

While waiting for the answer, I swung my Olympus to my face and clicked off a few shots of *Mr. Pleased.*

Sharif returned with my info: "He's the site supervisor for the security detail responsible for this market area."

I thought, *Hey, buddy, the site you're being paid to protect just got blown the fuck up. Maybe it's time to wipe the smug expression off your face.*

Sharif continued, "He has an unofficial title of sheik."

Most sheiks either were born with the title or got rich and bought it. Others were crooks and received the title by extorting local nationals. Whichever, locals viewed sheiks with great reverence, like a drug kingpin in the projects.

The camera got Mr. Pleased's attention, and his expression changed. I made the best of the situation and squeezed off a couple more photos, these full-face, an excellent likeness to accompany my written report.

The INP, Sharif told me, had been curious about me, suggesting I might be something other than a soldier.

"What did you tell him?" I asked.

"Said you were a *very* high-ranking soldier, supervisor of the entire scene."

I happily approached the INP who'd provided the intelligence on Mr. Pleased, clapped him on the shoulder, shook his hand, and thanked him profusely while crossing my heart with my right hand, a sign of respect.

It was my turn to feel my Spidey Sense tingling at the back of my neck. In my peripheral vision I saw another INP taking a photo of me shaking hands with our informant. I quickly turned away from the camera.

I pegged him as Iraqi Intelligence and gave Phoenix the heads-up. "We have company," I said. "Iraqi counterintelligence with camera. Maybe we should get going."

Before we could be compromised, we assembled back by the vehicles.

Back at the shop we compared notes. Mike D. ran down his deductions about what had happened from an EOD standpoint. Before we got there, the theory was that there had been two separate events, a blast in the market and another in the parking lot. Mike D. set that straight: one explosion, one flying fireball car traveling two hundred feet in the air.

I gave my HUMINT observations. I included the boy driving a red Volvo and fleeing, and Mr. Pleased.

I finished my written report, including Mr. Pleased photos, and gave it to intelligence/targeting officer Tony V. to be included with the Phoenix report. Tony said he was glad I photographed the guy, as he too had noticed his unusual affect.

The following day, Tony received an intelligence update from a captain with the 1-22 who was buddies with Mr. Pleased. He said we got it all wrong. Oh, sure, Pleased had once been a JAM cell leader—murdering, kidnapping, and planting roadside bombs to blow up American soldiers—but he had left that life behind years ago and now was an upstanding citizen. To bolster his argument, the captain said Colonel Buford also knew Pleased and vouched for him. Tony V., to his credit, stayed cool, and the conversation ended nice. Then our mouths dropped open.

When we tried to figure out what was going on, we learned of a process in Iraq known as "reconciliation." There is a theory that Iraq has so many warring factions that the only way to hold the country together as a unified state is to install a ruthless dictator. But since the whole cesspool got started because we wanted to remove a ruthless dictator, we were left with the mess. In a misguided attempt to keep everyone sort of happy, a mild form of judicial rehabilitation was used on politically connected criminals who should have been put to death.

It was true that Iraq was being held together with bubble gum. The government in power had been put there via a disputed election, and there was no recount process, just growing cracks of dissent. Adding to the madness, Prime Minister Nouri al-Maliki was a formerly exiled Shia leader who was now looking to exact revenge on any Sunni Iraqi.

As a police officer I understood the importance of immunity, excusing petty criminals on the path toward capturing a bigger and nastier fish. But this Iraqi business was offensive to civilized sensibilities. Known murderers were being allowed to roam the streets, and the army treated this practice as if it were completely normal. It sickened me not only because it was morally reprehensible but also because it amounted to a complete waste of American taxpayers' money.

The reporter we'd spotted at the bomb site painted a picture of "sectarian violence," a problematic assessment as both Sunni and Shia bought and sold at that market. The reporter also suggested the blast may have been an attempt to disrupt the Arbaeen pilgrimage that slowed our arrival to the scene. Trouble with that was, the bomb went off so far from the holy walk that walkers might not have noticed it but for the sound.

We didn't give up on Mr. Pleased just because we'd been told we were barking up the wrong tree. We continued to dig, and the story grew even more offensive. When Pleased learned that he was getting reconciliation for his past sins in hopes of a warm and fuzzy future, he celebrated by throwing a party: an event was staged to demonstrate the progress of the USCF and the emergence of a blossoming democracy in the region. Mr. Pleased invited members of the Fourth Infantry Division and a *New York Times* reporter who got free drinks and a fluffy human-interest piece out of the deal.

We built a case against the sheik, learning that he'd had several conversations with a known bomb-builder, a man later arrested for placing roadside bombs directed at USCF. We made a list of questions we wanted answered. Who authorized the removal of the barriers? Of those killed and injured, how many were Shia and how many Sunni? And what was the breakdown of Sons of Iraq security killed or injured versus civilians? We suspected this ratio was heavily skewed toward civilian casualties. If there was a lack of SOI among the casualties, this would be indicative of Mr. Pleased's involvement.

But we were wasting our time. Busting a sheik and "friend" would have been an embarrassment that no one was willing to face. Colonel Buford had been hell-bent to get Phoenix the fuck out of Iraq, and now we were getting an inkling as to why. We tended to lay bare the truth, and there was so much of the truth Big Army was trying to hide. There were elements of its work it simply didn't want scrutinized.

Our investigation did get the attention of someone in Washington, who decided to take a "serious look" at the case. But this too went nowhere. The military was adamant: Some folks were untouchable. Better to prevent "hurt feelings" than punish mass murderers.

Our minds boggled. Were we setting up a "true democracy" or not? With billions of dollars pouring into a sham government, couldn't we find a better way?

The knock never came at a good time. It was about two weeks later and I had just stepped out of the shower when Cole, one of our new intel guys, came knocking, "We've got a mission." I'd just finished eight miles on the treadmill and now had a long night ahead of me.

In the shop, the dry erase board said our supporting unit would be 1-22 TST, Sergeant Peluso and his boys. Our target, a man named *Ammar*, had recently surfaced. New signals intelligence indicated an imminent threat.

With an RIP/TOA (relief in place / transfer of authority) underway, I noted that elements of the security agreement, like warrants and sworn statements, suddenly didn't apply. That was OK by me. I'd always thought those elements were insane. We were in a war—self-protection needed to outweigh a terrorist's civil rights. The system had been set up in Washington, a political program that risked soldiers' lives in exchange for keeping favor with Congress. Some called it foreign policy. I called it cowardice and appeasement.

It would be one of our last missions with Sergeant Peluso and his crew. Working with them was always a treat. Dave saw it as a challenge when people called a task impossible, and his adrenaline was contagious. Point is, he sounded cruel, yet he was loved and respected. "Cruel to be kind," it's called. While other troops slept in their bunks or played video games, Dave rehearsed worst-case scenarios with his men to the point of exhaustion. When action came, they were ready. His crew revered his leadership.

After waiting five long hours, we moved forward to the target area. As we drove down a commercial street toward the objective, Dave called out commands, making the newer guys smile with admiration. In under a minute he established a security perimeter and advanced his sniper teams to the adjacent rooftops.

I spied a young soldier to my three o'clock position. He maneuvered his Humvee directly in front of a commercial business. He stood on the hood and, using the muzzle of his M4, broke the four-foot florescent tubes that illuminated our positions, another of Dave Peluso's TTPs (tactics, techniques, and procedures).

We sat inside our RG-33 for over an hour waiting for a signal indicating Ammar had been located.

Tony V. was losing faith. "A lot of time has passed. You think we lost him?"

I replied, "If anyone else was in charge, I'd worry about that. I think Dave's got this."

The words were just out of my mouth when Dave Peluso gave the signal. Target had been captured. Time to dismount.

"See what I mean, Tony?" I said—and we both laughed.

In the foyer of a commercial building, Tony and I assisted in the fingerprint and iris scan of Ammar. Our K-9 team, Mark and Joker, cleared the residence, allowing the rest of us to enter and commence our TSE.

Sharif and I walked Ammar to the second-story bedroom and removed his blindfold. I looked for a light switch and spotted a lamp on the bedside nightstand. In Iraq, electrical devices were crude, and this one flickered on like a relic from an old movie. Centered in the room was a space heater that also provided additional lighting.

I snapped a couple of photographs and gave Ammar a physical inspection. He had several scars to his chest and right forearm area.

"How did you get these scars?" I asked.

"In an automobile accident," he replied.

I showed him a photo. "You know who this is?"

"That's *Mr. Abbah*," he said without hesitation.

I stayed cool, but the confirmation of identity was huge. We'd been looking for Abbah for five months. I continued my questioning, changing the subject. The thing that threw me was Ammar's forthcoming nature. I was skeptical of his assertions. It was coming too easy.

"I would like to speak in private," Ammar said. There were INP around and he didn't want them to hear.

Once he had them out of earshot, he told me he was a confidential informant working for the USCF in a security element attached to a joint task force. I asked his handler's name and work locations. In great detail,

Ammar promptly filled in the blanks, saying he was a cooperator, not a criminal. He was a security officer within the Ministry of Defence and for six months, he said, personally involved in the investigation of Abbah, providing the good guys with counterintelligence and countersurveillance.

This raised a big question: If Ammar was being truthful, how did he, as a source, get on the targeting deck? Surely the army had safety mechanisms in place to prevent a potential CI from being compromised or killed. Fail-safe measures I would have assumed in place were absent. No code name, no code phrase, no simple cell phone number to verify he was an informant.

After policing up all the evidence, we prepared to leave the objective with Ammar in tow. Ammar had a request that I forwarded to Sergeant Peluso. Ammar wanted to kiss his newborn daughter and say good-bye to his family. I explained the gesture of goodwill would do wonders in follow-on interviews—but it was Dave's call.

Dave gave the OK. Ammar's blindfold was removed and he was allowed a brief conversation with his family. Ammar thanked me and gestured that he was ready to be re-blindfolded, after which he was transported back to the detention center.

Our teammate Artie was confused about our generosity to the subject. I explained that he was perhaps a source and the small kindness might pay dividends. "It's a cop thing, Artie," I said. "You wouldn't understand."

At the division HQ meet-and-greet I explained that Ammar claimed to be a source, that he knew Abbah, and that he was willing to help in Abbah's capture. I briefed intelligence guru Ryan, whose clearance allowed him access to high-side info from the SCIF. Better that Ryan present the info, as he had an excellent working relationship with the female lieutenant in charge of the unit.

Ninety minutes later, I was nearly done with my report and Ryan came back and confirmed that Ammar was "known by someone" but no one was actually laying claim to being his handler.

The army, Ryan added, wanted to "dust Ammar off and send him home."

"Just another example of how the army sucks at police work," I said.

"What's the over/under on Ammar's life expectancy?"

"Whatever it is, I'm betting the under," I said. Sending Ammar home too quickly placed a huge INFORMANT sign on his back, a death sentence.

Although individual soldiers were frequently warm-blooded human beings, "the army" as an entity was downright sociopathic, operating with a shallow charm but without conscience. The army as an entity slept fine with sending Ammar to his death. Again, I compared the situation to my experiences as a New York cop. If this had occurred in Brooklyn, not only would heads have rolled, but if the source was killed, people would go to jail. That wasn't likely to happen in Baghdad. In the army, life was cheaper in general, but Iraqi life was bargain basement.

I suggested to Ryan that even though the source had not been claimed, the reference to the possible unit and handler should be included in my report. The army apparently had established a connection with Ammar but was unwilling to take full ownership of him. I thought the rationale was obvious: if they admitted that Ammar was a bona fide source, they had to admit they intentionally withheld intelligence information that could have kept Ammar out of our targeting process. This failure put many lives at risk—the lives of Dave Peluso and his men—as they rolled up a Good Guy. Iraqi lives weren't the only ones cheapened by the army.

When confronted with that fact, the army laughed it off, calling it calculated risk assessment. They, in fact, were pissed off at us. Later that same day, I walked into the office and was greeted by Cole and James, another new intel specialist.

"We got a beef from the captain of the unit that handled Ammar," Cole said.

"Chris, he's frosted because you mentioned them in your written report," James added.

"I know the protocol," I said. "But in this particular case a formal request for acknowledgment of Ammar had been made and had received a CYA response." That meant *cover your ass.*

In dropping off the evidence captured from Ammar's residence, I spoke briefly to an intelligence officer who said he'd talked to the responsible captain. The intel officer said, "The guy admitted he was aware of the targeting of Ammar but thought we wouldn't be able to find him."

And there it was, the final act of "Fuck you." What if during the mission, one of Dave's men had been killed? What would be the fallout for such an egregious act of omission?

I was reminded of the Pat Tillman cover-up. Tillman was a true American patriot and hero who left a promising career in the NFL to join the Army Rangers in service of his country. The army initially reported Tillman KIA by the enemy in some courageous battle. After a formal inquiry, the army was compelled to come clean and admit that Tillman was killed by friendly fire. It was outrageous, but punishment was limited to a few formal letters of reprimand.

I knew many more soldiers' lives would be lost at the hands of a few incompetent jackasses, guys detached from reality, guys who never left the TOC, idiots who felt more regret at the personal loss of a mistress who was rotated back home to her husband than at the deaths of their own brethren.

What would Carl Solo, the top exec I met at Roswell, have said? Oh, that's right. *Ca-ching!*

My mind pushed back a few weeks to a mission in which we raided a house and found "secret" military peripherals in a dresser drawer. One of the house's occupants had access to the base through a woman interpreter. In addition, the subject's brother was an Iraqi police officer, very clean cut with a mustache.

Home decor in Baghdad always had an austerity budget feel to it. Walls were an industrial color, in this case puke green. If you didn't look outside, where the surroundings had "Middle East" written all over them, you might think you were in a poorly aging motel in the American Southwest, one that charged for the rooms by the hour.

Here's how the interrogation of the brother went:

Q: Your brother, he's never been involved in anything bad?
A: No, never.
Q: When was your brother arrested?
A: December 19.
Q: Have you seen him since? Did you go visit him?
A: Yes.
Q: What did he tell you he was arrested for?
A: He said they have been investigating him but they have nothing on him.
Q: What are they investigating him about?
A: I don't know.

It was the first week in March, moving day for Phoenix. Good-bye, FOB Falcon, hello, Camp Liberty. We had been hearing for a while that they were closing down FOB Falcon, but the date kept being set and canceled, set and canceled, and when it finally came time to evict us, we were caught not completely prepared. As it turned out, Falcon never actually closed—but that didn't change the fact that we had to move.

Why were we moving? The reason given was, and I paraphrase: because we had routed the insurgency in our area of operation, the army felt it best to move us to a more central location so we could aid more units. It didn't make sense, but what could you do?

It was only a seven-mile move, but it was complicated in myriad ways. Most of them were physical, breaking down equipment and packing it up, everything from the hefty to the minute, choosing what to take, what to toss. But there were psychological factors as well. Falcon had been my home for more than a year. I had my routine. I had less than two months left on my contract, and it seemed wrong that there should be upheaval this late into my program.

The other psychological factor was uncertainty. No one had adequately answered why we were moving. I suspected Ricky knew the reason and had questioned him about it, but his answers were never solid.

Here I am with an American flag just before going out on my one hundredth mission in Iraq.

The packing process had taken a solid week, and finally the last box was loaded into the CONEX, a transportable steel container like you might see loaded onto a flatbed freight train car.

Adoni and I tried to find Sergeant Dave Peluso at his workspace to say our last good-byes. Entering the hallway of the building, I spotted nine soldiers sitting in a zipper formation on the floor cleaning their weapons. I imagined Dave had ordered them to do so as a way of keeping all his men in one area and out of trouble so that he could concentrate on his own logistics and the impending transition stateside.

We asked the weapon-cleaning soldiers where Dave was and were told he was unavailable until later in the evening. Disappointed, I said, "When you see him, tell him Adoni and Chris came by to say good-bye."

A specialist said, "Not a problem, sir. I'll pass it on."

I made one last sweep of my bare room, stowed my shit at the office, learned my helicopter flight was still two hours away, and headed to the Green Bean for one last cup of coffee. I grabbed a few guys, said coffee

The gang at the Green Bean coffee shop on my last day.
The comforts of home provided by that place kept a lot of us sane.

was on me, and off we went. I smiled at Magish and Ganish and they correctly readied our orders from memory. I told them this was the last cup of coffee and pulled out a pencil to get the correct spellings of their names for the plaque I was going to have made thanking Magish and Ganish for being the unsung heroes of Phoenix's mission in Baghdad.

Ganish grinned as he took the pencil and paper and wrote everything down for me.

Walking back from the Green Bean, I spotted Sergeant Peluso coming at us head-on. With a warm handshake and hug, Dave said, "Hey, how about one last cup of coffee at the Green Bean, on me!"

We laughed, did an about-face, and went back into the coffee shop. During the second cup of coffee I felt my humor leaving me. I became morose. I realized the best days of the mission were behind me. I invited everyone to Roanoke when it was all said and done, said an awkwardly

It was Sergeant Dave Peluso's last day in Iraq. He (center, holding flag) was a fantastic asset outside the wire, and we were all going to miss him.

22

HOME AND AFTER

BY THE TIME OF OUR TRANSFER TO Camp Liberty in March 2009, the United States was well into planning its withdrawal from Iraq under the terms of the Status of Forces Agreement signed late the previous year. As a consequence, changes in the rules of engagement continued to pile up. Although the Iraqis weren't ready for Western-style law enforcement, the pinheads in Washington decided the army's approach should be kinder and gentler to the populace, requiring three-party affidavits sworn before an Iraqi judge before our soldiers could take action and target. Another new condition imposed on us was that missions were to be undertaken only during daylight hours. Sleepy Iraqis were pleased by this, as was the INP, who could now track us more easily. But for us the daylight rule was both dangerous and tactically unsound.

Phoenix's operations came to a screeching halt. Where we'd once gone on daily missions in search of terrorists and their weapons, the opportunities now presented to us were few and far between. March, April, and May 2009 were noteworthy primarily for the excessive downtime.

Then came the day when Ricky came to me and asked if I was going to re-up for another six-month rotation.

I wasn't happy when I said it, but I declined. "What we developed from the ground up can no longer operate as conceived," I said. "I came here to interrogate bad guys, not to help with nation-building, hand-holding, and the wholesale giveaway of taxpayer dollars in exchange for five-minute friends." I was saddened, disillusioned, and frustrated. But knowing I had done my best, I had no regrets leaving Iraq. The experience had taught me a lot.

Despite the frustration, as my mission came to end, I swelled with pride. For all the nonsense imposed by DC and Big Army, the adventure had been all I'd hoped for. The relationship that developed between me and the other members of Phoenix Team was one of unyielding loyalty. We shared not only the battlefield experience of facing down evil on its home ground but also the courage and brotherhood of a team in which independent contractors and army soldiers offered each other their full mutual trust and respect. Never before had a team with such a diverse set of war-fighting skills been so successful in countering a lethal insurgency. Our level of passion and true grit shattered the expectations of even the most jaded army officer and might never again be replicated. I hope it is, though. If a machine like Phoenix could be assembled once more, look out, bad guys!

On our last day in Iraq, I made a video of my soon-to-depart Phoenix teammates standing around a barbecue, drinking Jameson Irish whiskey out of an elk's horn. We took turns briefly testifying as to our experiences.

When it was my turn, I expressed gratitude. "I'm thankful that we were successful, that we did our thing and for a while we had many terrorist cells on the run. But most of all I'm thankful that we're all leaving—that is, going home—in one piece." I quaffed thirstily from the horn.

When I got to the airport, I didn't feel like stopping the party over something like a flight halfway around the world. So I upgraded my coach ticket to business class—just one row behind first class—and drank twelve-year-old scotch once we reached cruising altitude.

After landing in DC, I rented a car and called Debbie from the road. In Virginia, I went to both of my kids' schools and picked them up unannounced. It was very emotional—like what you see on TV all the time—with the teachers, kids, wife, and me all crying.

Daddy was home.

"I want you to make me a promise," Debbie said.

"What's that?"

"No more duty in the line of fire."

"It's a deal," I said.

What is it you always hear about turning an ending into a new beginning? After returning from Iraq in May 2009, I kept in contact with my program manager at NEK, Rob Lambert, who offered me several prospective jobs involving interrogation.

On August 26, 2009, two Virginia Tech students, Heidi Childs and David Metzler, were visiting Caldwell Fields park when an unknown assailant shot both of them to death, leaving their bodies in the parking lot. Heidi was the daughter of a Virginia state trooper and David was a doctor's son. The morning after the murders, the Montgomery County Sheriff's Office sent out a road crew of inmates who completely (although inadvertently) compromised the crime scene by picking up garbage from the surrounding area.

Unaware of the crime scene's destruction but disgusted by the heinous murders, I visited the sheriff's office to offer my assistance to the case detective pro bono, laying out my intentions and my investigative background. After leaving the sheriff's office, I called Rob and asked for NEK's help in providing analytical tools and a dedicated analyst to aid in the investigation. Rob was happy to provide the assistance.

On my second visit to the sheriff's office, I brought a huge platter of pastries and met with a man I'll call *Marcus*, who had taken over the case and was now married up with an FBI field team from St. Louis.

After looking around, I asked Marcus if he had done some basic investigation regarding the victims: locating and questioning known sex offenders within a 150-mile radius, prisoner debriefs, warrant sweeps, and conferral with known criminal informants. To my dismay, Marcus said no.

Inquiring about their existing analytical support and the analyst who was coordinating it, I asked if the software was organic. That meant, did they have immediate access through a dedicated line or were their requests for information being forwarded to another facility?

Marcus replied, "Well, the info we get we have to submit, and right now the computer system is down. The analyst is only here for the week and then rotates out and is replaced by a new guy."

"I would like to solve those intelligence gaps for you," I said.

"I am very interested," Marcus said. "But I have to pass this up to leadership."

When I followed up a couple of days later, Marcus said that while he was interested in the help, the FBI was against it. Even after offering to sign a nondisclosure agreement and pointing out that I had an active Top Secret security clearance, they were not interested.

The case remains unsolved to this day.

———

In January 2010, I got another call from Rob, this time to see if I was interested in providing interrogation training to a team of SEALs at the navy's Little Creek base in Virginia Beach. After expressing interest, I was put in touch with the program manager, *Jason W.*, who was also a former Navy SEAL.

SEALs were exceptional when it came to capturing and killing bad guys, but they weren't quite as proficient on the HUMINT collection side. I realized that my specialized expertise could be a huge benefit to them, helping them accomplish their missions while saving lives in the process.

"You interested, Chris?" Jason asked.

"Yes!" I said.

The program, like Phoenix, was classified. My sessions took place in a training area on base called a "kill house," a partitioned structure with breakdown plywood walls designed to simulate an urban combat environment. There were no ceilings in place, so instructors could observe the movements and actions of the SEALs from a catwalk spanning the entire first-floor footprint.

On the first day of training, I went over the basics of interrogation:

Sorting of Sources: When you arrive on target and there are multiple people in the house to interrogate—males, females, children—the idea is to determine which detainee will be the easiest to break in order to get the intelligence you're after. From there, you use the statements from each detainee to confirm or challenge the others in order to advance the interrogation and intelligence picture.

Behavioral Aspects: This applies to the Sorting of Sources when you're at the target, where one detainee looks terrified, one looks mad, one is crying. Essentially you're trying to locate the weakest link based on behavioral affect. It also applies to when you are in the box [interrogation room] running an interrogation and the subject is expressing an unconscious body language like eye movement, sitting position, leaning in when asked a question, leaning back, arms crossed, legs crossed, or mirroring (when the detainee adopts your body language, how you sit, etc.), all of which generally indicates engagement or active listening.

Physiology: Is the person breathing heavily, sweating? Is he afraid?

Mental and Physical Aspects: Is the detainee mentally fit to interrogate? While some detainees with formal resistance training can feign illness or injury, some are legitimately mentally challenged. Similarly, is the detainee injured, is he suffering a heart attack, does he require medical treatment or medicines?

Direct Questions: These are questions that ask for specific information: Where are the explosives? Who was with you when you placed the IED? Straight and to the point.

Indirect Questions: As an example, *Do you ever shop in Manhattan?* as opposed to the Direct Question, *Were you at the Century 21 store in Lower Manhattan?*

Logic Traps: *You said you never shop in Manhattan. How do you explain this picture of you buying clothes in Century 21?* It generally follows a series of questions during which the interrogator allows the subject to tell his story, lies and all, and then comes back with the Logic Trap to confront the detainee.

Shaming: Family shaming is the most often used, when the family name could forever be associated with killers of innocents such as children. Sometimes the questioning induced personal shame, like the time we were going through a detainee's phone and came upon a photo of a naked woman. "Is this your wife?" I asked. Of course, it was not. Did this mean he was not being a good Muslim, father, business owner from the community? What would the imam at your mosque have to say about this?

I also focused on key indicators that the subject was weakening and headed toward eventual submission. And since the SEALs' interrogations would take place in a war zone, I explained that site exploitation at the point of capture was critical. I emphasized evidence and psychological manipulation as key elements in breaking the will of a hardened terrorist insurgent.

I gave a role-play demonstration, using one of the SEALs as the subject. The interrogation started off slow and gradually grew in intensity. I alternated among direct questions, indirect questions, logic traps, family shaming, and so on.

As the training progressed, the SEALs were partnered up and tasked with interrogating a professional actor, who was allowed to take his responses in any direction he felt might mentally challenge the team. The training was viewed live via video and audio feed into the main classroom, where the remaining members could observe and learn.

On the third and final day of training, I gave a presentation on a captured Al Qaeda cell member who was a notorious bomb-maker in southern Baghdad. As I moved through the PowerPoint, the team's chief, *Ed Robinson*, nodded his head and smiled.

Usually I got right down to the nitty-gritty when instructing, but this case had a backstory that I liked a lot. I had been standing in line at the Green Bean at FOB Falcon when I noticed a young staff sergeant and second lieutenant in front of me. I motioned to Magish and Ganish that I wanted to buy the two soldiers their coffee. The staff sergeant thanked me and asked what I did. I told him that we processed POCs and created HUMINT reports based on battlefield interrogations.

Cut to three months later and I was in my office when the phone rang. Phoenix was asked to respond to a location in southern Baghdad. As soon as I got there, I was directed to the area for interrogation and began to work on the captured subject. The subject was a hardened true believer, willing to die for the cause.

After twenty minutes of questioning, the subject said, "You've got nothing. Let me know when you're finished."

Frustrated and feeling defeated, I eventually left the room, kicking a garbage pail into the street. After about ten minutes, one of my teammates ran up to me holding a bag filled with plug-and-play IED components.

In a perfect example of the use of evidence to break the will of the subject, I presented it to the subject and dumped it at his feet, saying, "I got nothing huh? Fuck. You. Asshole."

Walking outside, feeling much better than I had when kicking the trash can, I met up with a soldier wearing sunglasses. He said hi and I said hi back.

He removed his sunglasses and said, "You don't remember me, do you? We met in the coffee shop a while back and you said for me to give you a call if I needed help . . . so I called you."

I hugged the soldier and said, "Yes, I remember you now. Do you realize what you've got here? You've got the master bomb-maker. *The guy!*"

"Oh, the story gets better," the soldier said. "I was driving on point with the first sergeant when I spotted this guy, who I believed was from the Deck of Cards."

When the United States invaded Iraq, the Defense Department put out a deck of playing cards printed with the names and, where available, the photos of the top fifty-two most wanted Iraqis. Saddam Hussein was the ace of spades, of course.

"Since it was only a glance," the soldier continued, "I told the first sergeant and we squared the block and did a dynamic takedown in the middle of the street."

"That's fucking awesome, man," I said.

At SEALs training, I had just told my students this same story when Ed said, "I'm smiling because I had read your HUMINT report on that interrogation. But it wasn't until just now as you told it that I put two and two together."

After class, Ed approached me. I could tell he had something heavy on his mind. Then he said it: "We're getting ready to deploy in April for a six-month mission and would love to have you on the team."

"Where?"

"Afghanistan."

"I'm flattered," I said. "And grateful for the offer, but I just got back from a fifteen-month tour in Iraq and would need a serious kitchen pass from my wife."

"Well, let me know if you change your mind."

At the end of the course, we conducted live exercises that included assaulting a target, capturing a bad guy for interrogation, and performing TSE of the house for evidence. The idea was to test the SEALs' comprehension of the subject matter and combine all the techniques I was teaching to break down the bad guy and get him to divulge his objective and expose other bad guys.

On the last day of training, I'd been invited to a workout session that began at 5:00 AM. The workout was designed to demonstrate not only physical fitness but also unit cohesion. The workout, I must confess, was beyond me, which is why there aren't many forty-eight-year-old SEALs. Being a subject matter expert in interrogation was one thing, but being able to live in a war zone with a bunch of hardened men was another animal altogether. If I'd felt any urge at all to go to Afghanistan, that workout squelched it.

Besides, I had other plans. I'd started my own company, Intel Investigations. My idea was to travel around the country—or even to *other* countries, including some in the Middle East—and train police departments on counterterrorism strategies, including interrogation techniques.

In a real sense, I was wedding the experience I gained as a cop with everything I learned in Iraq and passing it on to others who were fighting the good fight. It's a good living. A meaningful one. It's honest and straightforward and I earn it on my own terms. The mission that took me from Brooklyn to Baghdad goes on.

CONCLUSION

MATT PUCINO

To CONCLUDE THE STORY, I want to back up a little bit and tell you more about a guy named Matt Pucino. I first met Matt in June 2008, when he was one of the FNGs who came in like the cavalry to rescue Phoenix Team from the incompetence of its previous leadership.

I remember the first time I saw Matt. The new team was entering the office. Our new team lead, Ricky Peterson, came in first, with Matt and the others right behind him. They took turns introducing themselves. Matt was a handsome guy, Italian features, in his early thirties, five ten, 190 pounds, thick, jet-black wavy hair, bright blue eyes, and an athletic build. He'd been the quarterback on the Bishop Stang High School football team.

When it was Matt's turn to introduce himself, there were other things that made him stand out. Matt had the heaviest Boston accent I had ever heard. Plus, he didn't have the appearance of an "intel weenie," who frequently look nerdy and in need of sunshine.

Matt quickly won over everyone on base, both team members and army personnel, and repaired the damage done by our previous intelligence analyst, Cunningham. He changed everything for Phoenix. Suddenly we were off and running like never before, doing five or six missions a week. In short, Matt turned out to be a miracle worker.

And the miracles didn't stop once he charmed us back into the army's good graces. Matt's genius as an analyst—and I don't use the word *genius* lightly—was his ability to not only see the big picture and develop targets for Phoenix but also play a crucial role in the combat missions that followed. Matt would give me the targeting package to read over and was able to answer any questions I had from memory. If the subject was an HVI, Matt would often accompany us on the missions. The beauty of this was that as I was interrogating the target trying to establish a positive identification—usually in hundred-degree heat in some filthy bathroom with a flashlight and huge Madagascar cockroaches running around—Matt would search the house and hand me evidence to use, good stuff with which I could psychologically manipulate the target.

Matt was confident in his abilities but not boastful and was always the first one in for the initial briefing and last one out after all the reports, pictures, and evidence were processed. He was also a Boston Red Sox fan, which made for some great humor. Matt brought out the humor in others. Funniest, I think, was interpreter Muaad, who would mimic Matt's accent and reduce everyone, including Matt, to tears. Matt and Muaad would recite lines from famous movies like *The Godfather* and *The Departed*, again and again demonstrating the subtle differences between Brooklyn and Boston accents.

As you might expect considering his movie-star looks, Matt was popular with the ladies. It was funny—there always seemed to be a small group of women soldiers following him around, vying for his attention. All you could say was "Wow." Many times, female soldiers would stop by the office and ask for Matt, and if he wasn't there they would turn around and leave.

Matt was very considerate and would go out of his way to help me on a particular target. He was the first to buy coffee from the Green Bean when I was beyond exhaustion writing my report. When Matt left, Phoenix was never the same. His personality and reputation were not transferable, and his replacement Tony V., hard as he tried, was not of Matt's caliber. Our workload immediately fell from five or six missions a week to one or none

Most of all, though, Matt was my friend. When he was killed in action, part of my heart died with him, and I'm not sure I'll ever fully recover.

Matt Pucino was a miracle worker and a genius, a guy who could both see the big picture and create intricate, workable plans, whether he was in a meeting room or in combat.

It was autumn 2009 and I was back stateside when I received the horrible news. Matthew Pucino had been on combat patrol near Pashay Kala, Afghanistan, when an IED struck his vehicle. His obituary said he had been assigned to B Company, Second Battalion, Twentieth Special Forces Group (Airborne) of the Maryland Army National Guard and was a Special Forces Operational Detachment Alpha intelligence sergeant. He'd earned multiple medals for heroism and meritorious service.

———————

I went to Matt's funeral, an evening service that I was certain would befit a true warrior. I was approaching the church when I spotted the flashing lights of a Massachusetts state trooper, a beacon to guide the way. They had the road coned off so access to the church was limited to funeralgoers. At the driveway entrance, another trooper stood, directing vehicles into the almost-full parking lot. I was an hour early and I took one of the last spots. Folks would soon be parking along the road.

In front and to the left of the church was a hook-and-ladder fire truck with a complement of firefighters in dress uniforms raising a tremendous garrison American flag illuminated by bright spotlights. The entrance was lined with members of Matt's Special Forces unit standing at attention. They were in full dress: spit-shined boots, bloused trousers, and green berets. Their faces were stoic, though I could tell some had been crying.

"Good evening, sir," they said.

A stiff breeze from the outside and my emotions on the inside battled for control of my face. Once inside the vestibule, I saw sharply dressed cops and soldiers standing by to usher. On a table was a display board featuring a collage of family and military photos. The dominant image in the middle was a photo of Matt with his radiant smile.

I spoke with a family friend, Lori. She knew who I was and referenced the beautiful letters and e-mails sent by Ricky, Adoni, and the rest of the team. She explained that Matt's family, including Lisa, his sister, were not available to greet guests because they were making last-minute preparations for the funeral service.

"I'll tell her I saw you," Lori said.

I took a seat in the back. A young man named Kane McManus, in a tartan kilt with bagpipes, came in the side door, took up his post at the side of the altar, and played "Amazing Grace." I noticed that a box of tissues had been placed at the end of every pew, and already mourners were grabbing for them. The pastor, Dr. Paul Jehle, escorted Matt's family to the front pews, said a few prayers, and introduced the dignitaries in attendance: Massachusetts governor Deval Patrick, state senate president Therese Murray, state representative Vinny deMacedo, and General Joseph Carter of the Massachusetts National Guard. There was a screen behind the altar, upon which were projected photos of Matt as a series of eloquent Matt experts addressed the gathering. Army chaplain Captain Shane Blankenship spoke of Matt's tremendous character as a soldier.

Matt's close friend Sergeant First Class Dan Dosier spoke of his Matt memories, all of which were funny. He recalled the time he spread a rumor among teammates and fellow soldiers that Matt, before his military career, had been an underwear model. Matt, for reasons he didn't understand, suddenly found himself getting weird smiles—from both men and women. The rest of that story was no doubt hysterical, but Sergeant Dosier didn't get to it, as he completely broke down and had a well-deserved cry.

"I can't believe this Green Beret is acting like a little boy," he managed, and everyone gave supportive applause.

He shifted gears and talked about his combat experience with Matt, how he was once shot in the leg and Matt rode along on the chopper ride to the hospital, cracking jokes to keep the mood light.

Phil Haglof, Matt's brother-in-law, took the pulpit. The photos being projected took on a family tone. I sensed that this was the last-minute change the family was taking care of. Someone had arrived with new slides, and they needed to be included in the presentation. We saw photos of Uncle Matt wrestling with his nephews Nicholas and Joshua. Haglof spoke of how much Matt loved being an uncle. He recalled the way Matt had explained how important it was for his nephews to look after his niece, their sister Katelyn, doing a Godfather impression. "If anybody messes with Kate you have to break their legs," he said.

There was appreciative laughter from everyone who well remembered Matt's Godfather impression, which he pulled out with great regularity in Iraq. Hell, he gave Muaad Godfather lessons!

Haglof told of a family trip to Disney World. Matt came along and tried to get past security with a pocketknife hooked onto his pants pocket. Matt attempted some sleight of hand to make it look like he was getting rid of the knife, when in reality he just pushed it down deep into his pants pocket. He was only a few feet into the park when a burly guy approached with long strides and put his hand on Matt's shoulder.

"I want you to know, sir, I saw what you did," the guy said—and he pulled out his gold security badge, which was *shaped like Mickey Mouse*! And so Matt was literally kicked out of an amusement park by a Mickey Mouse security guard. He was teased relentlessly. Could have been worse, could have been the Goofy Police, they said. Of course, Matt took it with good cheer.

After their dad, the Haglof kids took turns reading scripture, and Chaplain Blankenship offered closing prayers and remarks. The bagpipe played "Amazing Grace" again, and the family greeted us outside.

I told his sister Lisa that everything people said about Matt was true tenfold. "His work saved so many soldiers' lives," I said.

She gave me a hug and a kiss on the cheek. I could feel the pain in her heart and didn't want to let go—but I eventually did.

After the service, there was a get-together at the local VFW, but I didn't go. Instead I went to my hotel room, cleaned up a little, had some dinner, and went to the bar. There, still in my black suit, I ordered a Dewar's on the rocks. The bartender could tell where I was coming from and prepared my drink accordingly. She pretended not to look as I sat and sipped and wiped at the corners of my eyes with a paper napkin, thinking about Matt and Matt's family and the love they all shared.

God bless Matt and his family.

EPILOGUE

AND NOT A DAMNED THING HAS CHANGED

As I WRITE THIS, TEN YEARS HAVE PASSED since I arrived with Phoenix in Iraq, and during that time I would have hoped that US foreign policy in that nation would start to make sense, but it's every bit as broken as it ever was. And now our inability to rid the world of monsters is coming back to haunt us.

I was reminded of this recently when I read that Moqtada al-Sadr—the same radical Shia cleric who became a wanted man in 2003 after sparking bloodshed in Basra, whose JAM militia was targeting US coalition troops with IEDs, who should have been rolled up and disposed of long ago—was likely to come out on top in Iraq's May 2018 national elections. These were touted as the first parliamentary elections since the defeat of ISIS, and the Western world assumed the candidate it backed—incumbent prime minister Haider al-Abadi—would be reelected and that would be that. But the West has (predictably) failed to win the hearts and minds of the Iraqi people.

Al-Sadr did not become prime minister, since he did not run for the position himself, but he led a bloc of candidates opposed to the US-backed status quo. When they made major gains in the election, it gave al-Sadr veto power over the selection process, which meant al-Abadi was out. Scenes of al-Sadr's supporters celebrating in Tahrir Square in Baghdad were enough to make me sick.

ACKNOWLEDGMENTS

I'D LIKE TO THANK THE FOLLOWING PERSONS, without whose help this book would not have been possible:

My wife, Debbie, and children, Stephanie and Christian, whose love and support made *Brooklyn to Baghdad* a reality.

Writer Jim DeFelice, who not only called me back but connected me with his friend Jerome Preisler, who helped launch and cowrite *Brooklyn to Baghdad*. Thanks, Jim!

Cowriter Michael Benson, who allowed me tell the story my way.

Retired army first sergeant Dave Peluso of the 1-22 TST, whose leadership, vision, and support not only kept the entire Phoenix Team safe but was also instrumental in its success.

Retired sergeant first class Adoni Poledicha, a true friend and soldier, whose voice of reason kept Phoenix Team focused and safe.

My interpreters Muaad Kholi and Sharif Morsi, whose dedication made the Phoenix Team such a success.

My agent Doug Grad, for taking me on as a client, and for his tireless efforts in finding this book a good home.

My editor Jerry Pohlen, who gave a first-time author a chance.

Retired FBI special agent Tim Clemente, who not only hired me for the Phoenix Team mission but also suggested I write a book about my experiences in Iraq.

NYPD assistant chief David Barrere, who not only looked out for me when my son was sick but gave me the best career advice in pushing me to transfer into the Intelligence Division. A true gentleman and leader and one of the finest people I know.

Retired NYPD deputy inspector Vincent (Vinny) Marra, whose support and friendship continue to this day.

Retired NYPD sergeant Sean Gelfand, whose friendship, love, and sense of humor were never in short supply.

Retired NYPD sergeant Michael O'Neil, a true "street cop," mentor, and friend.

Retired NYPD detective first grade Thomas (Tommy) Dades, a true friend and mentor who showed me a better way and encouraged me to become an author.

Retired NYPD detective first grade Gerard Ahearn, whose life was taken too soon. RIP, my brother.

Retired NYPD detective second grade Jesus (Este) Estevez, whose friendship, loyalty, and love—for me and my family—has never once wavered.

Retired NYPD detective Freddy Rodriguez, a true friend and hilarious driver.

Retired NYPD detective Douglas (Doug) Gorman, an awesome undercover narcotics cop and brother marine, whose unshakable loyalty and friendship helped keep me sane throughout the process of writing this book.

Retired police officer Matthew Murray, a true friend whose care packages in Iraq really meant a lot.

John and Karen Lucas, true best friends who always managed to put out fires while I was away in Iraq.

Bianca Scola, our beautiful aspiring dancer and waitress at Del Frisco's Steakhouse in NYC, who helped celebrate the signing of *Brooklyn to Baghdad*. As promised, Bianca!

My faithful and loving companion Juneau, our Siberian huskie. We all love and miss you, girl.

My in-laws, Maryann and Stephen Improte, who always supported me and questioned neither my motives for going to Iraq nor the love I had for their daughter or grandchildren.

My grandparents Blanche and Millard Friday, whose love and Christian values brought me into the faith of Jesus Christ and fixed an otherwise broken moral compass. Love and miss you both!

My mother, Blanche, and father, Roy. I will always love you.

ABOUT THE AUTHORS

Photo by Stephanie Strom

Chris Strom is a former US Marine (honorably discharged) and retired twenty-plus-year veteran sergeant with the NYPD. He finished his police career in the Intelligence Division as a section leader in the citywide counterterrorism unit that responded to live (in-progress) terrorism incidents and conducted long- and- short-term counterterrorism investigations. In the course of his daily duties, Chris directed human and real assets during acts of terrorism, coordinating efforts with federal, state, and local law enforcement agencies alongside the Joint Terrorism Task Force.

In October 2007, Chris was recruited by the Joint Improvised Explosive Device Defeat Organization (JIEDDO), a government agency that devised top-secret strategies for combating the IEDs, or roadside bombs, that were killing US soldiers, other coalition forces, and innocent men, women, and children in Iraq and Afghanistan.

As the lead tactical debriefing officer, Chris applied his tradecraft to a lethal insurgency, participating in over 110 combat missions and 91 captures of high-value targets (HVTs) in southern Iraq and performing more than 200 battlefield interrogations.

Upon his return from Iraq, Chris started his own company, Intel Investigations LLC, a security services company that provides platform instruction to US Navy SEALs, law enforcement agencies, and global intelligence agencies, specializing in human intelligence collection (HUMINT), tactical site exploitation (TSE), and counterterrorism strategies. Currently, Chris serves as the lead interrogation instructor for a Middle Eastern intelligence organization.

Chris is married with two children and lives in Roanoke, Virginia.

Jerome Preisler is a native New Yorker who has written forty published books of fiction and narrative nonfiction, including all eight titles in the number-one *New York Times* bestselling Tom Clancy's Power Plays series. He is the author of the bestselling Net Force series (created by Tom Clancy and Steve Pieczenik).

His nonfiction titles include *All Hands Down: The True Story of the Soviet Attack on the USS Scorpion* (Simon & Schuster, 2008), *Code Name Caesar: The Secret Hunt for U-Boat 864 During World War II* (Berkley Caliber, 2012), *Daniel's Music: One Family's Journey from Tragedy to Empowerment Through Faith, Medicine, and the Healing Power of Music* (Skyhorse, 2013), *First to Jump: How the Band of Brothers Was Aided by the Brave Paratroopers of Pathfinders Company* (Berkley Caliber, 2014), *Game Face: A Lifetime of Hard-Earned Lessons On and Off the Basketball Court* (with NBA hall of famer Bernard King, Da Capo, 2017), and *Civil War Commando: William Cushing's Daring Raid to Sink the Invincible Ironclad C.S.S. Albemarle* (Regnery, 2020).

Michael Benson, originally from Rochester, New York, is one of today's most popular true-crime writers. His books—including *Escape from Dannemora*, *Nightmare in Rochester*, *Killer Twins*, and *The Devil at Genesee Junction*—tell vividly of today's most heinous criminals, and the clever and stalwart lawmen who bring them to justice. He has a BA with honors in communication arts from Hofstra University.